SEXUAL HARASSMENT

A Reference Handbook

SEXUAL HARASSMENT

A Reference Handbook

Lynne Eisaguirre

CONTEMPORARY WORLD ISSUES

ABC-CLIO

Santa Barbara, California
Denver, Colorado
Oxford, England

Library of Congress Cataloging-in-Publication Data

Eisaguirre, Lynne, 1951–
    Sexual harassment : a reference handbook / Lynne Eisaguirre
      p. cm.—(Contemporary world issues)
    Includes bibliographical references and index.
    1. Sex discrimination—Law and legislation—United States. 2. Sex discrimination—United States. I. Title.   II. Series.
    KFR4758.E36   1993   342.73'0878—dc20   [347.302878]   93-8805

ISBN 0-87436-723-9

99 98 97 96 95 94   10 9 8 7 6 5 4 3 2

Cover photo: Attorney Anita Hill takes the oath prior to her testimony before the Senate committee hearing on the nomination of Clarence Thomas to the Supreme Court. Hill's unproven allegations of sexual harassment against Thomas did not stop his appointment to the high court, but served to focus national attention on the issue of sexual harassment. Photo courtesy of AP/Wide World Photos.

ABC-CLIO, Inc.
130 Cremona Drive, P.O. Box 1911
Santa Barbara, California 93116-1911

This book is printed on acid-free paper ⊖.
Manufactured in the United States of America

For John

Contents

Preface

THE PURPOSE OF THIS BOOK IS TO PROVIDE ACCESS to the available information as well as the full range of thought on sexual harassment in employment and education. It is not intended to promote any particular view, except the view that all commentators should be heard and considered. Historical and factual background information is offered, along with resources for further exploration into the legal, social, psychological, and political aspects of sexual harassment. Because this work gathers together a wide array of information not available in any other single source, it may prove helpful to many different people—students, researchers, writers, journalists, historians, and activists, as well as individuals who are interested in clarifying their own thoughts and feelings about sexual harassment. In this fast-changing and evolving field, however, be aware that any single source mentioned may be out-of-date by the time you read this book.

A particular attempt has been made to include writers and activists who question the whole idea of the imposition of legal or social penalties for what is called sexual harassment. Such voices are few and have been difficult to identify, because there is a lack of expression of what seems to be an increasingly unpopular viewpoint.

Organization

Like other titles in the Contemporary World Issues series, this book is meant to serve as a complete resource and a guide to further research. Chapter 2 sets the historical context with a chronology that includes significant legislation, court decisions, trends, political events, and other relevant occurrences. This chronology is necessarily limited, as the term *sexual harassment* did not even come into the lexicon until the 1970s. Chapter 3 contains biographical sketches of some key persons in the field, including activists, lawyers, politicians, commentators, and others. Chapter 4 offers factual information about sexual harassment, including laws and policies, statistics, relevant studies, and a summary of important cases. Chapter 5 is an annotated directory of organizations, including activist groups, research organizations, educational organizations, legal defense funds, political lobbying groups, and support services. Chapter 6 is an annotated bibliography of print resources, such as bibliographies, anthologies, books and monographs, and loose-leaf services. Chapter 7 is an annotated listing of nonprint resources, including films and videocassettes. A glossary of important terms, a note on how to read legal citations, and an index complete the volume.

About the Language Used in This Book

Because the vast majority of sexual harassment claims are brought by women against men, this book uses the feminine pronoun in places where use of the words *he* or *she* seems awkward or incorrect. This is not meant to deny that women sometimes sexually harass men or that same-sex harassment occurs, but is simply an attempt to make the text easier to read.

In addition, much of the information about sexual harassment focuses on legal decisions. To avoid continually interrupting the text with complex discussions, many legal terms are used without explanation. Consult the glossary for any legal terms that are unfamiliar to you.

How To Read Case and Statute Citations

A CASE MAY BE REPORTED by several different reporting services. These books are generally found in law libraries. If a case is decided by the United State Supreme Court, it will be found first in a loose-leaf service entitled *U.S. Law Week* (U.S.L.W.), and then, later on, in either the *United States Reports* (U.S.) or the *Supreme Court Reporter* (S. Ct.). If it is a federal case decided by a court other than the U.S. Supreme Court (either a federal district or federal appeals court), you may find the case soon after it is decided in *U.S. Law Week* and then in either the *Federal Reporter, Second Series* (F.2d) or the *Federal Supplement* (F. Supp.)

Most state courts print their own official state reports. In addition, all published state court decisions are included in the West Reporter System. The West Company has divided the country into seven regions. A particular state's court decisions will be reported in the reporter for the region to which that state has been assigned. These reporters are as follows:

A. and A.2d The *Atlantic Reporter (First and Second Series),* which includes decisions from Connecticut, Delaware, the District of Columbia, Maine, Maryland, New Hampshire, New Jersey, Pennsylvania, Rhode Island, and Vermont.

N.E. and N.E.2d *Northeastern Reporter (First and Second Series),* which includes decisions from New York (except for decisions from New York appellate courts, which are published in a separate volume, *New York Supplement* [N.Y.S.]), Illinois, Indiana, Massachusetts, and Ohio.

N.W. and N.W.2d *Northwestern Reporter (First and Second Series),* which includes decisions from Iowa, Michigan, Minnesota, Nebraska, North Dakota, South Dakota, and Wisconsin.

P. and P.2d *Pacific Reporter (First and Second Series)*, which includes decisions from Alaska, Arizona, California (except California appellate decisions, which are published in a separate volume, the *California Reporter* [Cal. Rptr.]), Colorado, Hawaii, Idaho, Kansas, Montana, Nevada, New Mexico, Oklahoma, Oregon, Utah, Washington, and Wyoming.

S.E. and S.E.2d *Southeastern Reporter (First and Second Series)*, which includes decisions from Georgia, North Carolina, South Carolina, Virginia, and West Virginia.

So. and So. 2d *Southern Reporter (First and Second Series)*, which includes decisions from Alabama, Florida, Louisiana, and Mississippi.

S.W. and S.W.2d *Southwestern Reporter (First and Second Series)*, which includes decisions from Arkansas, Kentucky, Missouri, Tennessee, and Texas.

A case citation provides the names of the people, schools, government agencies, or companies on each side of a case (the plaintiff[s] and defendants[s]); the volume of the reporter in which the case can be found; the page number on which the case begins; and the year in which the case was decided. For example, in *Ellison v. Brady,* 924 F.2d 872 (9th Cir. 1991),Ellison and Brady are the names of the parties involved in the case. Ellison is the plaintiff and Brady is the defendant. The case is reported in volume 924 of the *Federal Reporter, Second Series,* beginning on page 872. The Ninth Circuit (a federal court of appeals) decided the case in 1991.

1

Introduction

ANTHROPOLOGIST MARGARET MEAD LAUNCHED one of the earliest and most direct volleys in the debate over the issue of sexual harassment. Writing for *Redbook,* she argued that "it isn't more laws that we need now, but new taboos." In 1978, at a time when nearly half of all adult women were working, Mead contended that we need a taboo saying clearly and unequivocally, "You don't make passes at or sleep with the people you work with." (Mead 1978)

Mead defined *taboos* as internalized prohibitions directed against behavior that "is unthinkable and which affirm what we hold most precious in our human relations." It has always been "the basic taboos—the deeply and intensely felt prohibitions against 'unthinkable' behavior—that keep the social system in balance." Although ancient taboos governed relations between men and women in the home, there were no comparable taboos governing relations between men and women on the job. According to Mead, we are in a period of transition that requires the development of "decent sex mores in the whole working world." Citing recent developments in coeducational dormitories, she noted that an informal taboo has developed: a prohibition against serious dating among those who live in the same dormitory. Such taboos, she submitted, are now necessary at work.

Some critics, however, find this view prudish and unrealistic. They argue that many people today expect to meet and marry someone from work. (Farrell 1993) In our modern society, workers move frequently and have severed many traditional family ties that fostered age-old ways of meeting and matchmaking. Work may be their major social contact; for many people, work is the only chance to find and court a suitable mate. Now that sexual harassment is also clearly a form of illegal sex discrimination in education, critics complain that even meeting someone in school or college may be a problem, since acceptable social interactions have become more complex.

Where natural courting runs into problems may be in the different expectations men and women bring to the workplace or to school. Out of the plethora of studies that have been conducted on this subject, one of the most interesting is that done by Barbara A. Gutek, currently a professor of psychology, business administration, and executive management at the Claremont Graduate School. In *Sex and the Workplace* (1985), summarizing studies conducted in the early 1980s, Gutek found that little is known about workers' attitudes about sexual overtures at work. There are even relatively few myths or stereotypes relevant to this issue, she contends. The stereotype that women go to college to find husbands was prevalent in the past, but the view that women seek jobs for the purpose of finding husbands is less common.

Perhaps the most common relevant stereotype is the idea that some women are willing to use their sexuality to advance their careers and thus gain an unfair advantage over men competing for the same job. Some persons in Gutek's studies expressed this concern, although she found virtually no evidence that women benefit in this way. Nevertheless, this belief may lead some people to attribute any advancement by women to their willingness to "put out." These stereotypes assume that women encourage and welcome sexual advances from men.

Yet these stereotypes are about women only. Comparable statements about men—that they "sleep" their way to the top or get jobs to find wives—are rare. Although some people believe that women use their sexuality as a resource at work, apparently few believe men do. While observing that none of these stereotypes have been studied empirically, what Gutek did find was a "giant gender gap" concerning people's attitudes and reactions to overtures from the opposite sex.

Sixty-seven percent of the men in Gutek's survey said that they would be flattered by a proposition made by a woman at work, but only *17* percent of the women said that they would be flattered by a proposition from a man. Whereas most women (62.8 percent) said that sexual advances are insulting to them, only a minority of men (15 percent) felt this way.

What makes this finding so astounding, Gutek observed, is that neither men nor women are aware of this gender gap. Both sexes are aware that men are flattered if a woman propositions them, especially if she is attractive. What is surprising, however, is that both men and women also report that women are complimented and flattered by advances from a man, especially an attractive man. Although both sexes assume that men are more complimented than women, they still report that they believe women are similarly complimented.

It is perhaps understandable that men believe women are complimented—after all, men are. Why shouldn't women be complimented too? Especially if, for various reasons, women do not directly tell men that they are angered, insulted, or disgusted by male advances, it is possible to understand how men who are not sensitive to women's responses might assume that women are complimented. Harder to explain is how women who report that they personally are insulted believe other women are flattered and complimented.

One possible explanation is that women, along with men, hold the general belief that being attractive to men is extremely important to women, and that overtures and advances are an indication of that attractiveness. This is a variation on the common theme that women take jobs in male-dominated fields because they are looking for sex or husbands. Work is simply one of those areas in which a woman's attractiveness can be "validated" by comments, overtures, and advances from men.

Why, then, are individual women insulted? Perhaps because those advances frequently have job-related consequences (such as a lighter or heavier work load, longer or shorter hours) and because women want their work, not their physical attractiveness, to be noticed and evaluated. In other words, in the workplace, indications of women's sexual desirability are less important than indications of their worth as employees.

Nevertheless, women somehow separate their own reactions from their views of other women's reactions. An individual victim may feel that she did nothing to encourage an advance and may be concerned that if she does not act flattered, her circumstances at work will suffer; yet, according to Gutek's findings, she apparently assumes that other women who receive advances must have welcomed or even encouraged them.

Men's and women's responses to other questions in Gutek's survey support this theory. For example, both sexes generally reported that both men and women, but especially women, dress to be attractive at work. (Gutek 1985) In addition, a majority of both sexes agreed with the statement that if a man or woman was propositioned at work, he or she could have done something to prevent it. In general, both men and women in the Gutek survey tended to blame or place responsibility on the recipient rather than to attribute advances to some outside societal force like sex role expectations. The responses of women to this whole issue appear to illustrate a classic case of a group endorsing a stereotype about itself. Gutek concludes that both men and women are apparently misinformed about women's reactions to sexual advances by men at work.

There is another, more compelling reason why women are insulted by sexual overtures, while men are complimented. For women, overtures more frequently lead to unpleasant and negative job or educational consequences, whereas there are few such results for men. (Gutek 1985)

The cluster of attitudes held by both sexes, at least in the early 1980s, was not consistent with the existence of widespread sexual harassment. The belief that both sexes could prevent overtures, overtly or covertly encourage propositions, and dress to be sexually attractive supports the idea that any social-sexual encounters must have been welcome rather than harassing. These attitudes help explain both why sexual harassment was overlooked in the past and why so much documentation was necessary before people would believe that the problem really exists.

Major studies have shown widely disparate results—anywhere from 15 to 88 percent—with regard to the amount of sexual harassment perceived to be occurring in the workplace. Much of this discrepancy can be tied to the lack of a definition for *harassment*; many studies have not been careful to ask questions based upon the legal definition, but have instead simply asked people for their own opinions, leaving the definition up to the individual. Furthermore, answers varied depending upon whether people responded voluntarily or were surveyed randomly.

What is clear is that the nomination hearings of Clarence Thomas during October 1991 and the Civil Rights Act (of 1991) served as wake-up calls to women and employers. Millions of Americans sat glued to their television sets for several days while the Senate Judiciary Committee struggled to determine if the sexual harassment charges of Anita Hill, a law professor from Oklahoma, against Thomas, the Supreme Court nominee, were true. Through these hearings, the nation participated in a giant "teach-in" on the law and social theory of sexual harassment. The Equal Employment Opportunity Commission reported a surge in formal sexual harassment complaints following the Thomas hearings. Formal complaints increased 70 percent over the previous year; informal inquiries were up 150 percent in the nine months following the hearings. (Solomon 1992) The intense television coverage of the Thomas hearings dramatically increased awareness of what sexual harassment is and the rights of victims. According to two ABC News polls, conducted before and after the hearings, the percentage of women reporting that they had been sexually harassed more than doubled.

Another action in that same year—enactment of the Civil Rights Act of 1991—changed the law to allow up to $300,000 in compensatory and punitive damages, in addition to the preexisting remedies of reinstatement, back pay, and injunctive relief. The act also now allows jury trials in sexual harassment cases. Because juries may be more likely than judges to decide against employers and award plaintiffs substantial monetary settlements, lawyers are now much more actively pursuing harassment cases in an attempt to gain compensation for the victims. Employers can be found liable for sexual harassment even though they prohibited such conduct and were unaware that it was happening. Both the dramatic Thomas hearings and the new Civil Rights Act led to a growing national debate on the entire issue of sexual harassment.

Several other stories in the news in 1992 also contributed to the rise in public awareness. At the Tailhook convention in Las Vegas, a group of women (some of them Navy officers) accused Navy fliers of sexual harassment and assault during a drunken convention party, leading to an investigation of sexual harassment in the Navy and the resignation of several high-ranking officers. Three U.S. senators were accused of sexual harassment by current or former staffers. The United States Supreme Court jumped into the fray in 1992 by deciding a case concerning sexual harassment in schools, settling a decade of legal debate over whether the schools themselves can be liable for monetary damages for sexual harassment by employees or students. In the 1990s, suddenly, sexual harassment was no longer an issue confined to the interest of feminist scholars or social scientists. Employers, educators, workers, and students were all forced to decide what they thought about the issue.

To date, feminists, courts, legal theorists, and management have had different responses to this problem. There has been no organized opposition to the movement to make sexual harassment illegal. Perhaps this is because private employers have been quick to realize that sexual harassment directly affects their profitability in terms of lost productivity and morale, as well as legal fees and damage awards if a complaint is filed. A study of Fortune 500 companies estimated that sexual harassment costs each company over $7 million per year in worker turnover and decreased productivity. (Klein 1988)

The public sector may have been slower to recognize the problem. Some writers noted that the most serious, pervasive complaints come from public institutions. (Paul et al. 1991) Perhaps, these writers speculate, workers with the relative security of a government paycheck can afford to take time off for such unprofessional behavior and, because of civil service protections, face fewer management sanctions if they do.

Over the past 15 years in the United States, the impact of sexuality at work and at school has become the concern of four different groups, each approaching the issue from a different point of view. These different perspectives on the issue include a feminist perspective, a legal perspective, a management perspective, and the male response. Oddly absent is any organized perspective of men—the group primarily charged, in 90 to 95 percent of the cases, with perpetrating sexual harassment. These points of view are neither independent nor mutually exclusive. For example, some men are feminists, many feminists are managers, and some lawyers are managers.

The feminist perspective argues that fundamental social changes are necessary to eliminate sexual harassment. The legal and managerial perspectives tend to seek solutions through less sweeping changes in the workplace, such as establishing regulations about personnel behavior or sanctions for misusing power. Each perspective is presented in this text in its strongest form; not all feminists, lawyers, or managers would agree with the views exactly as they are outlined here. It is difficult to address the issue in a way that satisfies all four groups. Understanding the divergent perspectives is important because the way the problem is framed drives the proposed solutions.

The Feminist Perspective

The feminist viewpoint sees sexual harassment as an expected consequence of sexism in society. It is both a cause and an effect. Sexual harassment exists because women are considered the inferior sex. Men can and do exploit women, without sanctions, in the workplace, in school, and outside these institutions.

One of the ways gender stereotypes are maintained is by emphasizing sex role expectations. Being a sex object is part of the female sex role. Sexual harassment is a reminder to women of their status as sex objects; even at work or at school, women are sex objects. Feminists contend that even when women behave in a seductive manner at work or at school or are willing to exchange sexual favors for promotions or grades, they do so because they are rewarded more for that behavior than for professional or academic competence.

Because sexual harassment is an outgrowth of society's gender expectations, its occurrence in organizations may be viewed as normal or expected by nonfeminists. At the very least, handling sexual harassment may be viewed by nonfeminists as a woman's responsibility. If a woman wishes to venture into the world of work or into educational institutions dominated by men, she should expect sexual overtures from men and be able to handle them. The general attitude of managers who responded to a survey sent to readers of the *Harvard Business Review* was that women should be able to handle whatever comes their way.) (Collins and Blodgett 1981) Feminists, therefore, contend that sexual harassment is difficult to treat because it is not always viewed as a problem. Accordingly, they are committed to documenting the existence of harassment and exposing it as a form of male domination over women.

(Because the feminist perspective sees sexual harassment as an outgrowth of sexism in society, commentators from this viewpoint have had relatively little to say about workplaces or educational institutions themselves. The workplace or school is just another sphere of male domination and another arena—like marriage—where men can exert their power over women.)

The Legal Perspective

Still in the process of development, the legal perspective on sexual harassment currently parallels the legal approach to sex discrimination. The United States Supreme Court has determined that sexual harassment is a form of sex discrimination in the workplace and in school and is, therefore, illegal; yet many other legal questions—such as whether the victim's perspective should be that of the reasonable man or the reasonable woman—remain. In determining whether sexual harassment has occurred, courts will focus on the *effects* rather than the *intent* of harassment. Sexual harassment impacts an employee's or a student's performance, mental and physical health, and job or school satisfaction. One type of sexual harassment occurs when submission to sexual requests serves as a basis for employment or educational decisions, such as employee selection, grades, graduation, performance appraisal, merit increases, promotions, or tenure. Sexual harassment also occurs when the workplace or educational institution is so permeated with sexual behavior or innuendoes that the environment is hostile or intimidating. Any particular behavior is considered harassment when it leads to negative consequences for the worker or student or puts members of that worker's or student's group—in most cases women—at a disadvantage relative to other groups, usually men.

Although the legal perspective recognizes that society influences sexual harassment, it focuses on behavior in the work and educational environments rather than on broader social changes. Thus, in the law's view, complying with the legal requirements simply necessitates some changes in regulations and actions in the workplace or schools. Employers and educators must attempt to create an environment free of harassment through written policies and training and must respond promptly and vigorously to complaints of sexual harassment.

The Management Perspective

The management perspective—either in the workplace or in educational institutions—comes in two variants, one old and the other relatively new. (Gutek 1985) The older view does not take the existence of sexual harassment very seriously: sexual interactions are seen as personal matters that occasionally get out of hand. For example, perhaps a woman cannot handle the office "Don Juan," or perhaps he becomes too aggressive with one too many female employees. This point of view also tends to see an allegation of sexual harassment as an outgrowth of a lovers' quarrel or the result of misunderstandings or misperceptions. A woman may be insulted by a remark that a man meant as a compliment. Women's complaints of sexual harassment arise from their own inability to handle men who are too friendly, their own sensitivity or prudishness about sexuality, or their own retaliatory anger over a rejection by the man they have accused.

From this point of view, protecting the reputation of the senior employee—almost always a man—from false charges that could damage his career may be the organization's primary concern. Allegations of harassment are usually handled informally because they are viewed as personal matters. The accuser may be transferred or fired; sometimes the harasser may be moved or fired. Because the organization is primarily concerned with keeping the services of the most valuable of the two employees, the high-status person usually stays. Thus, even when the accuser is acknowledged to have a legitimate case, the accuser may be transferred or asked to leave.

The second, newer management point of view takes sexual harassment more seriously. Harassment is viewed as an interpersonal problem, but one that is also the organization's business, as it leads to decreased morale and productivity. Sexual harassment is viewed as an expression of personal preferences in a damaging way, when a person misuses the power associated with his or her organizational position. As such, it is unproductive and unprofessional behavior.

An organization maintaining this perspective may use classes, seminars, and written statements to emphasize that harassing behavior is unprofessional and will not be tolerated. The organization may also establish an office to formally handle cases of sexual harassment, to provide counseling to the harasser and to the harassed, or to discipline offenders.

The Male Response

Although women sometimes sexually harass men, and there is some evidence of same-sex harassment, 90 to 95 percent of all sexual harassment claims are brought by women against men. Despite this, men in the workplace and educational institutions are curiously unorganized and silent, as a group, in the face of the recent barrage of charges. Men have not banded together to protest the imposition of liability for sexual harassment of women by men. A few individual voices have been raised, however, to question whether the charges are fair and whether the sanctions are appropriate or necessary; some individuals have revealed a fear of false charges. (Farrell 1993; Paul et al. 1991) Yet, beyond some sporadic grumbling about wasting time on sexual harassment training classes at work or school, most men have remained mute.

Another question left open for future resolution is the issue of backlash. Will the increasing number of sexual harassment claims, more intensive training, and a growing male fear of false charges make men in power more reluctant to hire, teach, travel with, or promote women? Virtually no discussion of this issue has yet emerged in the literature or the case law.

Today, what is clear is that sexual harassment is illegal—and the legal definition is expanding. More and more companies and schools are creating sexual harassment policies and training programs. Whether this trend will continue remains uncertain. The number of claims and the continued prevalence of office and school romances indicate that we are still a long way from Mead's suggestion of a new taboo against sex at work or at school.

References

Collins, Eliza G. C., and Timothy B. Blodgett, "Sexual Harassment: Some See It ... Some Won't," *Harvard Business Review* 59, no. 2 (March-April 1981): 76–96.

Farrell, Warren, *The Myth of Male Power* (New York: Simon & Schuster, 1993).

Gutek, Barbara A., *Sex and the Workplace* (San Francisco: Jossey-Bass, 1985).

Klein, Freada, *The 1988 Working Woman Sexual Harassment Survey Executive Report* (Cambridge, MA: Klein Associates, 1988).

Mead, Margaret, "A Proposal: We Need Taboos on Sex at Work," *Redbook* (April 1978): 31–33, 38.

Paul, Ellen Frankel, Lloyd R. Cohen, Linda C. Majka, Alan Kors, Jean Bethke Elshtain, and Nicholas Davidson, "Sexual Harassment or Harassment of Sexuality?," *Society* 28, no. 4 (May/June 1991): 4–39.

Sandroff, Ronni, "Sexual Harassment: The Inside Story," *Working Woman* (June 1992): 47–51.

Solomon, Alisa, "One Year After Anita Hill . . . Has America's Crash Course in Preventing Sexual Harassment Made a Difference?," *Glamour* (November 1992): 238–311.

2

Chronology

A FEW IMPORTANT CASES AND LEGISLATIVE DEVELOPMENTS have substantially changed the legal complexion of sexual harassment, often wiping out all the decisions and developments that came before. When doing research on sexual harassment, some of the older resources may provide interesting historical perspectives, but check the following dates to be sure that the information offered on specific points has not become obsolete.

Pre–Twentieth Century

Although the term *sexual harassment* did not come into the lexicon until the 1970s, the problem is ancient. As far back as Genesis 39, the master's wife "casts her eyes upon" the servant Joseph and demands that he "lie with" her as an implied condition of his employment. Joseph refuses, somehow leaving his clothes behind in his rush to flee from his amorous employer. In retaliation, the wife uses the garments as evidence that Joseph tried to attack her, and the master shows his wrath by throwing innocent Joseph into prison.

Until the late twentieth century, victims of sexual harassment in employment or education had no recourse unless the attack rose to the level of an assault and battery. Usually, to prevail in such a case, a victim had to allege that she had been beaten, seriously molested, or raped. As early as 1875, however, in *Croaker v. Chicago & Northwestern Railway*, 36 Wis. 657 (1875), a court awarded a woman $1,000 in damages in an assault and battery claim for both mental suffering and "being wronged" when a male train conductor thrust his soiled hand into the muff she wore to keep her hands warm and then kissed her several times.

Early Twentieth Century

Despite the 1875 *Croaker* case, most early courts remained leery of sexual harassment claims. As summarized by Petrocelli and Repa (1992), "[w]hen evaluating evidence of outrageous and sometimes brutal attacks by a male co-worker, court opinions would quaintly ponder for pages whether a man had 'put his hands upon a woman with a view to violate her person.'"

Women factory workers in the early 1900s, wherever they worked, were sexually harassed by male workers, foremen, and bosses. In fact, learning to tolerate this abuse was one of the first lessons on the job. Male supervisors or employers commonly demanded sexual favors from women workers in exchange for a job, a raise, or a promotion. (Hymowitz and Weissman 1978)

Mid– to Late Twentieth Century

1934   A group of female servants publishes a notice in the *New York Weekly Journal* that announces, "We think it reasonable we should not be beat by our mistresses' husbands, they being too strong and perhaps may do tender women mischief." (Clark 1991)

1964   In July, Congress considers the Civil Rights Act, which would outlaw discrimination in employment and create the Equal Employment Opportunity Commission. Ironically, as it is originally introduced in Congress, the Act only prohibits discrimination in employment based on race, color, religion, or national origin. Discrimination based on gender is attached to the bill at the last moment, when conservative Southern opponents introduce an amendment prohibiting discrimination on the basis of sex; they assume that adding sexual equality is so preposterous

1964
cont.
that the amendment will scuttle the entire bill. Although the very idea of prohibiting sex-based discrimination engenders mirth on the floor of Congress and the editorial pages of major newspapers, the Johnson administration wants the Civil Rights Act passed so badly that it decides not to oppose the amendment. Although some members laughingly argue that men can now sue to become Playboy bunnies, the virtually all-male Congress passes the bill.

1974
Lin Farley, a 29-year-old women's movement activist teaching an experimental course on women and work at Cornell University, discovers that many of her students were the targets of unwelcome advances during their summer jobs. All had been so affected that they had been forced to leave.

Around the same time, Carmita Woods, a 44-year-old administrative assistant, leaves her job with a Cornell physician to escape his sexual overtures and files for unemployment compensation. Farley and two Cornell colleagues, Susan Meyer and Karen Sauvigné, find a lawyer for Wood and invent a name for her claim: *sexual harassment.*

1975–
1978
In the mid-1970s, several early sexual harassment cases begin to wend their way through the courts. All of the first women to file suits claiming sexual harassment lose at the lower court level—Jane Corne, Geneva DeVane, Paulette Barnes, Margaret Miller, and Adrienne Tomkins. In the earliest decided case, a Washington, D.C., federal judge rejects the argument that sexual harassment constitutes a cause of action under Title VII of the Civil Rights Act, holding that "the substance of plaintiff's complaint was that she was discriminated against not because she was a woman but because she refused to engage in a sexual affair with her supervisor." *Barnes v. Train (Costle),* 13 Fair Empl. Prac. Cas. (BNA) 123, 124 (D.D.C. 1974).

In *Corne v. Bausch & Lomb,* 390 F. Supp. 161 (D. Ariz. 1975) and *Miller v. Bank of America,* 418 F. Supp. 233 (N.D. Cal. 1976), the courts determine that sexual harassment is not sex discrimination because the acts complained of are not sufficiently tied to the workplace. In Corne's case, the sexual advances are seen as "a personal proclivity, peculiarity or mannerism"; in Miller's case, the "isolated misconduct" is not considered attributable to employer "policy." In *Corne,* the court quoted *Barnes* to find again that the behavior is not "based on sex"

1975– within its legal meaning: "The substance of plaintiff's com-
1978 plaint is that she was discriminated against, not because she was
cont. a woman, but because she refused to engage in a sexual affair
with her supervisor."

1975 In May, the Cornell group holds a "speakout" in a community
center in Ithaca, New York. A questionnaire reveals that a large
number of the women present have been victims of the newly
identified problem, sexual harassment. (Brownmiller and Alexander 1992)

Eleanor Holmes Norton, then chair of the New York City Commission on Human Rights, holds hearings on women and work.
Lin Farley arrives to testify, half expecting to be laughed out of
the hearing room. "The titillation value of sexual harassment
was always obvious," Farley recalls (Brownmiller and Alexander
1992), but Norton takes the issue seriously. Reporter Enid
Nemy covers the Human Rights Commission hearings for *The
New York Times*. Her story, "Women Begin to Speak Out Against
Sexual Harassment at Work," may be the first in a major publication. It appears on August 19, 1975, and is syndicated nationally. Thousands of responses pour in from women around the
country.

Around 1975, Sauvigné and Meyer set up the Working
Women's Institute in New York City to serve as a clearinghouse
for inquiries, to develop a data bank with an eye toward public
policy, and to assist women in finding legal counsel and tracking
important cases.

Carmita Wood loses her case; the unemployment insurance
appeals board rules that her reasons for quitting were personal.

1976 As in *Corne* and *Miller*, the lower court in *Tomkins v. Public
Service Electric & Gas Co.*, 422 F. Supp. 553 (D.N.J. 1976), considers sexual harassment neither employment-related nor sex-
based, but a personal injury properly pursued in state court as
a tort. The *Tomkins* court holds that a firing for a complaint
about sexual harassment is not discriminatory.

In April, a Washington, D.C., judge other than the one who
decided *Barnes* becomes the first to recognize sexual harassment
as a form of sex discrimination, in allowing a lawsuit by a black

1976
cont.
public information specialist in the Department of Justice. The employee claimed that her supervisor harassed her and then fired her after she refused to have sex with him. This is the first case to find sexual harassment to be treatment "based on sex" within the meaning of Title VII, although it leaves the employment-relatedness of the incidents to be determined at trial. *Williams v. Saxbe,* 413 F. Supp. 654 (D.D.C. 1976).

1977–
1979
By 1977, three of the early cases rise to the appellate level, and the results are different from those in the lower courts. All three appellate courts rule that a harassed woman has a right, under Title VII of the Civil Rights Act, to sue the corporate entity that employed her. *Barnes v. Costle (Train),* 561 F.2d 983 (D.C. Cir. 1977); *Miller v. Bank of America,* 600 F.2d 211 (9th Cir. 1979); *Tompkins v. Public Service Electric & Gas,* 568 F.2d 1044 (3d Cir. 1977). The *Tompkins* case contains the clearest statement that the courts will no longer view harassment as a personal problem, but as sex discrimination. In *Barnes,* the Court of Appeals for the District of Columbia holds that making sexual compliance a "job retention condition" is sex-based differentiation, under the circumstances, because it imposes an employment requirement upon a woman that would not be imposed upon a man.

Also in the late 1970s, Freada Klein and a group of feminists form a Boston area advocacy group called the Alliance Against Sexual Coercion. Soon, the term *sexual coercion* is abandoned and the term *sexual harassment* dominates the movement. Several leading women's magazines run stories on the issue in the late 1970s, including a survey in 1976 by *Redbook* and a *Ms.* speakout and cover story in 1977. Even anthropologist Margaret Mead leaps into the fray with a 1978 article in *Redbook* in 1978 entitled "A Proposal: We Need Taboos on Sex at Work."

1977
The first student brings a claim of sexual harassment under Title IX of the 1972 Education Act Amendments. Ronnie Alexander, a female undergraduate at Yale, claims that her professor offered her an A in his course in exchange for sex and told her that if she refused, she would receive a C. In *Alexander v. Yale,* 459 F. Supp. 1 (D. Conn. 1977), Alexander asks that the grade be removed from her record. Four other students and a faculty

1977
cont.
member join in the suit. The district court holds that sexual harassment may constitute sex discrimination under Title IX, stating, "It is perfectly reasonable to maintain that academic advancement conditioned upon submission to sexual demands constitutes sex discrimination in education, just as questions of job retention or promotion tied to sexual demands from supervisors have become increasingly recognized as potential violations of Title VII's ban against sex discrimination in employment."

1978
Lin Farley's groundbreaking book, *Sexual Shakedown: The Sexual Harassment of Women on the Job,* is published by McGraw-Hill after being rejected by 27 other publishers. "I thought my book would change the workplace," Farley said. "It is now out of print." (Brownmiller and Alexander 1992)

1979
Following close behind Farley, Catharine MacKinnon, a young lawyer who followed the early cases while a student at Yale Law School, publishes *Sexual Harassment of Working Women,* a book that provides the first legal theoretical analysis of the issue.

Without much publicity, the courts continue to broaden the definition and scope of unlawful harassment. As the number of women in the workplace grows, new cases go beyond the situation of bosses suggesting sex for jobs. A court decision in Minnesota establishes that co-worker harassment also poisons the workplace and is illegal; a New York court holds that a receptionist should not be required to wear revealing clothes that bring her unwanted attention.

A clerk-typist named Karen Nussbaum starts to organize women office workers through a national network she calls 9 to 5. Jane Fonda—an old friend from the antiwar movement—visits Nussbaum's headquarters in Cleveland with the idea of making a movie about underpaid and harassed secretaries.

1980
Ronnie Alexander's suit is ultimately dismissed, because she has graduated from Yale and thereby mooted the issue. The university, however, establishes a sexual harassment grievance procedure for dealing with complaints, and the *Alexander* case stands for the proposition that sexual harassment is illegal in education as well as employment.

1980
cont.
The movie *9 to 5,* starring Jane Fonda, Lily Tomlin, and Dolly Parton, is produced by Fonda's IPC Films. Parton plays a secretary dodging the advances of an amorous boss. The movie, which is a commercial success, uses comedy to fuel the public consciousness about the issue of sexual harassment in employment.

On 10 November, in the last days of the Carter administration, Eleanor Holmes Norton, the chair of the EEOC, issues a set of federal guidelines on sexual harassment in a single-page memorandum. The guidelines were published earlier, in the spring, and subjected to public discussion and debate. The guidelines declare sexual activity as a condition of employment or promotion to be a violation of Title VII.

A federal district court allows a suit over an "atmosphere of discrimination." *Brown v. City of Guthrie,* 22 Fair Empl. Prac. Cas. (BNA) 1627 (W.D. Okla. 1980). Even though the plaintiff woman cannot show a loss of tangible job benefits, she does establish that the harassment created a hostile, offensive, and unbearable work environment. *Brown* is the first court opinion to cite the 1980 EEOC guidelines, quoting Section A, that sexual harassment is a violation of Title VII when "such conduct has the purpose or effect of substantially interfering with an individual's work performance or creating an intimidating, hostile, or offensive work environment."

1981
Following shortly after *Brown,* in *Bundy v. Jackson,* 641 F.2d 934 (D.C. Cir. 1981), another circuit court rules on the basis of an atmosphere of discrimination and also cites the EEOC guidelines. This court holds that the phrase "terms and conditions of employment" protected by Title VII means more than tangible compensation and benefits.

The Merit Systems Protection Board releases the results of a random survey of 20,100 federal employees, revealing that 42 percent of the government's female workers experienced an incident of sexual harassment in the previous year. This is the first survey to use a reliable methodology for its study.

In July, homosexual advances at work are found to be within the purview of the Civil Rights Act. *Wright v. Methodist Youth Services, Inc.,* 551 F. Supp. 307 (N.D. Ill. 1981).

1982–
1983
During this two-year period, two federal circuit courts of appeal adopt their own standards for sexual harassment cases, identifying two kinds of sexual harassment: (1) harassment in which a supervisor demands sexual considerations in exchange for job benefits ("quid pro quo") and (2) harassment that creates an offensive environment ("condition of work" or "hostile work environment" harassment). *Henson v. City of Dundee,* 682 F.2d 897 (11th Cir. 1982); *Katz v. Dole,* 709 F.2d 251 (4th Cir. 1983). The *Henson* court establishes four elements that a plaintiff must prove to establish a case of quid pro quo sexual harassment: (1) he or she belongs to a protected group (that is, is male or female); (2) he or she was subjected to unwelcome sexual harassment; (3) the harassment complained of was based on sex; and (4) the employee's reaction to the harassment complained of affected tangible aspects of the employee's compensation, terms, conditions, or privileges of employment. The *Henson* case also reverses the lower court's holding that the plaintiff must show some tangible job detriment in addition to the hostile work environment created by sexual harassment. The *Katz* court lists the same four elements as required for quid pro quo sexual harassment, but adds the requirement that the employer knew, or should have known, of the harassment in question and failed to take prompt remedial action.

In September 1982, a federal judge in Wisconsin upholds a verdict in favor of a male social services worker who claimed that he was sexually harassed by his female supervisor. *Huebschen v. Health & Social Services Department,* 547 F. Supp. 1168 (D. Wis. 1982).

1986
In June, the U.S. Supreme Court decides its first sexual harassment case and issues an historic ruling that harassment is sex discrimination and illegal under Title VII of the Civil Rights Act, even if the victim suffers no economic loss. *Meritor Savings Bank v. Vinson,* 477 U.S. 57 (1986). Hired by the bank as a teller-trainee, Mechelle Vinson advanced on the basis of her abilities to the position of assistant branch manager before her ultimate termination for excessive use of sick leave. About a year later, Vinson sued the bank and Sidney Taylor, her supervisor, alleging hostile-environment sexual harassment. Vinson claimed that, during her four years at the bank, she had sex with Taylor some 40 or 50 times. He allegedly also followed her into the ladies' room, fondled her in front of co-workers, and raped her several times. Although the bank had an antidiscrimination

1986
cont.

policy and a stated complaint procedure, Vinson did not use the internal process, claiming that she feared reprisals. In their defense, Taylor and the bank alleged that the ongoing relationship was entirely voluntary and that no liability should attach because there was no notice to the employer. Despite the length of the relationship and the lack of notice, the Supreme Court allows Vinson's hostile-environment claim in a landmark decision with far-reaching implications for employers.

The Court holds that "the language of Title VII is not limited to 'economic' or 'tangible' discrimination and the phrase 'terms, conditions or privileges' of employment in the law indicates a congressional intent to 'strike at the entire spectrum of disparate treatment of men and women,' " including harassment that creates a hostile work environment. Quoting *Henson*, the Court finds that

> [s]exual harassment which creates a hostile or offensive environment for members of one sex is every bit the arbitrary barrier to sexual equality at the workplace that racial harassment is to racial equality. Surely, a requirement that a man or woman run a gauntlet of sexual abuse in return for the privilege of being allowed to work and make a living can be as demeaning and disconcerting as the harshest of racial epithets.

The Supreme Court's important holdings are:

Sexual harassment is a form of sex discrimination illegal under Title VII of the 1964 Civil Rights Act

Sexual harassment is illegal even if the victim suffers only a hostile work environment and not the loss of economic or tangible job benefits

Employers are not automatically liable for sexual harassment by their supervisors

Lack of knowledge of the harassment does not automatically relieve the employer of liability for a supervisor's harassment

The complainant's consent to the behavior does not relieve the employer of liability. The question is not the "voluntariness" of the complainant's participation, but whether her conduct indicates that the behavior was unwelcome

The complainant's behavior, such as provocative speech and dress, may be considered in determining whether the complainant found particular sexual advances unwelcome

1988   One of the first cases of "paramour preference," *Broderick v. Ruder*, 685 F. Supp. 1269 (D.D.C. 1988), is decided by a judge in Washington, D.C. The plaintiff, a staff attorney at the Securities and Exchange Commission, alleges that several supervisors were involved in sexual relationships with secretaries and a staff attorney and rewarded them with promotions, cash, and other job benefits. Broderick also alleges isolated instances of harassment directed at her. (In one, a drunken supervisor untied her top and kissed her at an office party.) The court finds that a hostile environment was created, even though all of the relationships were entirely consensual. The court emphasizes that the sexual activity in the office was widespread and that it formed the basis for decisions on the terms and conditions of employment. When the plaintiff made it clear that she would not participate, the quality of her work assignments changed.

1990   In March, the EEOC issues new guidelines on how to define and prevent sexual harassment, updating the guidelines it issued in 1980. This new publication reflects agency and court decisions since the first guidelines' issuance in 1980.

A number of studies and surveys are conducted and their results published. In September, the Pentagon releases the largest military survey ever on sexual harassment, showing that of 20,000 military respondents worldwide, 64 percent of the women and 17 percent of the men reported that they have been sexually harassed.

In business, estimates continue to run from 15 to 40 percent of women and 14 to 15 percent of men reporting that they have experienced sexual harassment. In education, 40 to 70 percent of female students report experiencing harassment, mostly from other students.

Women's groups and others push a bill through Congress that would allow an employee to sue for compensatory damages for personal injuries in a sexual harassment case. Under the previous law, damages were limited to lost wages. President George Bush vetoes the bill.

1991   In January, an appellate court in Florida rules that nude pinups in the workplace could lead to a "hostile work environment" and constitute illegal sexual harassment. *Robinson v. Jacksonville Shipyards*, 760 F. Supp. 1486 (M.D. Fla. 1991). Robinson, a female shipyard welder, wins this first case to find that such

1991
cont.

pictures are sexual harassment in and of themselves; in other cases, courts had found that pornographic pictures merely contribute to an atmosphere of sexual harassment. In this case, the plaintiff claimed that she had told her co-workers that their behavior was sexual harassment and that they had then subjected her to new ridicule. The *Robinson* court finds that the employer and two of its employees were directly liable for the harassment and rejects what it calls their "ostrich defense." (They claimed to be unaware of the victim's complaint.) The judge holds that the shipyard maintained a "boys' club" atmosphere with a constant "visual assault on the sensibilities of , female workers." Some of the pictures posted on the walls in *Robinson* included close-ups of female genitals. The judge finds that the sexualized atmosphere of the shipyard had the effect of keeping women out of the workplace, and he orders the employer to institute a sexual harassment policy written by the National Organization for Women's Legal Defense and Education Fund, which brought this case to trial.

About a week after *Robinson,* an appellate court for California recognizes that, in considering what qualifies as sexual harassment, the behavior should be evaluated by the "reasonable woman standard," as opposed to the reasonable man standard that was formerly applied. *Ellison v. Brady,* 924 F.2d 872 (9th Cir. 1991). In *Ellison,* the employer's response to the harassment was to counsel the harasser, instructing him to leave the woman alone, and to transfer him to a different facility for four months. The court finds that the employer should have consulted the victim about the harasser's return to the office and should have taken some other kind of disciplinary action. With regard to the reasonable woman standard, the court finds:

An understanding of the victim's perspective requires an analysis of the different perspectives of men and women

A female employee may state the basics of a case of hostile-environment sexual harassment by alleging conduct that a reasonable woman would consider sufficiently severe; however, the employer does not have to accommodate the idiosyncrasies of a hypersensitive employee

The reasonable woman standard is not static, but will change over time as the views of reasonable women change

There can be unlawful sexual harassment even when harassers do not realize that their conduct creates a hostile working environment

1991
cont.

The facts upon which the court decided *Ellison* are significant because many critics use this case to argue that the courts have gone too far in enforcing sexual harassment claims. Ellison was an IRS agent who accepted an invitation to lunch with a fellow employee, Gray. A few months later, he asked her out again and she refused. Gray then started to write her love letters. Ellison testified that she was frightened by his attentions and filed a complaint with her employer, who then transferred Gray. Three months later, the IRS, without consulting Ellison, allowed Gray to return. When Ellison learned that Gray was returning to her workplace, she requested and received a transfer. She then filed suit. The trial judge dismissed the case, ruling that, under the reasonable person standard, Gray's actions were "isolated and genuinely trivial." The Ninth Circuit reverses and orders a trial, ruling that a hostile work environment must be judged from the perspective of the victim, in this case the "reasonable woman."

In October, law professor Anita Hill charges Supreme Court nominee Judge Clarence Thomas with sexually harassing her when she worked with him. At first, the United States Senate Judiciary Committee decides to ignore the charges and vote on the nomination. A delegation of congresswomen, led by Representative Pat Schroeder, marches into the Senate hearing from the House and demands a more thorough investigation. After receiving thousands of calls and letters from outraged constituents, the committee votes to hold hearings. The televised proceedings before the United States Senate Judiciary Committee fuel a dramatic leap in public awareness about sexual harassment on the job. Despite the accusations, the all-male committee votes in favor of confirmation, as does the full Senate.

In one of the most quoted statements on the Hill/Thomas controversy, Molly Yard, president of the National Organization for Women, in a 10 October 1991 plea to members to help finance campaigns of women for Congress, writes:

> They just don't get it. Those men just don't understand how injurious, how demeaning and how frightening sexual harassment really is. So it took a massive eruption of outrage from women across America—and across party lines—to shock those senators into delaying the vote on Thomas so that the charge could be investigated. (Petrocelli and Repa 1992, 1/24)

In the wake of the Thomas hearings, the issue of amending the Civil Rights Act is again brought before Congress. Although the Bush administration still opposes allowing employees to sue for

1991
cont.
damages, at the last minute, bowing to political pressure, it agrees to a compromise bill. An employee can now sue for compensatory damages, in addition to lost wages, but a strict limit is placed on the total amount the employee can recover: $50,000 to $300,000, depending on the number of employees in the company.

Women's groups and others point out that no other group is subject to such severe limits on the amount of damages that may be recovered in a personal injury action. Faced with the alternative of staying with the old law that would allow no compensatory damages, however, women activists reluctantly support the bill. The act passes and becomes part of the Civil Rights Act of 1991.

Several other federal courts follow *Ellison* and adopt the reasonable woman rule during 1991 and 1992.

1992
In February, the Supreme Court decides the first case relating to sexual harassment in schools. In *Franklin v. Gwinnett County Public Schools,* 112 S. Ct. 1028 (1992), a high school student alleges that she was sexually harassed by her sports coach and teacher. After the school became aware of the harassment, it conducted an investigation. The teacher resigned on the condition that all matters pending against him be dropped. Franklin's suit was dismissed by the court of appeals on the basis that Title IX (which prohibits sex discrimination in educational institutions that receive federal funds) does not authorize an award of money damages. The Supreme Court disagrees. It determines that Title IX allows compensatory damages to be awarded to the student, even though the school investigated and the teacher resigned.

A group of at least 26 women, half of them Navy officers, claim that they were sexually harassed at a party of Navy pilots at the "Tailhook" convention in Las Vegas in late 1991. The Navy conducts only a cursory investigation until one of the women, an admiral's aide named Lieutenant Paula Coughlin, continues to press the issue. Feeling the heat of congressional and media pressure in early 1992, the Pentagon and the House Armed Services Committee conduct in-depth investigations of the incident. In June of the same year, several high-ranking officers are forced to resign, including Navy Secretary Lawrence Garrett and Admiral John Snyder. The investigations of at least 69 other officers continue.

Three senators are accused of sexual harassment by current or former staff members or other women. Senator Bob Packwood,

1992 R-Oregon, issues an apology after the *Washington Post* publishes
cont. a story in late November 1992. It states that he had harassed as
many as ten staffers and former staffers over the years. Packwood
was reelected to a new six-year term earlier that month, before
the story broke. Also during 1992, Senator Daniel Inouye,
R-Hawaii, is accused by his long-time hair stylist and several
other women of molestation. Senator Brock Adams, D-Washing-
ton, does not seek reelection in 1992 after the daughter of a
family friend accuses him of drugging and molesting her, and
a newspaper publishes similar allegations by several other
women. Congress is forced to investigate all three incidents.

References

Brownmiller, Susan, and Dolores Alexander, "From Carmita Wood to Anita
Hill," *Ms.* (January/February 1992).

Clark, Charles S., "Sexual Harassment," *CCQ Researcher* 1, no. 13 (August 9,
1991): 539–545.

Hymowitz, C., and M. Weissman, *A History of Women in America* (New York:
Bantam, 1978).

MacKinnon, Catharine A., *Sexual Harassment of Working Women* (New Haven, CT
and London: Yale University Press, 1979).

Omilian, Susan M., *Sexual Harassment in Employment* (Wilmette, IL: Callaghan,
1987).

Petrocelli, William, and Barbara Kate Repa, *Sexual Harassment on the Job: What It
Is and How To Stop It* (Berkeley, CA: Nolo Press, 1992).

Webb, Susan L., *Step Forward: Sexual Harassment in the Workplace* (New York:
Mastermedia, 1991).

3

Biographical Sketches

TO LIST ALL THE PEOPLE WHO HAVE CONTRIBUTED to the debate on the issue of sexual harassment or related gender discussions would be impossible, because many people have written just a few important articles or given several speeches on the issue, rather than making the subject of sexual harassment the focus of a career. This is particularly true of those who criticize the idea of making sexual harassment a legally actionable wrong. It has been difficult to identify representatives on all sides of the issue, as there is currently no organized opposition to either the legal or social movements to eliminate sexual harassment. Therefore, because an attempt is made in this book to present all points of view, some critics of sexual harassment laws and policies may be featured more prominently in these biographies than might appear warranted by their involvement in the issue. Conversely, some proponents of the movement to make sexual harassment illegal have been necessarily omitted. The list is not meant to be comprehensive, but rather represents a sample of persons related to the issue. The following list profiles some of the important writers, researchers, attorneys, politicians, lawsuit plaintiffs, political activists, and others who have figured in the issue.

Stephen F. Anderson (1947–)

Stephen Anderson began conducting training sessions on the issue of sexual harassment while serving in the Air Force in the 1970s, as a result of his volunteer work in a sexual assault clinic.

Before that time, he had also worked as a trainer on the issue of race relations for the Air Force. In 1980, after reading Lin Farley's book *Sexual Shakedown,* he designed a training program on sexual harassment for private companies. In doing so, he became one of the first corporate and government trainers to focus exclusively on the issue. Over the past 12 years, he developed a variety of training programs, manuals, videotapes, and other materials on the issue of sexual harassment. In his training programs and materials, Anderson has focused on what he calls "subtle sexual harassment," actions that may not rise to the level of a legal claim, but which may, if allowed to expand without question in the workplace, lead to a lawsuit for hostile work environment. Anderson's company has trained over 100,000 management personnel and other employees in 500 organizations and educational institutions. In addition to sexual harassment training, his company provides workshops in team building, working with irritating people, and other workplace issues. Anderson also serves as an expert witness in sexual harassment cases. He emphasizes that "[i]n sexual harassment situations, it is the *impact[,] not the intent[,]* of the behavior that creates interpersonal conflicts and legal and financial liabilities." Anderson holds a bachelor's degree in psychology and a master's degree in personnel administration.

In 1992, Anderson reported, the issues women face are the same issues of subtle sexual harassment that they confronted in 1980 when he first began conducting harassment training. Anderson has noticed a new form of sex discrimination developing, a new excuse to discriminate against women: men claim that they fear false sexual harassment claims and therefore refuse to work with women. He sees "a lot of backlash and distancing" when he conducts training in today's corporate environments.

Stephen A. Bokat (1946–)

As vice-president and general counsel of the U.S. Chamber of Commerce, Stephen Bokat has represented the business and management point of view on the issue of sexual harassment in *amicus curiae* (friend of the court) briefs before the United States Supreme Court and other federal courts, as well as serving as a speaker, panelist, and counselor to management on the issue. In the case in which the Supreme Court first addressed the issue of sexual harassment, *Meritor Savings Bank v. Vinson,* the Chamber, under Bokat's direction, took the position that sexual advances without any loss or threatened loss of tangible job benefits did not state a case of sexual harassment under Title VII; that an employer should not be strictly liable under Title VII for a supervisor's advances when the employer neither knew nor reasonably could have known of the advances; that evidence relating to the plaintiff's behavior and dress should be admissible (a position adopted by the Court); and that the Court should establish guidelines for analysis of sexual harassment cases.

Bokat is frequently called to represent the management perspective on sexual harassment cases on educational panels or in media interviews. He also conducts training programs on sexual harassment. He believes that most businesses are now receptive to training on the issue because sexual harassment "doesn't improve anyone's bottom line. It doesn't improve productivity and it has no place in the work place." Bokat sees problems when employers are not informed about the law or where some people are overly sensitive. During the Clarence Thomas nomination hearings, he was interviewed on radio and television shows daily. The Chamber supported Thomas's nomination.

As general counsel of the U.S. Chamber of Commerce, Bokat is in charge of the Chamber's legal department. He also serves as executive vice-president of the National Chamber Litigation Center, a public policy law firm associated with the U.S. Chamber and established to represent business before the courts and federal regulatory agencies. He joined the Chamber in June 1977, after serving as an appellate litigator for the Occupational Safety and Health division of the Solicitor's Office of the U.S. Labor Department. Earlier, he served as attorney-advisor to the chairman of the Occupational Safety and Health Review Commission and to a member of the National Labor Relations Board. A graduate of Adams State College, he received his law degree from the George Washington University Law School in 1972. Bokat is coeditor-in-chief of *Occupational Safety and Health Law* (1988), published by the Bureau of National Affairs.

Catherine A. Broderick (1953–)

Catherine Broderick was an attorney with the Securities and Exchange Commission (SEC) when she filed a lawsuit based on the allegation that she was the subject of a hostile work environment because other women in her department were given promotions as a reward for sexual relationships and favors. (This case is discussed in chapters 1 and 3.) The atmosphere, she has since reported, was "all ingrown and festering." Broderick sued only after she was threatened with termination for complaining about the environment in her office. The case garnered national media attention on the new claim of "paramour preference," and Broderick has been interviewed by a number of national radio and television programs. As a result of her legal victory, she was awarded a choice of jobs in the agency. She now works in the general counsel's office on appellate litigation, where she describes the work environment as "very professional."

Broderick has been employed by the SEC since 1979; currently, she serves as counsel to the assistant general counsel. Before that assignment, she was the senior attorney of corporation finance, where she supervised the staff review of antitakeover proposals in proxy statements. She also served as an attorney in the division of enforcement, where she worked on litigation and compliance. Before joining the Securities and Exchange Commission, she was in private practice in New York. Broderick has an LL.M. in securities from Georgetown University Law Center. She received her J.D. from the New York University School of Law, her M.A. in English from the same university, and a B.F.A. from Carnegie-Mellon University in 1972.

Lloyd R. Cohen (1947–)

Lloyd Cohen is an associate professor of law at Chicago-Kent College of Law in Chicago. He has written and lectured widely on questions of ethics and law. Recently, he is one of the few legal scholars to write and speak out as a critic of laws and regulations governing sexual harassment. Cohen's articles on this subject have appeared in *The New York Times, Society,* and *Academic Questions,* a publication of the National Association of Scholars. His basic thesis has been that the workplace is one of the central or primary places in our society where women and men can meet romantic partners. In his *New York Times* piece, entitled "Fear of Flirting," he argued that "[a]t work they can flirt and in other ways get things rolling in a largely unthreatening environment. Should this be substantially limited by regulations, the lives of those affected will be diminished." He has also been a critic of so-called harassment speech codes on campus—including those designed to prevent sexual harassment—because he fears that they will lead to infringement on the First Amendment and interfere with the university's role as the "temple of thought, discourse, and intellectual dispute."

Cohen has taught at the University of Chicago Law School and the California Western School of Law. In addition to a law degree with honors from Emory University, he holds a Ph.D. in economics from SUNY-Binghamton. He graduated from Harpur College with a major in economics in 1968. Before starting his career as a law professor, he served as special counsel to the vice-chairman of the U.S. International Trade Commission.

Frances Krauskopf Conley (1940–)

Frances Conley, M.D., made national headlines when she resigned as a professor of surgery (neurosurgery) at Stanford University School of Medicine, alleging that she could not work under the newly appointed chairman of her department because he was a perpetrator of sexual harassment against her and other women. Going public with her reasons for the resignation, Conley stated

> I resigned my professorship because, under his stewardship, my professional work environment was truly hostile and because I wanted no part of an institution that proved incapable of recognizing that its actions were diametrically opposed to those beliefs it publicly articulated. Just because I had chosen to close my eyes to inappropriate behavior and remarks in my quest for success did not mean that I should continue to facilitate the career of one who is offensive and who, perhaps more importantly, would subject yet another generation of women and minorities to the same abuse.

As a result of Conley's resignation, the university commenced an investigation. Two days before its effective date, Conley rescinded her resignation and returned to her faculty position, convinced that her presence might force the medical school to remedy the problem. The supervisor Conley accused of sexism was ultimately asked to step down, as the investigators found that "it would not be in the interests of the school for him to continue in the position of acting chair." The doctor, Gerald Silverberg, agreed to participate in training and counseling programs focused on gender and sensitivity and agreed to a procedure to monitor his behavior. In a press release on the subject, he apologized to "anyone I may have offended." Silverberg went on to state that "[i]t was never my intention to demean or insult any women, but it is now clear to me that some things I said or did in jest or from affection were taken as signs of disrespect."

Frances Conley was educated in California public schools, attended Bryn Mawr College, received a B.A. in biology with distinction from Stanford, and went on to obtain both an M.D. degree and an M.S. in management from Stanford. A tenured faculty member at Stanford, she has been the recipient of many honors, is board certified in neurological surgery, and has published numerous writings in her field. She was the nation's fifth woman to be certified in neurosurgery. Now a frequent speaker on the issue of sexual harassment, Conley notes that, after years of accepting sexual harassment in her male-dominated field, she "sinned twice" against the male status quo, "[f]irst by refusing to play the game anymore and refusing to keep silent and then by going public" with her reasons for dropping out.

Paula Anne Coughlin (1962?–)

Lieutenant Paula Anne Coughlin, a Navy aviator, made national headlines when she complained to her superiors about sexual harassment at a 1991 meeting of the Tailhook Association in Las Vegas. At that meeting, 26 women—half of them military officers—claimed that they had been sexually assaulted while being pushed down a gauntlet of drunken naval aviators in a hotel hallway. Just days before Anita Hill testified in the Senate, Paula Coughlin filed her complaint with the Navy. Later, when interviews with some 1,500 men at Tailhook turned up only two names of men on the gauntlet, she went public, "putting a name and a face to this." Her courage was instrumental in forcing the Pentagon to reopen the investigation. The final report blasted the Navy for its handling of the scandal, concluding that the men in charge were more worried about covering the Navy's tail than uncovering Tailhook. The investigation eventually led to the resignation of Navy Secretary Lawrence Garrett and several other top Navy officials. After the investigation, the Pentagon engaged in a new push to halt sexual harassment; the program includes a videotape on the subject that now accompanies training packets sent to every U.S. Naval command.

Coughlin, the daughter of a retired Naval officer, has stated about the incident, "I've been in the Navy almost eight years and I've worked my ass off to be one of the guys, to be the best Naval officer I can be and prove that women can do whatever the job calls for. And what I got, I was treated like trash. I wasn't one of them." A graduate of Old Dominion University and a native of Virginia,

Coughlin was commissioned in the United States Naval Reserves and began her service in the Hampton Roads Naval Reserve Officers Training Corps unit in 1984. Lieutenant Coughlin worked as an aide to the commander in the Naval Air Test Center, and has flown more than ten different models of aircraft. Designated as an unrestricted aviator in 1987, Lieutenant Coughlin has been awarded one Navy Commendation Medal, two Navy Achievement Medals, three Meritorious Unit Commendations, the Armed Services Defense Medal, and two sea service ribbons. She is currently training to fly the H-53 helicopter at NAS Norfolk, Virginia.

Peggy Crull (1946–)

Peggy Crull served as both the research director and the executive director of the Working Women's Institute (WWI) from 1977 through 1985. WWI was probably the first institute devoted exclusively to combating sexual harassment in the workplace. As research director, Crull instituted some of the first studies ever conducted on the issue. When publicity about the institute started to reach women, Crull was "flooded with mail and phone calls" from sexual harassment victims who wanted to share their experiences. Crull realized that the letters represented a "goldmine" of original research material on a subject that had not been extensively documented. From that data, she published the first study on the incidence of sexual harassment in the workplace. She went on to direct research and write articles on the stress effects of sexual harassment, as well as pursuing original research work on the issue of sexual harassment of women in blue-collar and other nontraditional jobs. She remembers that it was difficult to obtain funding for research on the issue in those early days because, unlike rape or other forms of physical assault against women, "sexual harassment was not a criminal offense."

Since the 1970s, Crull has continued to develop her expertise on the issue, testifying in sexual harassment cases and serving on the New York Governor's Task Force on Sexual Harassment. She was one of a number of women who sought to convince members of the Senate Judiciary Committee, during the Thomas hearings, that they needed to consider expert testimony on sexual harassment, especially on such issues as whether it is common for victims not to report the harassment at the time it occurs, a major issue in the Hill testimony. (The senators could not understand why Hill had waited ten years to come forward with her story.) Currently,

Crull serves as the research director of the New York Commission on Human Rights; in that role, she has helped organize hearings on harassment in the construction industry.

Warren Farrell (1943–)

Dr. Warren Farrell is the author of *Why Men Are the Way They Are, The Liberated Man,* and the new book, *The Myth of Male Power,* which includes an entire chapter on the issue of sexual harassment. The first book was a national best-seller, won two national awards, and was published in more than 51 countries in 8 languages. The *New York Post* called it "the most important book ever written about love, sex, and intimacy." Over a period of 20 years, Farrell has worked with hundreds of men's and women's groups on gender issues and relationships between the sexes. He is the only man to have been elected three times to the Board of the National Organization for Women in New York City; he has also served on the boards of the National Organization for Changing Men and the National Congress for Men. The *Chicago Tribune* described Farrell as "the Gloria Steinem of Men's Liberation."

More recently, Farrell has been criticized by some women activists since he began to write and speak out on the subject of men's liberation, challenging the feminist assumption that society's problems are caused by the power men have over women. He argues that male power is a myth, because most men have little control over their lives, are required in our society to support families, to work in dangerous occupations, and serve in the armed forces. On the issue of sexual harassment, especially in his new book, *The Myth of Male Power,* Farrell argues that many claims are the result of the mixed signals women send out in the workplace; many women expect to meet and even marry men they meet at work. He also argues that allowing such claims will lead to a new form of discrimination against women, as some men—leery of false claims of sexual harassment—will be reluctant to hire, travel with, or promote women to close working relationships. What is called sexual harassment, Farrell also argues, is the result of our society's expectations that men will take the lead in sexual relationships.

A frequent commentator on television and radio shows on gender issues, Farrell has written for numerous magazines and professional journals. Although his original Ph.D. was in political science, he has also taught at the college level in the departments of psychology, sociology, sexual politics, and public administration at several universities, including the School of Medicine at the University of California and Georgetown University. Currently, Farrell conducts workshops across the country on men's roles and other gender issues. He stresses in these workshops that although women have valid complaints that they are "sex objects," men are treated as "success objects."

Barbara Gutek (1949?–)

Barbara Gutek is one of the pioneering researchers on the incidence of sexual harassment and other issues relating to sex in the workplace. Author of the widely read book, *Sex and the Workplace,* published in 1985, Gutek conducted one of the first random-sample studies on the issue of sexual harassment. In that 1985 book, she reported that her studies have revealed that sex at work is a problem for up to half of all workers, and that "[i]t is a mistake to assume that sex at work is simply a product of biological attractions between men and women and that none of it has work related consequences." Gutek has also consulted on or designed a number of other major studies. She has served as a faculty member at several universities in the schools of psychology, sociology, management, and business. She received her Ph.D. from the University of Michigan, specializing in organizational psychology. Currently a professor of management and policy at the California Institute of Technology, she has also taught at the University of Arizona, Claremont Graduate School, and a number of other institutions.

In addition to her work in the field of sex and work, she has studied the issue of computer use and learning at work, women managers and entrepreneurs, and other workplace issues. The recipient of numerous fellowships, she has consulted with major corporations and government entities on sexual harassment and other workplace issues, as well as serving as an expert witness in cases involving equitable promotion systems, sexual harassment, and survey research methods. She is the author of many books and articles on the issues of women and work.

Anita Faye Hill (1956–)

Born the youngest of 13 children in a poor black farm family, Anita Hill graduated from Oklahoma State University in 1977 with honors. In college she was a National Merit Scholar, a

University Regents Scholar, and a member of the president's and dean's honor roll. After receiving her law degree from Yale, she worked in private practice at a large and prestigious Washington, D.C., law firm before working for Clarence Thomas in the Office of Civil Rights at the Department of Education. She then followed Thomas to the EEOC. After leaving the EEOC, Hill became a law professor at Oral Roberts University in Tulsa and then taught at the University of Oklahoma Law School, where she was awarded tenure after four years.

Hill worked far from the public eye in all these endeavors until her accusations in 1991 against then-Supreme Court nominee Clarence Thomas. Her claim that Thomas sexually harassed her when she worked with him ten years before his nomination stunned the Senate and the country. Despite her charges and the nationally televised hearings that mesmerized and divided the American people on the issue of sexual harassment, the Senate Judiciary Committee voted to confirm Thomas.

Since that time, Hill has received more than 40,000 letters and 1,000 speaking requests. Despite critics' predictions that she would use her notoriety for personal gain, she has not written a sensational book, sold her story for a television movie, or appeared on the talk-show circuit. She refuses to pose for photos and turns down nearly all media requests. Hill has now begun a sabbatical from her usual duties of teaching commercial law, in part to analyze the prospects for founding an institute devoted to researching racism and sexism. When she does speak, she avoids rehashing the charges against Thomas and instead discusses the history and effect of sexual harassment and discrimination. "Sexual harassment is used as a tool of exclusion," she tells her audiences. In a speech before the Women Judges Fund for Justice, she noted that "the nation's courts often misunderstand women victims. . . . One of the things that became quite evident last year during the hearings was the Senate did not grasp the seriousness of sexual harassment and the pervasiveness of it. And unfortunately, it was because of a lack of perspective."

Public opinion polls have shown an increase in the number of people who believe Hill's allegations about Thomas. A *Wall Street Journal*-NBC poll taken in September 1992 found that 44 percent of those surveyed believed Hill, up from 24 percent in 1991. Belief in Thomas's testimony dropped from 47 percent to 34 percent.

Freada Klein (1952–)

Dr. Freada Klein has worked on issues of discrimination and diversity since the early 1970s. In 1976, she co-founded the Alliance Against Sexual Coercion in Boston, one of the first organizations in the United States to offer comprehensive services, training, and consultation on the topic of sexual harassment to both the private and public sectors. She assisted in the formation of similar organizations in Connecticut, Ohio, and Canada. She is the author of a number of articles and co-authored the book, *Fighting Sexual Harassment: An Advocacy Handbook,* one of the first manuals about sexual harassment. The Alliance Against Sexual Coercion was founded because Klein and three associates who had worked in rape crises centers recognized that most women had complaints about what Klein decided to call "sexual coercion" in their workplaces—including requests for sex in return for jobs and actual assaults.

More recently, Klein has consulted with dozens of organizations to help them develop harassment policies, grievance procedures, and training programs, including General Motors Corporation and Harvard University. Her research on discrimination and diversity surveys for corporations and universities included the first large, methodologically sound study on the issue for the Merit System Protection Board. She was also a consultant on the first major Defense Department study, the *Harvard Business Review/Redbook* study, and many others. She received a fellowship from the Social Science Research Council for her doctoral dissertation on sexual harassment. In 1988, Klein completed a survey of the Fortune 500 manufacturing and service firms for *Working Woman* magazine to determine the effectiveness of corporate efforts to address sexual harassment. Klein frequently speaks to professional associations and conferences, and guest lectures in educational institutions on sexual harassment issues. She also serves as an expert witness in sexual harassment litigation. Recently Klein was invited to testify in hearings before the U.S. House of Representatives' Labor and Education Committee on the proposed Civil Rights Bill of 1991, during which she provided data from the results of various surveys. During the Senate confirmation hearings of Clarence Thomas, Klein was asked to provide commentary on several television shows and she was quoted extensively in press reports on the subject.

Formerly the Director of Organizational Development for Lotus Development Corporation, Klein currently heads Klein Associates, Inc., in Cambridge, an organizational development and human resource consulting firm. Klein holds a Ph.D. in social policy and research from Brandeis University, where she concentrated on employment policy. She received her B.A. in criminology with highest honors from the University of California at Berkeley.

Judith Ellen Kurtz (1948–)

As the managing attorney for Equal Rights Advocates, Inc. (ERA), a nonprofit legal and educational corporation whose purpose is to end sex discrimination, Kurtz has been involved in a number of important legal cases of sexual harassment and other kinds of discrimination against women. She also contributed to the plaintiff's Supreme Court brief in *Meritor Savings Bank v. Vinson*. Today, ERA continues to bring important test cases concerning the issue of sexual harassment, including a recent action against the City of San Francisco Police Department.

After graduation from Hastings College of Law, Kurtz began her career in private practice by specializing in domestic relations and criminal law. She has worked as an attorney with Equal Rights Advocates since 1978, where she was promoted to managing attorney in 1986. In addition to sponsoring complex litigation, ERA provides advice and counseling for employees and employers, along with public education and community outreach. As the senior staff attorney, Kurtz oversees the litigation as well as the counseling and educational activities of the staff. The office has a hotline for sex discrimination cases; Kurtz reports that sexual harassment complaints still account for more calls than any other category of discrimination complaint.

A frequent speaker on the issue of sex discrimination around the country, Kurtz has also served as an instructor at San Francisco State University, teaching a course on women and the law. She is a graduate of the State University of New York at Buffalo and co-author of *Bargaining for Equality,* a guide to legal and collective bargaining solutions for workplace problems that particularly affect women.

John Leo (1935–)

John Leo is the widely read "On Society" columnist for *U.S. News & World Report.* His column is syndicated nationally by Universal

Press. In that position, he has written numerous columns addressing the issue of sexual harassment, rape, sexual discrimination, and other gender issues. With regard to the issue of sexual harassment, he has taken what he calls a "yes but" position. Admitting that the issue is an important one that can do serious harm to victims and their careers, he has argued that some programs, authors, and judges have gone too far. He has criticized campus programs that address the issue of sexual harassment and other gender issues as examples of a new wave of "political correctness on campus," a movement he finds dangerous to the role of academic freedom and free speech. He has also criticized the reasonable woman standard articulated by some recent cases as placing sexual harassment "in the same category as violations of college speech and behavior codes, which often turn on the feelings of the aggrieved rather than any objective and definable offense. . . . [I]f feelings are trumps, how do we know when sexism and harassment end and hypersensitivity begins?" He has written that "the reasonable-woman standard is insulting to women because it shrinks what ought to be a universal standard of fairness into a merely tribal one." Leo has also been critical of the feminist perspective on rape, arguing that it is not an act of bias against women.

Before joining *U.S. News* in September 1988, Leo covered the social sciences and intellectual trends for *Time* magazine and the *New York Times.* He also reported on religion for the *Times,* and wrote essays and humor. Leo is a former associate editor of *Commonweal* magazine, former book editor of the sociology magazine, *Society,* and a former deputy Administrator of New York City's Environmental Protection Administration. He launched the "Press Clips" column in the *Village Voice,* and is the author of a book of humor, *How the Russians Invented Baseball and Other Essays of Enlightenment* (1989). He earned a degree with honors from the University of Toronto in 1957 in philosophy and history.

Judith L. Lichtman (1940–)

Judith Lichtman is the president of the Women's Legal Defense Fund, an organization whose mission is to assert women's legal rights. Since the 1970s, she has been involved in crafting legal arguments and influencing public policy on the issue of sexual harassment and other discrimination issues. She was one of the attorneys involved in one of the first federal cases to consider the issue of sexual harassment, *Barnes v. Costell (Train)*. She also appeared as an advocate before the EEOC to convince that agency to promulgate its first guidelines on the issue of sexual harassment and successfully lobbied Congress on the 1991 Civil Rights Act to expand the damage provisions relating to sexual harassment. She testified against Clarence Thomas's nomination to the Supreme Court.

Prior to assuming her position as president of the Women's Legal Defense Fund in 1988, Lichtman served as the executive director of the fund. Before that, she was the legal advisor to the Commonwealth of Puerto Rico, a consultant and senior attorney at the U.S. Commission on Civil Rights, a staff assistant at the Urban Coalition, and an instructor in the history and political science departments at Jackson State College. A long-time civil rights activist, Lichtman has served on the Glass Ceiling Commission for the Labor Department under Lynn Martin, been the co-chair of the Leadership Conference on Civil Rights, and acted as a member of many other groups. She was a founding member of the Women's Law and Public Policy Fellowship Program and of the Alliance for Justice, as well as serving on the Advisory Committee of the ACLU Women's Rights Project. She has won a variety of public service and legal awards, including the Association of Trial Lawyers of American Humanitarian Award, the American Bar Association Silver Gavel Award, and many others. Lichtman was named as one of the 100 Most Powerful Women of Washington in 1989 by *Washingtonian* magazine and as one of America's 100 Most Important Women by *Ladies Home Journal* in 1988.

She has published widely on the areas of sex discrimination. She recalls that she went to law school because, "for me, being a lawyer meant having a license to be an activist." A tireless advocate of women's rights, she asserts, "I define a feminist as somebody who believes in the equality of all people and has a commitment to equal justice, somebody who has a vision of everyone being able to be economically independent and treated fairly."

Catharine A. MacKinnon (1946–)

Catharine MacKinnon is a central figure in feminist legal thought and the author of the pioneering work, *The Sexual Harassment of Working Women*. As such, she has been a frequent target of critics such as columnist John Leo, who lambasted her "pinched view" of sexuality as eroticized male power. MacKinnon was the first to articulate in a comprehensive book the argument that sexual harassment is sex discrimination and a violation of Title VII. She is the author of numerous articles in scholarly journals on feminist theory, pornography, and the law in women's lives. MacKinnon has participated as both an expert witness and with expert briefs in major sexual harassment and women's rights cases, including *Thoreson v. Penthouse,* a case in which she argued that punitive damages should be available for sexual harassment in cases involving women and pornography. She also assisted with the case of *Alexander v. Yale,* arguing that sexual harassment in education violates Title IX. MacKinnon has served on various legal committees, testified before the U.S. Senate on the Pornography Victims Protection Act, written ordinances against pornography, and given extensive public lectures, workshops, speeches, media appearances, and interviews on the issues of sexual equality and the law. During the Clarence Thomas hearings, she provided extensive commentary on one of the major networks. Currently, she fields two to three speech requests per day. MacKinnon now focuses her efforts on pornography issues rather than sexual harassment. Pornography, she believes, will be a much more difficult battle for women because businesses make money on pornography, while "sexual harassment costs business."

A tenured professor of law at the University of Michigan, MacKinnon has also been a visiting professor of law at Yale Law School, Harvard Law School, Stanford, the Chicago Law School, and several others. In addition, she has served as a visiting scholar at the Institute for Research on Women and Gender at Stanford University. She has authored nine law-course casebooks on subjects such as sex equality, feminism and/or socialism, sexuality and legality, and pornography. She received her J.D. from Yale Law School in 1977 and her Ph.D. in political science in 1987. Her undergraduate degree was from Smith College. Among her academic honors are the Smith Medal from Smith College, the Honorary Doctor of Laws from Harverfore College, and the Doctor of Humane Letters from Reed College.

Eleanor Holmes Norton (1937–)

Congresswoman Eleanor Holmes Norton, a fourth-generation Washingtonian, currently serves as the Washington, D.C., representative to Congress. Previously, she held the office of chair of the Equal Employment Opportunity Commission under President

Jimmy Carter, the only woman to hold that position. Under her direction, the Commission in 1980 drafted the first guidelines on sexual harassment. The guidelines affirmed that sexual harassment was unlawful discrimination because of sex. As a member of Congress, Norton has also urged the House and the Senate to endorse a sexual harassment policy based on the guidelines she wrote in 1980. She herself has signed the policy and mandated its terms in her own congressional office. She spoke out from the floor of the House on the Anita Hill charges against Clarence Thomas, stating that "I feel obligated because I am a black woman who cannot help but share some of the lonely pain Professor Anita Hill has courageously chosen to bear. . . . I cannot know where the truth lies, but I cannot imagine why Professor Hill would have chosen to invent a story she knew would submit her to public torment." Norton was also one of several congresswomen who demanded that the Senate investigate Hill's charges. She has spoken and written about the controversy, most notably in *Ms.* magazine.

In addition to her service at the EEOC, Norton served as the chair of the New York City Commission on Human Rights, where she held what may have been the first public hearings on the issue of sexual harassment in the late 1970s, and as a tenured professor of law at Georgetown University. A nationally recognized commentator, writer, civil rights and women's rights leader, and the recipient of 50 honorary degrees, Norton has been named one of the 100 most important women in America by *Ladies Home Journal* and one of the most powerful women in Washington by *Washingtonian* magazine. Norton received her B.A. from Antioch College, and then simultaneously earned a master's degree in American studies from Yale Graduate School and a law degree from Yale Law School. She has served on the boards of three Fortune 500 companies and the board of the Rockefeller Foundations, as well as the Board of Governors of the D.C. Bar Association and as a trustee of many professional, civic, and civil rights organizations.

Michele A. Paludi (1954–)

Dr. Michele Paludi was one of the first, and remains one of the foremost, researchers on academic and workplace sexual harassment. She is the editor of *Ivory Power: Sexual Harassment on Campus* and co-author of *Academic and Workplace Harassment: A Resource*

Manual and the forthcoming *Working 9 to 5: Women, Men, Sex, and Power. Ivory Power* was selected as the Outstanding Book in Human Rights by the Gustavus Myers Center for Human Rights. For five years, Paludi facilitated a research laboratory on sexual harassment located at Hunter College, where she was a full professor of psychology. Her most recent research focuses on the academic sexual harassment of women of color. She has gained national media attention for her work on the psychological impact of sexual harassment and is the host of the new City University of New York and Schenectady, New York, television program *Gender Matters.* Currently, Paludi offers education and training in issues related to sexual harassment and gender to private corporations, government, and educational institutions. She has received several awards for her research work, including the 1992 Progress in Equity Award from the New York State chapter of the American Association of University Women. The author of numerous scholarly papers on sexual harassment, Paludi has presented her findings to several professional conventions, including the American Psychological Association.

Paludi takes a feminist stance in her work. In *Ivory Power,* for example, she wrote that "[s]exual harassment, like rape, incest, and battering, represents male expressions of power and dominance over women." She emphasizes that "[s]exual harassment is not simply an annoyance or flirtation. It can mean the difference between passing a college course and failing one, between being given a raise or being fired. . . ." Her research has focused on exploding myths such as the idea that the victim invited the harassment or that only attractive women are harassed.

Mary P. Rowe (1936–)

When Mary Rowe started working as a special assistant to the president of the Massachusetts Institute of Technology (MIT) in 1973, she began to notice a surprising trend: about one-fifth of all the problems students brought to her involved some aspect of sex bias or other gender issues. She began meeting with groups of students and eventually developed a training program relating to these issues. Her early work with those students led to her becoming a nationally recognized expert in the field of sexual harassment problems and training. Currently, she serves as an MIT ombudsman, where she is designated as an impartial counsellor and informal complaint-handler. Anyone in the MIT community may contact her for any reason; they are encouraged to do so by MIT's complaint policy and by booklets for students and employees called "Tell Someone."

Rowe believes that MIT is the first major employer in the country to have "named" harassment as a problem and to have developed procedures to deal with concerns. She authored *Stopping Sexual Harassment: A Guide to Options and Resources at MIT*, which has served as a guide for other employers. Because of her role in developing the MIT sexual harassment program, she is also involved in consulting, teaching, research, and writing for other organizations on the issue. In addition, she also serves as a consultant to other ombudsman programs. She is the author of numerous articles on such issues as the role of women and work, child care, and the role of corporate ombudsmen. Rowe is also the past president of the Corporate Ombudsman Association. She believes that with the increasing diversity in the U.S. workforce, lawmakers and corporate decision makers will need to prevent and deal with sexual and racial harassment. A corporate ombudsman, she finds, can help resolve those complaints. Rowe holds a Ph.D. in economics from Columbia University and a B.A. in history (international relations) from Swarthmore College.

Karen Lee Sauvigné (1948–)

Karen Sauvigné was a co-founder and the executive director, from 1976 to 1983, of the Working Women's Institute (WWI), the pioneering organization that may have been the first to focus on sexual harassment in employment. The institute was established in 1975 to bring national attention to the widespread, but theretofore unspoken, problem of sexual harassment in employment. Sauvigné designated and implemented the institute's program of research and public education on sexual harassment and other equal employment issues. A recognized authority on sexual harassment, she has appeared on television, testified before congressional hearings, conducted workshops, and served as a policy consultant for government agencies, corporations, labor unions, educational institutions, and community groups. She has written articles and delivered speeches on sexual harassment in various publications and before various groups, including a presentation at the U.N. Decade for Women Forum in Nairobi, Kenya.

Sauvigné now serves as the associate director of continuing legal education, training, and consultation at CUNY Law School at

Queens College. Before assuming that position, she was the director of development at the law school. She has also served on the faculty and as a research director at Cornell University in the Human Affairs Program. Early in her career, she worked as the field coordinator for the College for Human Services and was the assistant national director of the Civil Rights Research Council. Sauvigné has received a number of awards, including the *Mlle* Award from *Mademoiselle* magazine for outstanding achievement and the Susan B. Anthony Award from the National Organization for Women. She was also designated as one of Eighty Women to Watch in the Eighties by *Ms.* magazine. She has served on the Board of the New York University Public Interest Law Foundation and the Institute for Women and Work of the New York State School of Industrial and Labor Relations/Cornell, and the Asian American Legal Defense and Education Fund. She holds a master's degree in comparative history from Rutgers University.

Phyllis Schlafly (1924–)

Born Phyllis MacAlpin Stewart in 1924 in St. Louis, Missouri, Phyllis Schlafly has been a leader in various conservative movements for 30 years. Considered to be a major force behind the defeat of the Equal Rights Amendment in many states, she is the president and founder of a conservative organization called the Eagle Forum. Her *Phyllis Schlafly Report* has been published monthly for 25 years. She is a lawyer, author of 13 books, syndicated columnist, and radio commentator. Her radio commentaries are heard on 270 stations, and her weekly live radio program on education is heard on 45 stations. Schlafly has testified before more than 50 congressional and state legislative committees, advocating her conservative agenda on such on topics as the Equal Rights Amendment, treaties, nuclear weaponry, education, child care, comparable worth, parental leave, and federal spending. One of her books, *A Choice Not an Echo* is one of the ten best-selling conservative books of all time. Schlafly is a Phi Beta Kappa graduate of Washington University and of Washington University Law School. She also received a master's degree in political science from Harvard University. Schlafly is the mother of six children and lives in Alton, Illinois.

On the issue of sexual harassment, Schlafly led an unsuccessful effort to repeal the EEOC guidelines during the Reagan administration, testifying at 1981 Labor Commission hearings that "sexual harassment is not a problem for the virtuous woman, except in the rarest of cases. When a woman walks across the room, she speaks with a universal body language that most men intuitively understand." In a November 1991 *Phyllis Schlafly Report* entitled *Feminism Falls on Its Face,* she wrote that "[t]he confirmation of Clarence Thomas was a personal victory for an honorable man who was the victim of a savage eleventh-hour ambush by feminists in special-interest groups and in the media." Claiming that the hearings were the result of a conspiracy between feminist and liberal politicians who would have been willing to use any tactic to defeat Clarence Thomas, Schlafly went on to write that "unscrupulous feminists and liberals will conspire to use false charges of sexual harassment to destroy a man who stands in their way." Schlafly doubted that a law school graduate could be a victim of sexual harassment, observing that the "very nature of being a lawyer is to thrive in a hostile environment. A lawyer complaining about this is like a doctor complaining about working in a 'bloody environment.' "

Patricia S. Schroeder (1940–)

Patricia Scott Schroeder, a Democrat, represents the First Congressional District of Colorado, comprising most of the city and county of Denver. Schroeder was elected in 1972 and reelected 9 times, winning by 64 percent in 1990 and an even higher percentage in 1992. Schroeder is the dean of the Colorado Congressional Delegation, as well as the most senior woman in Congress. She has served in the House leadership as a Democratic Whip since 1978, and was appointed Deputy Whip in 1987. Schroeder, who in 1987 explored a bid for the presidency, was rated in a 1988 Gallup poll as one of the six most respected women in America.

On the issue of sexual harassment, in the fall of 1991, Schroeder made headlines when a picture of her marching a group of congresswomen from the House to the Senate was published in newspapers around the country. She was instrumental in galvanizing the group to force the Senate Judiciary Committee to hold public hearings on the claim of Professor Anita Hill that she was harassed by Clarence Thomas. In addition, she persuaded the House to hold hearings in 1992 on the question of sexual harassment in the Navy after the Tailhook incident, and helped force the Navy to conduct a more thorough investigation. As a result, a Navy group displayed a lewd picture of her at one of its meetings;

with typical Schroeder wit, the congresswoman displayed the image during the House hearings, using the incident as evidence of the need for sexual harassment policies and trainings in the military. As a member of the House Armed Services Committee, Schroeder has long been an advocate of women in the military, working to prevent all kinds of sex discrimination in that institution.

Throughout her congressional tenure, Schroeder has made women's rights issues, family issues, women's health issues, and defense burden sharing her top priorities. She is the leading House sponsor of the Family and Medical Leave Act, which gives workers a right to a job-guaranteed unpaid leave for family emergencies such as birth, adoption, or serious illness. Schroeder played a major role in the passage of the Voting Rights Act extension and the Civil Rights Act of 1984. She was also a sponsor of the Civil Rights Act of 1991. In 1989, she introduced legislation to increase the federal commitment to birth control and infertility research, which was incorporated in the Women's Health Equity Act. She is a House sponsor of the Freedom of Choice Act, a bill that would put into federal law the principles of *Roe v. Wade*, securing a woman's right to choose to terminate her pregnancy.

Schroeder was born in Portland, Oregon, attended grade school in Texas, junior high in Ohio, and high school in Iowa. She graduated magna cum laude from the University of Minnesota, where she was a member of the Phi Beta Kappa honor society. Schroeder received her J.D. from Harvard Law School in 1964. Prior to her election to Congress, Schroeder practiced law and lectured at Denver colleges.

Joseph M. Sellers (1953–)

Joseph Sellers was one of the lead attorneys for the plaintiff, Mechelle Vinson, in the Supreme Court case establishing that sexual harassment did indeed violate Title VII of the Civil Rights Act. He has also served as counsel in a number of other important sexual harassment cases, including *Delgado v. Leeman*, a case establishing important precedent on gender-based harassment and hostile work environment. In an area of the law where many cases settle before trial, Sellers estimates that he has actually litigated 10 to 12 sexual harassment cases and receives around 1,000 requests to litigate EEOC-related claims each year.

Currently, Sellers is the director of the Equal Employment Opportunity Program of the Washington Lawyers' Committee for

Civil Rights Under Law. In this capacity, he had litigated dozens of civil rights cases on behalf of several thousand plaintiffs before various federal and state courts and administrative agencies. The claims in these cases have alleged discrimination on grounds ranging from race and color to sexual harassment to disability and family responsibility. In addition, he oversees the operation of an EEO Intake Program through the Washington Lawyers' Committee.

Sellers has also served as legal counsel to two civil rights testing programs. In the first, he assisted in the development of a professional program to test the delivery of taxi service in the District of Columbia and later served as counsel to plaintiffs in the only litigation challenging the discriminatory practices committed by taxi companies. In the second, he assisted in the development of the first Equal Employment Testing Program and acted as counsel to the plaintiffs in the first EEO cases filed in the courts based upon EEO testing evidence. Sellers has also testified, on a number of occasions, before committees of the United States Congress regarding various civil rights matters. He has chaired a two-year study of the federal EEO complaints processing system, the results of which were presented to the Subcommittee on Employment and Housing of the House Government Operations Committee. He has also lectured on various equal employment and other civil rights subjects, ranging from the design of affirmative actions programs and managing a diverse workforce to the evaluation and litigation of various types of civil rights claims. He is a graduate of Brown University and Case Western Reserve School of Law, where he served as research editor of the *Law Review*. Sellers has also been active in political campaigns and privately practiced law.

Anne E. Simon (1950–)

Anne Simon tried the case of *Alexander v. Yale,* one of the pivotal cases on sexual harassment which established the legal precedent that sexual harassment in universities is a violation of Title IX of the Civil Rights Act. About that case, Simon stated that she expected other follow-up cases and was "astounded that universities all gave in right away." As a result of *Alexander,* most colleges and universities now have policies against sexual harassment. Simon also served as a staff attorney for the NOW Legal Defense and Education Fund, where she counseled women on sexual harassment and other employment issues. A magna cum laude graduate of Radcliffe College, she received her J.D. degree from Yale Law School in 1976. She has written on the issue of sexual harassment and other women's rights issues, including the chapter on sexual harassment in *Every Woman's Legal Guide* (along with P. L. Crocker), and currently serves as the chief administrative law judge for the Massachusetts Department of Environmental Protection. She has also worked as a staff attorney for the Center for Constitutional Rights in New York City, where she focused on civil rights, international human rights, and public education. She taught at the New York University School of Law, where she conducted a seminar on women and the law. Early in her career, she had a general practice with the New Haven Law Collective, where she focused on sex and race discrimination, family law, nonprofit corporations, housing, and consumer law.

Arlen Specter (1930–)

Senator Arlen Specter, a two-term Republican moderate and former prosecutor, made an indelible impression upon the public consciousness when he grilled Anita Hill as the designated Republican questioner during the Clarence Thomas confirmation hearings. Viewed by many observers as an unnecessarily relentless and probing examiner, Specter's role in the drama was ironic, since, before that time, the senator had had a reputation as a lifelong advocate of civil rights, a man sensitive to many women's issues, and a pro-choice Republican. His role in the Judiciary Committee hearing debates earned him a touchy reelection contest against Lynn Yeakel, a political unknown who, because of the hearings, came out of nowhere to oppose Specter at the Democratic convention, telling a national television audience, "I can no longer stand by after this senator humiliated American women with his shameless performance last fall." During a five-way Democratic primary, without the party endorsement, Yeakel aired a television ad that ignored her primary opponents and aimed instead directly at Specter. In the ad, Specter's voice asked Hill a question, then Yeakel's voice asked voters: "Did this make you as angry as it made me?" Evidently it did. Yeakel shot from 1 percent in state polls in March to a decisive primary win in April, but lost narrowly to Specter in November 1992.

A former district attorney, Specter has shown agility on two conservative Supreme Court nominees. In 1987, right *after* he was reelected to the Senate, he angered Pennsylvania right-wingers by blocking Reagan nominee Robert H. Bork. Then, in 1991, he eagerly supported Bush nominee Clarence Thomas, pleasing the political right *before* seeking reelection this year. "I call them as I see them," Specter stated.

Specter has run for office nine times within the last four decades, losing almost as often as winning. He failed in bids for Philadelphia mayor, for a third term as district attorney, for the Republican nomination to the Senate, and for the Republican nomination for governor. Then, in 1980, he won the Senate race.

Arlen Specter was born to immigrant parents in Wichita, Kansas, and grew up in the small town of Russell. After graduating Phi Beta Kappa from the University of Pennsylvania in 1951, he served in the Air Force's Office of Special Investigations for two years during the Korean War. He attended Yale Law School, where he was an editor on the *Yale Law Journal.* Specter began his public service career as assistant district attorney of Philadelphia, obtaining the first national conviction of labor racketeers. He quickly attained a reputation as a tough and effective prosecutor, which led to an appointment in 1964 as assistant counsel to the Warren Commission to investigate the assassination of President Kennedy. He is credited with a major role in the investigation and with developing the single-bullet theory. In Congress, he serves as the ranking Republican member of the Veterans Affairs Committee, the Appropriations Committee's Subcommittee on Labor, Health and Human Services, the Education Committee, and the Judiciary Committee's Subcommittee on the Constitution.

Nan D. Stein (1947–)

Nan Stein was the first researcher in the United States to define and survey student-to-student sexual harassment in high schools and grade schools. Her pioneering curriculum and resource guide for schools, *Who's Hurt and Who's Liable: Sexual Harassment in Massachusetts Schools,* first published in 1979, has been used nationally as a model for a sexual harassment curriculum. Her focus has been on sexual harassment of students at the elementary and secondary levels. Currently, Stein directs the Center for Research on Women at Wellesley College, where she is at work on a national research project on sexual harassment and child sexual abuse in schools. In cooperation with *Seventeen* magazine and the NOW Legal Defense Fund's Project on Equal Education Rights, Stein designed the first nationwide survey of sexual harassment and teens. The survey questionnaire was published in the magazine in September 1992 and the results will be available in 1993. Stein reports that letters arrived by the hundreds every day in response to the magazine's poll, screaming to be read; "Open," "Urgent," "Please Read," were scribbled on the envelopes.

Stein became interested in the subject in the late 1970s when she worked alongside a group of high school students at the Massachusetts Department of Education. At the time, she thought the problem of sexual harassment took place when someone in power bothered someone of lesser authority. In watching boys work with girls in her office, however, she realized that the boys were constantly recounting sexual conquests, cornering the girls, or telling sexual jokes. The girls "were getting very disturbed by this." After talking with the students, Stein found that they said it "goes on all the time." This discovery led to a career of studying, writing, and speaking about the issue. Sexual harassment in schools, Stein believes, is a serious problem because it can escalate into assault and battery—a phenomenon she sees increasing. She has discussed the subject on national television and consulted with schools around the country. Stein holds a B.A. in history from the University of Wisconsin, an M.A.T. from Antioch College Graduate School of Education, and a doctorate in education from Harvard University.

Nadine Taub (1943–)

Nadine Taub is a professor at Rutgers School of Law and is the director of the Women's Rights Litigation Clinic, an influential program that has been responsible for litigating a number of important women's rights cases. Taub was the lead attorney in one of the first cases to establish that Title VII provided a case of action for sexual harassment, *Tompkins v. Public Service Electric & Gas Co.* After the decision on the law was issued, Taub negotiated a highly favorable settlement that included a substantial monetary award, attorney's fees, a change in the company's policy, the institution of grievance procedures, and a company-conducted information program concerning laws against discrimination. She has also worked on significant sexual harassment cases such as *Keil v. Toys R Us* (hostile environment) and *Thoreson v. Penthouse* and on the appeal in *Yale v. Alexander*. She is one of the authors of the forthcoming *Sex Discrimination Law: Cases and Materials* (the second edition of a casebook first issued in 1974). Taub has also written a number of articles on discrimination and reproductive rights issues, including sexual harassment.

A frequent lecturer on the subject of sexual harassment, discrimination, and other women's rights issues, Taub emphasizes that "it's important to recognize that litigation may not always be the most appropriate way to address the problem." She recommends that women organize in groups to fight sexual harassment and that they confront their employers. Having worked closely with women who have brought sexual harassment claims, she recognizes their ambivalence about collecting damage awards. These women sometimes feel that "to bring the case is to say I'm worth money for sex." Currently, Taub and her center are investigating the new area of sexual harassment in housing.

Clarence Thomas (1948–)

Clarence Thomas was nominated by President George Bush as Associate Justice of the United States Supreme Court and took the oath of office on October 23, 1991. Prior to his service on the high court, he had served on the U.S. Court of Appeals for the District of Columbia Circuit since March 12, 1990. His confirmation hearings before the Senate Judiciary Committee in October 1991 fueled a national debate on the issue of sexual harassment when Anita Hill, a professor at the University of Oklahoma School of Law, charged that he had sexually harassed her when she worked for him at the Equal Employment Opportunity Commission and the Department of Education.

Thomas was born in Pinpoint, Georgia, to a teenaged mother in a house with dirt floors, no plumbing or electricity, and newspapers for wallpaper. In accepting Bush's nomination to the Supreme Court, he recalled that "as a child, I could not dare dream that I would ever see the Supreme Court—not to mention be nominated to it." Raised as a Catholic, Thomas attended Conception Seminary and Holy Cross College, where he graduated cum laude in 1971. After receiving his degree from Yale Law School in 1974, Thomas served as Assistant Attorney General of Missouri, was briefly in private practice, and worked as a legislative assistant to Senator John C. Danforth of Missouri before being appointed as Assistant Secretary for Civil Rights with the U.S. Department of Education. He served as chairman of the U.S. Equal Employment Opportunity Commission from 1982 through

1990, before being appointed by President Bush to the D.C. Circuit Court.

Professor Anita Hill's charges resulted in extensive televised hearings before an all-male Senate Judiciary Committee. Thomas totally denied the charges, stating that he had "been racking my brains and eating my insides trying to think of what I may have said or done to Anita Hill to lead her to allege that I was interested in her in more than a professional way" and claiming that he was the victim of a "high tech lynching." Indignantly, Thomas declared that the hearings were "not American; this is Kafkaesque." At one low point, he stated that "no job is worth what I have been through." Despite several days of hearings on the issue, Thomas was confirmed by the committee and later the full Senate. Millions of Americans watched the televised proceedings, however, and read the extensive press coverage. The debate introduced many, for the first time, to the issues of sexual harassment.

Karen (K. C.) Wagner (1951–)

K. C. Wagner was the counseling, program, and executive director for Working Women's Institute from 1980 through 1987, where she helped coordinate a brief bank and conducted research. The institute may have been the first organization in the country to focus on the field of sexual harassment. In commenting on the history of the drive to raise awareness on the issue of sexual harassment, Wagner emphasized that it was a diverse, "grass roots movement." Currently, she is a counselor, corporate trainer, and consultant specializing in the prevention of sexual harassment and gender bias in employment and academia. Wagner has addressed these issues as they relate to traditional and nontraditional work environments for women in over 150 corporations, unions, nonprofit, and public service organizations and academic institutions. Wagner provided testimony as an expert on sexual harassment in two significant cases, *Broderick v. Securities & Exchange Commission* and *Robinson v. Jacksonville Shipyards*. She has also appeared on numerous television shows as an expert on the issue of sexual harassment and has been interviewed by many national newspapers and magazines on the subject. Wagner co-authored a study entitled "Results of a Survey on Gender Bias and Sexual Harassment in the Federal Aviation Administration Eastern Region" and other articles on gender issues. She is currently on the EEO Studies Staff at Cornell University's New York State School of

Industrial and Labor Relations. She holds a master's of social work degree from Hunter College School of Social Work and graduated cum laude from the University of Pennsylvania.

Susan L. Webb (1948–)

Webb is the president of Pacific Resource Development Group, Inc., a Seattle-based consulting firm specializing in human relations issues and offering consulting and training in the area of sexual harassment. She is the editor of the *Webb Report*, the only national newsletter on the subject of sexual harassment. She has written three books, including the recent *Step Forward: Sexual Harassment in the Workplace*. Frequently interviewed on television, for magazines, and on radio about the issue of sexual harassment, Webb also provides expert witness testimony on sexual harassment and conducts investigations of sexual harassment complaints.

Webb reports that the first sexual harassment workshop she conducted was for 30 men in the Street and Sewer Maintenance Division of a public works department in 1981. They called it "the good ol' boy department." Five years later, she conducted another workshop for a similar group. When she went up to the front of the training room, she found that one of the men had taped a tampon, colored with red ink so it appeared bloody, to the overhead projector. When she asked him why, "he said he'd heard that 'I was a bitch.' " Since that time, she has seen the interest in sexual harassment training "run the gamut, from high interest to outright hostility to support and understanding." Yet, she reports,

> the problem that bothers me the most is that in all these workshops, whether in 1981 or 1991, the same questions keep coming up over and over. The lack of knowledge and understanding . . . is appalling and sometimes discouraging to anyone who works in the field. There is so much more work to do even to make a dent in the problem.

Webb received her bachelor's degree in economics and a master's degree in human relations from the University of Oklahoma.

Reference

Phelps, Timothy M., and Helen Winternity, *Capital Games* (New York: Hyperion, 1992).

4

Facts and Statistics

THIS CHAPTER PROVIDES GENERAL FACTS AND STATISTICS relating to sexual harassment, so that readers may evaluate what they see and hear about sexual harassment from other sources. Because the laws and the whole issue of sexual harassment are still relatively new and evolving, these facts and statistics are necessarily limited. The information given is as factual as possible, but in this rapidly changing field, the reader should be aware that even this information may soon be outdated. The significance or meaning of any particular fact or statistic will of course vary, depending on the individual point of view. Because the presentation of facts is necessarily brief, suggestions for further reading are included where appropriate. This chapter consists of an overview of the law, including statutes and important cases; future trends in sexual harassment law; and statistics and surveys relating to sexual harassment.

Overview of the Laws on Sexual Harassment in Employment

Three categories of laws cover sexual harassment in the workplace: (1) the United States Civil Rights Act, administered by the United States Equal Employment Opportunities Commission (EEOC); (2) state fair employment practices (FEP) statutes; and (3) common law tort principles. Each is separately considered in this section.

The Civil Rights Act and the EEOC

Title VII of the Civil Rights Act (Title VII) prohibits discrimination on the basis of sex. Sexual harassment has been found by the courts to be a form of sex discrimination in employment under this law. The law applies to most employers in the United States, if they employ 15 or more employees. The EEOC administers this federal statute.

The EEOC is charged with the responsibility of investigating employee harassment and discrimination complaints. The agency has subpoena power to compel the employer and others to turn over evidence. Generally, the EEOC negotiates with the employer in a process called *conciliation* to protect the harassed employee's rights. If negotiation fails, the agency has the power to file suit. Because of the number of claims and the limited resources of the agency, however, in most cases the EEOC issues a "right-to-sue" letter to the employee, allowing her to file a lawsuit to enforce her rights under the Civil Rights Act. Filing a claim with the EEOC is a necessary first step before the employee may start her own lawsuit.

The Civil Rights Act provides for five kinds of relief, if an employee is successful:

1. *Reinstatement and promotion.* The court may order the company to rehire the employee or promote her.
2. *Back pay and benefits.* The court may award any salary and benefits the employee lost because she was fired or forced to leave, demoted, or passed over for a promotion.
3. *Money damages.* The court may award money for any personal injuries the employee is able to prove, such as physical problems as the result of an actual assault or any stress-related problems. The amount awarded is limited to out-of-pocket losses, such as medical expenses and other damages, up to a limit—which varies depending on the number of people employed—of between $50,000 and $300,000.
4. *Injunctive relief.* A court may direct the company to revise its polices to prevent harassment in the future, conduct sexual harassment training, or any other relief the court deems appropriate.
5. *Attorney's fees.* A court may order the company to pay the employee's attorney's fees.

Legal Definitions of Sexual Harassment

Legal definitions of *sexual harassment* vary from state to state, but almost every state extends the minimum protection found in the regulations of the U.S. Equal Employment Opportunity Commission (EEOC). EEOC definitions and standards are the most often used throughout the United States in defining sexual harassment.

The EEOC definition of *sexual harassment* is found in 29 Code of Federal Regulations (CFR) 1604.11(a):

> Harassment on the basis of sex is a violation of [the law]. Unwelcome sexual advances, requests for sexual favors and other verbal or physical conduct of a sexual nature constitute sexual harassment when:
>
> 1. submission to such conduct is made either explicitly or implicitly a term or condition of an individual's employment,
> 2. submission to or rejection of such conduct by an individual is used as the basis for employment decisions affecting such individual, or
> 3. such conduct has the purpose or effect of unreasonably interfering with an individual's work performance or creating an intimidating, hostile or offensive working environment.

The EEOC regulations stress that most sexual harassment cases must be resolved by looking at all the facts in context (29 CFR 1604.11(b)):

> In determining whether alleged conduct constitutes sexual harassment, the [EEOC] will look at the record as a whole and at the totality of the circumstances, such as the nature of the sexual advances and the context in which the alleged incidents occurred. The determination of the legality of a particular action will be made from the facts, on a case-by-case basis.

The terms *quid pro quo* and *hostile environment* are frequently used in the cases and literature about sexual harassment. These are the two major types of sexual harassment cases. *Quid pro quo* harassment occurs when an employee is confronted with sexual demands to keep her job or obtain a promotion. In other words, she has to do "this" to get "that." *Hostile environment* is used to describe other types of cases in which the threat is not as direct. This frequently involves sexually offensive conduct that pervades and poisons the workplace, making it difficult or unpleasant for an employee to do her job.

Although decisions vary, most government investigating agencies or courts consider four factors to determine whether sexual harassment has occurred:

1. Was the behavior sexual in nature?
2. Was the behavior unreasonable?
3. Was the behavior severe or pervasive in the workplace?
4. Was the behavior unwelcome?

BEHAVIOR OF A SEXUAL NATURE   Behavior of a sexual nature that a court or the EEOC may determine to be sexual harassment includes:

1. Sexual advances, propositions, or attempts to obtain sexual favors from an employee.
2. Hostility toward women employees or a particular woman employee. These types of situations range from pranks, threats, and intimidation to highly dangerous physical attacks.
3. Sexual or pornographic pictures, language, and jokes permeating the workplace, creating an environment that is offensive. The sexual commentary and humor in such cases need not be directed at the particular employee, yet she may nevertheless find the atmosphere to be intimidating and offensive. Such an environment places her at a distinct disadvantage with respect to her male co-workers and is therefore discriminatory.

Because courts look at the kind of behavior closely to determine what is illegal sexual harassment, each type of sexual conduct is discussed in more detail here.

SEXUAL ADVANCES OR DEMANDS   Unwelcome sexual advances and propositions are one of the most common forms of sexual harassment. Whether a particular sexual advance is illegal sexual harassment usually depends on who is making the advance.

Sexual advances from a supervisor or other person in authority will be scrutinized more closely than those of co-workers because of the strong possibility of intimidation. Supervisors are in positions of power in the workplace. It is usually presumed that the employer has knowledge of any sexual harassment committed by supervisors, so the employer is almost automatically responsible for its supervisors' actions—whether or not the employer had actual knowledge.

Sexual advances by supervisors frequently involve the classic sex-for-jobs situation. The EEOC regulations state that sexual advances under these circumstances are unlawful if they are "explicitly or implicitly a term or condition of an individual's employment." In other words, if a woman must put up with these demands as part of her job (whether or not she accedes to them), they may qualify as harassment.

In a supervisor-worker relationship, little conduct of a sexual nature is needed to support a finding of harassment. Even a relatively polite request for a date by an employer or supervisor can be the basis of a sexual harassment charge if future work assignments, promotions, or raises appear to depend on acceptance of the demand.

Sexual harassment can arise from unwanted sexual advances even if the person in authority makes a favorable employment decision on behalf of the employee. If a woman submits to an unwelcome sexual advance because of a promise from her supervisor, he is guilty of sexual harassment—whether he delivers on his promise or not. It is the act or threat of using sexual conduct as the basis for making employment decisions that constitutes the sexual harassment. The same rules apply to anyone with power over the employee who threatens to use such power to make an employment decision, even if the person in authority is not the employee's supervisor.

Unwelcome sexual advances or demands from a co-worker can also be the kind of conduct giving rise to sexual harassment claims. Because these cases do not involve a supervisor or someone with power, however, the threat to the woman employee is lessened. In these cases, the courts take a deeper look at all the surrounding circumstances.

In addition, with a supervisor or someone in authority, the company is presumed to know what is going on and therefore is legally responsible for the situation. This presumption of knowledge, however, does not apply to co-workers.

If the sexual solicitation comes from a co-worker and management is not involved, directly or indirectly, the focus is on the nature of the sexual advance. The emphasis is less on the "who" and more on the "how." Many facts are important in determining whether a co-worker has crossed the line from friendly flirting into sexual harassment: the frequency of the solicitation, the nature of the proposition, the language used, the physical gestures, and the behavior of the co-worker. There is no hard-and-fast rule as to how far is too far.

An employer can also be legally responsible for sexual harassment if it creates or allows a situation in which an employee will be sexually harassed by customers, salespersons, visitors, or even passersby. This can happen when the employer places an employee in a situation where it knows or should know that unwelcome sexual advances are likely to occur. A company may, for example, require an employee to dress in sexy clothing, but it is then responsible if customers or passersby make sexual advances or remarks to her. A more serious situation occurs when the employer tries to force an employee to have sex with a client or someone else it wants to please.

A sexual harassment claim may also arise when sexual advances are made to two or more women with differing results. For example, if a supervisor denies a promotion to one employee because she will not sleep with him and then gives the same promotion to another because she will, both women have experienced sexual harassment. The first employee would have a sexual harassment claim based upon the improper denial of her promotion by a person in authority in a sex-for-jobs situation. The second would also have a claim if his sexual advances were unwelcome and she submitted only out of fear of losing the promotion.

In addition, if a supervisor has a mutual affair with one of his employees and gives her promotions and raises in preference over other employees, this type of relationship (especially when combined with abusive behavior toward other employees) can be a form of sexual harassment. These types of cases have come to be known as "paramour preference."

HOSTILITY RELATED TO GENDER   Hostile acts related to an employee's gender are another type of suspect conduct of a sexual nature, even though they may not involve sexual overtures at all. This type of claim involves harassment *because* of a person's gender, rather than sexual harassment as that term is sometimes understood.

Many cases of sexual harassment are based on outright animosity toward a particular woman employee or toward women employees in general. Often the hostility surfaces when a pioneer enters a previously all-male occupation. Other times it comes from a scorned lover. Alternatively, a supervisor may be hostile toward a particular woman employee right from the start and indulge his hostility in ways that he would not think of doing if she were a man.

Some employers have tried to argue that sexual harassment is not involved if a co-worker treats a woman employee with hostility. Sexual harassment, they argue, requires some evidence of sexual overtures to the female employee who registered the complaint. The courts have rejected this argument, finding instead that sexual harassment can exist without explicit sexual misconduct.

Plaintiffs have argued, and some courts have agreed, that hostile conduct is often a thinly disguised effort to force a woman employee out of the workforce. It is sometimes easier to analyze cases involving overt hostility as sexual discrimination cases rather than sexual harassment ones. If a supervisor subjects his female employees to abuse because he would prefer to have men working for him, he is treating them differently than he treats his male employees and is, therefore, discriminating against women. Yet the conceptual difference between a sexual discrimination case and a sexual harassment case is not important, because both are subject to the same legal prohibitions. In fact, the laws against sexual harassment are largely derived from the laws against sexual discrimination.

PORNOGRAPHIC MATERIAL AND LEWD BEHAVIOR   Both the EEOC and the courts are beginning to recognize that pornographic material and lewd behavior in the workplace can create a hostile working environment or "sexually poisoned" workplace for women. The offensiveness is not always directed at a specific individual. Often it is the result of the total effect of many offensive acts that may seem relatively mild when viewed in isolation. The main injurious result of this type of sexual conduct is a working environment that is hostile to working women as a group. The sexually poisoned workplace creates a situation in which discrimination against women flourishes. Plaintiffs have argued—often successfully—that lewd behavior is frequently sexist and woman-hating, revealing discrimination on the job and a different standard of judging male and female employees.

UNREASONABLE CONDUCT   The second legal factor in a sexual harassment case is unreasonableness. The law prohibits only *unreasonable* sexual conduct in the workplace. This is a requirement many critics miss when they argue that trivial or unjust claims of sexual harassment will be allowed by the courts. Some harassing conduct is obviously unreasonable. If a supervisor makes sexual demands on an employee as a condition of getting a job or a raise, for example, this is clearly unreasonable under the legal standard. It is also always unreasonable for an employer to physically assault or attack women employees.

Reasonableness is more difficult to determine when the conduct may be ambiguous or subject to misinterpretation. Courts want to make sure that the employee bringing the case is not complaining about conduct that other people would find trivial. As the *EEOC Compliance Manual* (the handbook for personnel investigating harassment) states, the law should not "serve as a vehicle for vindicating the petty slights suffered by the hypersensitive."

Courts traditionally have used an objective test to determine if conduct is reasonable: Would a "reasonable person" find the subject behavior or occurrence offensive? Recently, however, courts have begun to recognize that there is often a difference in how men and women perceive the same conduct. As one court submitted: "A male supervisor might believe, for example, that it is legitimate for him to tell a female subordinate that she has a 'great figure' or 'nice legs.' The female subordinate, however, may find such comments offensive." *Lipsett v. University of Puerto Rico,* 864 F.2d 881 (1st Cir. 1988). The *EEOC Compliance Manual* urges that the conduct be judged from the viewpoint of the woman employee: "The reasonable person standard should consider the victim's perspective and not stereotyped notions of acceptable behavior." Some courts have begun to agree. As one court noted:

> [M]any women share common concerns which men do not necessarily share. For example, because women are disproportionately victims of rape and sexual assault, women have a stronger incentive to be concerned with sexual behavior. Women who are victims of mild forms of sexual harassment may understandably worry whether a harasser's conduct is merely a prelude to violent sexual assault. Men, who are rarely victims of sexual assault, may view sexual conduct in a vacuum without a full appreciation of the social setting or the underlying threat of violence that a woman may perceive. *Ellison v. Brady,* 924 F.2d 872 (9th Cir. 1991).

This area of the law is still evolving. Ultimately, the Supreme Court may have to settle the debate over whether the standard should be that of a reasonable woman or the traditional reasonable man.

SEVERE OR PERVASIVE BEHAVIOR   The third factor to consider in evaluating sexual behavior is whether it is so severe or so pervasive throughout the workplace that it creates an intimidating, hostile, or offensive working environment. This requirement also guards against the possibility of trivial claims.

This factor is often assumed by the courts in certain types of cases. For example, if a co-worker physically assaults a woman employee, the situation is obviously severe.

EEOC GUIDELINES ON BEHAVIOR   The *EEOC Compliance Manual* sets out guidelines for investigators to follow in determining whether any sexual behavior is severe or pervasive. According to the EEOC, investigators should consider:

Whether the conduct was verbal, physical, or both

How frequently the conduct was repeated

Whether the conduct was hostile and obviously offensive

Whether the alleged harasser was a co-worker or a supervisor

Whether others joined in perpetuating the harassment

Whether the harassment was directed at more than one individual

The *EEOC Compliance Manual* also outlines how conduct should be evaluated using these factors. According to the EEOC, unless there is a single, "quite severe" incident, the investigator should use a weighing process to determine whether the conduct gives rise to a sexual harassment claim. No weighing process is necessary in a quid pro quo situation, however, because the EEOC says that "a single sexual advance may constitute harassment if it is linked to the granting or denial of employment benefits." Cases involving invasive touching or fondling are also usually considered severe, whether or not the incident involved a supervisor. In general, the EEOC considers physical actions to be much more serious than words, because "even a single unwelcome physical advance can seriously poison the victim's working environment." The *EEOC Compliance Manual* takes the position that "the more severe the harassment, the less the need to show a repetitive series of incidents. This is particularly true when the harassment is physical."

THE TOTALITY OF THE CIRCUMSTANCES   In the case of persistent sexual advances from co-workers or a sexually hostile workplace, courts will consider the totality of the working environment. No one fact may be decisive, but the sum total of them all might be. According to one court: "A play cannot be understood on the basis of some of its scenes but only on its entire performance; similarly, a discrimination analysis must concentrate not on individual incidents but on the overall scenario." *Robinson v. Jacksonville Shipyards,* 760 F. Supp. 1486 (M.D. Fla. 1991).

UNWELCOME BEHAVIOR   The EEOC regulations prohibit "unwelcome sexual advances, requests for sexual favors and other verbal or physical conduct of a sexual nature." The sexual conduct must actually be unwelcome and offensive to the employee bringing the complaint. In a quid pro quo situation, the supervisor or employer frequently claims that the employee welcomed the sexual advances at the time and that the relationship was purely consensual. Likewise, in the case of the sexually hostile workplace, an employer often argues that the employee was a willing participant in the jokes and sexual banter. A court will look at several factors to determine whether the conduct was unwelcome.

For example, employers have argued that if a woman voluntarily submits to her employer's sexual advances, she has consented to them. Courts have ruled, however, that a woman welcomed the sexual advance or conduct only if it can be shown that it was something she wanted to do at the time. The best example of this situation is *Meritor Savings Bank v. Vinson*, 477 U.S. 57 (1986), in which the employee appeared to submit voluntarily to her boss's advances but later argued successfully that she had done so in order to keep her job.

In the *Vinson* case, the U.S. Supreme Court also found that a court can consider evidence of the employee's "sexually provocative speech or dress," along with other facts, in determining whether the employee really welcomed any sexual advances. Many women activists have criticized this rule. It is virtually impossible to know what might be provocative speech or dress for any particular person; provocation is in the eye of the beholder.

Similarly, employers may argue that a woman welcomed the conduct because she failed to complain. Speaking out against harassment, however, is not always easy or possible; frequently, the employee is afraid of retaliation if she does. A woman faced with harassing conduct in the workplace often adopts a coping strategy. Such behavior sometimes gives the appearance that she is a willing participant, but in fact may only be her way of dealing with an unpleasant situation. These strategies may come back to haunt her when she files suit and the employer argues that she welcomed the conduct. An employee also does not forfeit her legal right to protection from sexual harassment if she was once romantically (and consensually) involved with a co-worker, but she has to make it clear to him that any further sexual advances are unwelcome.

Employers frequently argue that an employee has welcomed certain sexual advances or conduct because she willingly participated in some similar type of activity, citing instances in which the woman told a sexual joke as evidence that she must have no objection to the working environment. Yet mild jokes may escalate to hard-core pornography and dangerous threats that go well beyond the type of conduct she tolerated. By ignoring certain types of mild sexual conduct, a woman does not waive her right to challenge other, more serious forms of sexual harassment.

Even if a woman is hired to do a job that is based on sexual stereotypes, she does not give up her right to object to other forms of sexual conduct. The leading case on this point involved a woman hired as Pet of the Month by *Penthouse* magazine. Her job involved video and personal appearances in highly sexualized settings. Even so, the magazine and its publisher were held liable for forcing her into having sex with business associates and others that the publisher wanted to impress. *Thoreson v. Penthouse International, Ltd.,* 563 N.Y.S.2d 968 (N.Y. Sup. Ct. 1990).

A Special Note on the Law in Schools and Colleges

Sexual harassment in schools and colleges is illegal, according to the U.S. Civil Rights Act, Title IX of the Federal Education Amendments, which prohibits sexual discrimination in education. Title IX may be enforced through private litigation, the U.S. Education Department's Office of Civil Rights, or state departments of human rights. Under Title IX, educational institutions are required to maintain a grievance procedure that allows for prompt and equitable resolution of sex discrimination. The definitions of *sexual harassment* used by the courts are usually the same as those under Title VII, as outlined earlier in this chapter. The courts and agencies will look to the legal decisions in the area of sexual harassment in employment to decide a particular case involving harassment in education. The Office for Civil Rights, United States Department of Education—the agency responsible for administering and enforcing Title IX—has stated that "sexual harassment consists of verbal or physical conduct of a sexual nature, imposed on the basis of sex, by an employee or agent of a recipient that denies, limits, provides differently, or conditions the provision of aid, benefits, services or treatment protected under Title IX."

Title IX has had a limited enforcement history. Therefore, the case law in the area of education is not as well developed as in that of employment. In 1992, in *Franklin v. Gwinnett County Public Schools,* 112 S. Ct. 1028 (1992), the U.S. Supreme Court unanimously ruled that sexual harassment in schools is a violation of

Title IX and that students who suffer sexual harassment and other forms of sex discrimination can seek monetary damages from schools and school officials for a violation of civil rights.

Earlier, in *Alexander v. Yale*, 631 F.2d 178 (2d Cir. 1980), *aff'g* 459 F. Supp. 1 (D. Conn. 1977), a federal district court ruled that, in a university setting, sexual harassment could be sex discrimination under Title IX. It was the first court to do so, but the court of appeals later dismissed the case, ruling that it was moot because Alexander had graduated and that Yale University had adequately addressed Alexander's concern by setting up a sexual harassment grievance procedure.

Sexual harassment in schools may also be a criminal offense under state child abuse laws. In the area of sexual harassment and schools, however, many legal issues have yet to be addressed.

State Fair Employment Practices Statutes

In most states, victims of sexual harassment also have rights to sue under state fair employment practices (FEP) statutes. Most state FEP laws prohibit sexual harassment in that state. A few states, such as Alabama and Arkansas, have no FEP statutes. In states with FEP laws, smaller companies that might not be covered under the 15-employee minimum of the federal Civil Rights Act are usually included.

Most states have adopted a definition of *sexual harassment* similar to that in the EEOC guidelines. (See pages 67–89.) Usually, these same states also have agencies structured like the EEOC to investigate claims. The procedures and remedies offered to harassed employees under each state FEP law differ. State laws differ especially as to whether an employee may recover money damages for personal injuries suffered as a result of the harassment. The following document includes a summary of each state's FEP laws. (Because state laws change frequently, the reader should research any particular law in that state's official statute reporter before relying upon the information presented here.)

Common Law Torts

Lawsuits based on common law torts may include intentional infliction of emotional distress and assault and battery. These suits provide a remedy, in some sexual harassment cases, based on the common law of each state, rather than any statute or governmental agency regulation.

State Fair Employment Practices Laws

Reprinted with permission from *Sexual Harassment on the Job* by attorneys William Petrocelli and Barbara Kate Repa, published by Nolo Press, Berkeley, CA. Copyright © 1992 by William Petrocelli, Barbara Kate Repa, and Nolo Press.

How To Use These Listings

The information here is divided into a number of categories.

Statute. The legal citation to your state FEP law, if there is one.

State agency. The name, address and phone number of the state organization responsible for administering and enforcing the FEP law. Only the main office is listed here. There may also be local offices that are more convenient. Call the state agency for information on how and where to file a claim.

Exclusions. Groups who are not entitled to the protections of the state FEP law.

Time limits. The time within which you must file a claim. Unless otherwise indicated, the time limit starts with the incident of harassment. So, for example, in Alaska, an employee would have 300 days from the date she was harassed to bring a claim with the Commission. If she tried to bring a claim after 300 days, she would not be allowed to do so. It is very important to keep on top of these limits. Call your state agency if you have questions about when to file. When in doubt, file early.

Exhaustion. Whether you must file a claim with your state agency before bringing a private lawsuit based on the state FEP law. The term is shorthand for "exhaustion of administrative remedies." Some states require you to follow all available administrative procedures before you can resort to a lawsuit. If there is a "yes" listed for your state, you must file a claim with the state agency as a prerequisite to a lawsuit. If there is a "no" listed, you are not required to file a claim before bringing a lawsuit. Some states follow a procedure like the EEOC. They require you to file a claim with the state agency, but they will give you permission to bring a private lawsuit—either through a right-to-sue letter or by some other method—after a certain number of days.

Monetary damages. The kinds of damages that can be awarded under the state FEP law. We specify here whether these damages are available from an administrative hearing, a private lawsuit, or both. Unless otherwise indicated, all states will award job-connected losses, such as back pay and lost benefits. In addition, some states award:

- compensatory damages, or money to compensate for personal injuries, pain and suffering, mental distress and humiliation, and

- punitive damages, or money to punish the harasser for particularly heinous behavior.

Administrative procedure. Some details about how your state agency works. Unless otherwise indicated, every agency will investigate your claim and make an attempt to reach a settlement between you and your employer. Some agencies will also hold an administrative hearing, like a court case. Many agencies provide an attorney to argue for your complaint at this hearing; others require that you hire your own attorney. Some states will also award attorney's fees.

Private lawsuit. The requirements for bringing a private lawsuit based on state law. Some states don't allow you to bring a lawsuit at all. Others require you to obtain a right-to-sue letter before bringing a lawsuit or impose other limitations.

Note: An asterisk (*) indicates that the state agency has not been designated by the EEOC. This means that there is no guarantee of the quality of the agency's work, and your claim will probably not be dual-filed automatically.

ALABAMA
No state FEP law.

ALASKA
Statute: Alaska Stats. §§18.80.010-300
State agency: Alaska State Commission for Human Rights
    800 A Street, Suite 202
    Anchorage, AK 99501
    (907) 276-7474
Exclusions: Domestic employment, social clubs and nonprofit religious, fraternal, charitable or educational organizations
Time limits: 300 days
Exhaustion: No
Monetary damages: Compensatory damages can be awarded in a private lawsuit, but not by the administrative agency.
Administrative procedure: If you choose to bring your complaint to the Commission, an administrative hearing is available. The complaint will be represented by the Commission, but you can also hire your own attorney. Attorney's fees are available.
Private lawsuit: You can bring a lawsuit directly in state court. You must file this suit within two years.

ARIZONA

Statute: Arizona Rev. Stats. §41-1461 to 1465, 1481 to 1484
State agency: Arizona Civil Rights Division
 1275 West Washington Street
 Phoenix, AZ 85007
 (602) 542-5263
Exclusions: Employers of fewer than 15 employees, the United States,
 Native American tribes, bona-fide tax exempt private membership
 clubs, appointed staff of elected officials
Time limits: 180 days
Exhaustion: Yes. After 90 days, if the Division has not completed its
 administrative process, you can request a right-to-sue letter.
Monetary damages: No compensatory or punitive damages are available
 under state law.
Administrative procedure: The Division does not hold an administrative
 hearing. If, after investigation, the Division decides that there is
 reasonable cause to believe that harassment took place, the Division
 can bring an action on your behalf in state court against your
 employer, but it is not required to do so.
Private lawsuit: You can bring a private action only with a right-to-sue
 letter. If the Division decides not to bring a lawsuit itself, you can
 bring your own lawsuit starting 90 days after the complaint was
 originally filed. You can apply for a court-appointed attorney to
 represent you in this suit, or can petition the court for permission to
 begin the action without paying fees or court costs. Attorney's fees
 are available.

ARKANSAS

No state FEP law.

CALIFORNIA

Statute: Cal. Govt. Code §§12900 to 12996
State agency: California Dept. of Fair Employment and Housing
 2014 T Street, Suite 210
 Sacramento, CA 95814
 (916) 739-4621
Exclusions: Nonprofit religious groups
Time limits: One year
Exhaustion: Yes. If the Department has not completed its administrative
 process after 150 days, you can request a right-to-sue letter.
Monetary damages: Compensatory and punitive damages can be
 awarded in a private lawsuit, but the Department cannot award
 compensatory or punitive damages.
Administrative procedure: The Department will hold an administrative
 hearing. At this hearing, an attorney for the Department will
 represent the complaint.

Private lawsuit: You can bring a lawsuit for up to one year after receiving a right-to-sue letter.

COLORADO

Statute: Colorado Rev. Stats. §§24-34-301 to 406
State agency: Colorado Civil Rights Commission
  1560 Broadway Suite 1050
  Denver, CO 80202
  (303) 894-2997
Exclusions: Domestic employment, religious organizations not supported by public taxes
Time limits: 180 days
Exhaustion: Yes. If the complaint is dismissed after a finding of no probable cause, you can bring a private lawsuit within 90 days. You can also bring a private lawsuit if there has been no administrative hearing 180 days after you filed your complaint, or 120 days after your employer was notified that it would have to respond to your complaint in a hearing.
Monetary damages: No compensatory or punitive damages can be awarded under state law.
Administrative procedure: The Commission will hold an administrative hearing. The complaint will be represented by an attorney for the Commission.
Private lawsuit: You can bring a private lawsuit only under the circumstances listed above, under Exhaustion.

CONNECTICUT

Statute: Conn. Gen. Stats. §46a-51 to 99
State agency: Connecticut Commission on Human Rights and
  Opportunities
  90 Washington Street
  Hartford, CT 06106
  (203) 566-4895
Exclusions: Employers with fewer than three employees, domestic employment, those employed by their parent, spouse or child
Time limits: 180 days
Exhaustion: Yes. After 210 days, you can request a right-to-sue letter if the Commission has not completed its administrative process.
Monetary damages: Compensatory damages can be awarded both by the Commission and in private lawsuit. Punitive damages cannot be awarded under state law.
Administrative procedures: The Commission will hold an administrative hearing. The complaint will be represented by the Commission. You can hire your own attorney if you wish. Attorney's fees are not available from the Commission.
Private lawsuit: You can bring a lawsuit only with a right-to-sue letter.

DELAWARE
Statute: 19 Del. Code Ann. §§710 to 718
State agency: Delaware Department of Labor, Anti-Discrimination Section
   820 North French Street, 6th Floor
   State Office Building
   Wilmington, DE 19801
   (302) 571-3929
Exclusions: Employers with fewer than four employees, agricultural
   workers, domestic employees, those employed by their parent,
   spouse or child, those who live with their employers as part of
   their job
Time limits: 90 days
Exhaustion: Yes
Monetary damages: No compensatory or punitive damages can be
   awarded under state law.
Administrative procedure: If the Department finds that there is cause
   to believe harassment took place, there will be a hearing before the
   Equal Opportunity Review Board. Once this Board issues a ruling, the
   employer has 30 days to comply or appeal to the state court. If the
   employer does not comply, the Department will file an action in state
   court to enforce the ruling. You may request an attorney from the
   Commission or hire your own attorney, but no attorney's fees are
   available from the Board.
Private lawsuit: You cannot bring a private lawsuit.

DISTRICT OF COLUMBIA
Statute: D.C. Code §1-2501 to 2557
State agency: D.C. Office of Human Rights
   2000 14th Street, NW, 3d Floor
   Washington, DC 20009
   (202) 939-8740
Exclusions: Domestic employment in the employer's home, those
   employed by their parent, spouse or child
Time limits: One year
Exhaustion: No
Monetary damages: Compensatory and punitive damages can be
   awarded both by the Office and in a private lawsuit.
Administrative procedure: The Office will hold an administrative
   hearing, called a fact-finding conference. You can hire an attorney for
   this conference, but you are not required to have one. If you do get
   an attorney, attorney's fees are available.
Private lawsuit: You can bring a lawsuit directly in district court.

FLORIDA
Statute: Fla. Stats. Ann. §760.01 to .10
State agency: Florida Commission on Human Relations

325 John Knox Road
Building F, Suite 240
Tallahassee, FL 32399
(904) 488-7082

Exclusions: Employers with fewer than 15 employees

Time limits: 180 days

Exhaustion: Yes. After 180 days, you may withdraw your complaint and bring a private lawsuit.

Monetary damages: No compensatory or punitive damages can be awarded under state law.

Administrative procedure: The Commission will hold an informal hearing, at which attorneys are ordinarily not present. You may request a more formal hearing before the Department of Administrative Hearings; the Commission suggests that you hire an attorney for this hearing. Attorney's fees are available.

Private lawsuit: You can bring a lawsuit only after withdrawing your complaint from the Commission.

GEORGIA

Note: Only applies to employees of the state of Georgia

Statute: Code of Georgia Ann. §45-19-20 to 45.

State agency: Georgia Office of Fair Employment Practices
156 Trinity Avenue, SW; Suite 208
Atlanta, GA 30303
(404) 656-1736

Exclusions: Employees of private employers, appointed staff of elected officials

Time limits: 180 days

Exhaustion: Yes

Monetary damages: No compensatory or punitive damages can be awarded under state law.

Administrative procedure: Only state employees are protected, and they are limited to this state remedy. All actions are confidential. The Office holds an administrative hearing, at which you will be represented by an appointed attorney.

Private lawsuit: You cannot bring a private lawsuit.

HAWAII

Statute: Hawaii Rev. Stats. §368-1 to 17, §378-1 to 9

State agency: Hawaii Civil Rights Commission
888 Mililani Street, 2d Floor
Honolulu, HI 96813
(808) 586-8655

Exclusions: The United States, domestic employment

Time limits: 180 days

Exhaustion: Unclear. You probably should file a complaint with the Commission first, to be safe.

Monetary damages: Both compensatory and punitive damages can be awarded by the Commission. The damages that can be awarded in a private lawsuit are unclear, as workers' compensation may severely limit any recovery in state court. You should talk to an attorney if you are planning to bring a lawsuit.

Administrative procedure: The Commission will hold an administrative hearing. If you choose to hire an attorney for this hearing, attorney's fees are available.

Private lawsuit: State law is unclear as to whether you can bring a private lawsuit directly.

IDAHO

Statute: Idaho Code Ann. §67-5901 to 5912

State agency: Idaho Human Rights Commission
450 West State Street
Boise, ID 83720
(208) 334-2873

Exclusions: Employers with fewer than five employees, private clubs not open to the public, domestic employment

Time limits: One year

Exhaustion: No

Monetary damages: No compensatory damages can be awarded under state law. Punitive damages of up to $1,000 can be awarded if you or the Commission bring a lawsuit on your behalf in state court.

Administrative procedure: The Commission has no administrative hearing. If there is cause to believe that sexual harassment has occurred, the Commission will bring a lawsuit on your behalf in state court. You may hire your own attorney, if you are bringing claims that do not fall within the state statute, such as a common law tort action. Attorney's fees are available.

Private lawsuit: You can bring a lawsuit directly in state court. You must file the suit within two years.

ILLINOIS

Statute: Ill. Ann. Stats., chapter 68, §§1-101 to 2-105, §7A-101 to 104, §8-101 to 105, §8A-101 to 104

State agency: Illinois Department of Human Rights
100 West Randolph Street, 10th Floor
Chicago, IL 60601
(312) 814-6245

Exclusions: Domestic employment, appointed staff of elected officials, nonprofit religious groups, administrative officers of state and municipal governments, evaluees or trainees in vocational rehabilitation facilities

Time limits: 180 days

Exhaustion: No

Monetary damages: Compensatory damages can be awarded both by the

Commission and in a private lawsuit, but no punitive damages can be awarded under state law.

Administrative procedure: The Commission will hold an administrative hearing. You can hire an attorney for this hearing, and attorney's fees are available.

Private lawsuit: You can bring a lawsuit directly in state court.

INDIANA

Statute: Indiana Stats. Ann. §22-9-1-1 to 13, §22-9-4-1 to 6

State agency: Indiana Civil Rights Commission
32 East Washington Street, Suite 900
Indianapolis, IN 46204
(317) 232-2612

Exclusions: Employers with fewer than six employees, domestic employment, those employed by their parent, spouse or child, nonprofit fraternal or religious groups, clubs that are exclusively social

Time limits: 90 days, or 90 days from the end of a valid company or union grievance procedure

Exhaustion: Yes

Monetary damages: No compensatory or punitive damages can be awarded under state law.

Administrative procedure: The Commission will hold an administrative hearing. An attorney will be provided for you. No attorney's fees are available.

Private lawsuit: You cannot bring a private lawsuit.

IOWA

Statute: Iowa Code Ann. §601A.1 to .19

State agency: Iowa Civil Rights Commission
Grimes State Office Building
211 East Maple Street, 2d Floor
Des Moines, IA 50319
(515) 281-4121

Exclusions: Employers with fewer than four employees, domestic employment, employment for personal services

Time limits: 180 days

Exhaustion: Yes. After 60 days, you can request a right-to-sue letter. However, you can't get a right-to-sue letter if there has already been a finding of no probable cause, if a conciliation agreement has already been reached or if notice of the administrative hearing has already been issued.

Monetary damages: Compensatory damages can be awarded, both by the Commission and in a private lawsuit, but not punitive damages.

Administrative procedure: The Commission will hold an administrative hearing. The complaint will be presented by a Commission attorney. You can also hire your own attorney. Attorney's fees are available.

Private lawsuit: You can bring a lawsuit only with a right-to-sue letter.

KANSAS

Statute: Kan. Stats. Ann. §44-1001 to 1311

State agency: Kansas Commission on Human Rights
Landon State Office Building, Suite 851-S
900 S.W. Jackson Street
Topeka, KS 66612
(913) 296-3206

Exclusions: Employers with fewer than four employees, domestic employment, those employed by their parent, spouse or child, non-profit fraternal or social associations

Time limits: Six months

Exhaustion: Yes. After 30 days, you can request a right-to-sue letter.

Monetary damages: The Commission can award compensatory damages, but only up to $2,000. It is unclear whether compensatory or punitive damages can be awarded in a private lawsuit.

Administrative procedure: The Commission holds a public hearing if there is probable cause to believe discrimination has taken place. You will be provided with an attorney at this hearing.

Private lawsuit: You can bring a private suit only after receiving a right-to-sue letter.

KENTUCKY

Statute: Ky. Rev. Stats. §344.010 to .450

State agency: Kentucky Commission on Human Rights*
701 West Muhammed Ali Boulevard
P.O. Box 69
Louisville, KY 40201
(502) 588-4024

Exclusions: Employers with fewer than eight employees, domestic employment, those employed by their parent, spouse or child

Time limits: 180 days

Exhaustion: No

Monetary damages: Compensatory damages can be awarded both by the Commission and in a private lawsuit, but punitive damages cannot be awarded under state law.

Administrative procedure: If there is probable cause to believe that discrimination has occurred, there will be an administrative hearing. You can hire an attorney for this hearing, but the Commission will provide an attorney for you, if you wish. Attorney's fees are available, in the Commission's discretion.

Private lawsuit: You can file your own lawsuit directly.

LOUISIANA

Statute: La. Rev. Stat. Ann. §23-1006

State agency: None

Exclusions: Employers of fewer than 15 employees, religious organizations, non-profit corporations

Time limits: None indicated. If you are planning to bring a lawsuit, consult with an attorney about the appropriate statute of limitations.

Exhaustion: No, because there is no administrative procedure.

Monetary damages: Compensatory damages can be awarded in a private lawsuit.

Administrative procedure: None

Private lawsuit: You must bring a private lawsuit.

MAINE

Statute: Maine Rev. Stats. Ann., title V, §4551-4632

State agency: Maine Human Rights Commission
Statehouse Station 51
Augusta, ME 04333
(207) 289-2326

Exclusions: Those employed by their parent, spouse or child

Time limits: Six months

Exhaustion: No. However, civil penal damages and attorney's fees are only available if you filed a complaint with the Commission that was dismissed after a finding that there were no reasonable grounds to believe that discrimination took place, or that could not be conciliated within 90 days of a reasonable grounds finding.

Monetary damages: Compensatory damages are available in state court. Punitive damages of $10,000 for the first violation, $25,000 for the second violation and $50,000 for the third violation, can be awarded in a private lawsuit if you initially filed your complaint with the Commission, or if the Commission brings a lawsuit on your behalf.

Administrative procedure: There is no administrative hearing. After investigating and attempting to conciliate, the Commission will refer the case to its attorneys, who will bring a lawsuit on your behalf in state court. If the Commission cannot bring a lawsuit within a reasonable time, you will be given the right to sue. Attorney's fees are available.

Private lawsuit: The same remedies are available as through the administrative process if you initially filed a complaint with the Commission (see Exhaustion). If you did not bring a complaint, no attorney's fees or punitive damages are available.

MARYLAND

Statute: Ann. Code of Md. Article 49B, §1 to 39

State agency: Maryland Commission on Human Relations
20 East Franklin Street
Baltimore, MD 21202
(301) 333-1715

Exclusions: Employers with fewer than 15 employees, bona-fide private membership clubs, appointed staff (not civil service) of elected officials

Time limits: Six months

Exhaustion: Yes

Monetary damages: No compensatory or punitive damages can be awarded under state law.

Administrative procedure: The Commission will hold an administrative hearing. You can hire an attorney if you wish, but no attorney's fees are available.

Private lawsuit: You cannot bring a private lawsuit.

MASSACHUSETTS

Statute: Ann. Laws of Mass. chapter 151B, §§1 to 10

State agency: Massachusetts Commission Against Discrimination
One Ashburton Place, Room 601
Boston, MA 02108
(617) 727-3990

Exclusions: Employers of fewer than six employees, domestic employment, those employed by their parent, spouse or child, nonprofit clubs, associations or fraternal organizations

Time limits: Six months

Exhaustion: Yes. However, if you want to bring a private lawsuit, you may request a right-to-sue letter at any time. After 90 days, you can bring a private lawsuit even without a right-to-sue letter.

Monetary damages: Compensatory damages can be awarded by the Commission, and both compensatory and punitive damages can be awarded in a private lawsuit.

Administrative procedure: You can file your complaint anonymously if you wish. The Commission will hold an administrative hearing. An attorney will be provided by the Commission.

Private lawsuit: You can bring a lawsuit only after initially filing with the Commission.

MICHIGAN

Statute: Mich. Compiled Laws Ann. §37.2101 to .2804

State agency: Michigan Department of Civil Rights
Executive Plaza Building
1200 6th Street
Detroit, Ml 48226
(313) 256-2615

Exclusions: Those employed by their parent, spouse or child

Time limits: 180 days

Exhaustion: No

Monetary damages: Compensatory damages can be awarded, both by the Department and in a private lawsuit. No punitive damages can be awarded under state law.

Administrative procedure: The Commission will hold a hearing. An attorney from the Commission will represent you, but you can also hire your own attorney if you wish. Attorney's fees are available.

Private lawsuit: You can bring a lawsuit directly in state court.

MINNESOTA

Statute: Minn. Stats. Ann. §363.01 to .15

State agency: Minnesota Department of Human Rights
Bremer Tower
Seventh Place and Minnesota Street
St. Paul, MN 55101
(612) 296-5665

Exclusions: Domestic employment, those employed by their parent, spouse or child

Time limits: One year

Exhaustion: No. However, if you do file with the Commission, you must wait 45 days before bringing a private lawsuit.

Monetary damages: Unlimited damages can be recovered for mental suffering. In addition, you can recover up to three times the amount of your actual damages, and up to $8,500 in punitive damages. These damages can be awarded both by the Commission and in a private lawsuit.

Administrative procedure: The Commission will investigate and attempt to conciliate and will often hold a fact-finding conference. After 180 days have passed since the complaint was filed, you can request that the case be heard by the Department of Administrative Hearings. The Commission will pay your costs, but you must get your own attorney.

Private lawsuit: You can bring a lawsuit directly in state court.

MISSISSIPPI

Statute: Miss. Code Ann. §25-9-149

Although there is a state law prohibiting discrimination against state employees, no damages, exclusions or other specifics are mentioned in the statute.

MISSOURI

Statute: Vernon's Ann. Missouri Stats. §213-010 to .130

State agency: Missouri Commission on Human Rights
3315 West Truman Boulevard
P.O. Box 1129
Jefferson City, MO 65102
(314) 751-3325

Exclusions: Employers with fewer than six employees, religious groups

Time limits: 180 days

Exhaustion: Yes. You can request a right-to-sue letter 180 days after the harassment occurred if the Commission has not completed its administrative process.

Monetary damages: Compensatory damages can be awarded, both by the Commission and in a private lawsuit. Punitive damages are available in a private lawsuit only.

Administrative procedure: The Commission will conduct an administrative hearing. At this hearing, the complaint will be presented by the attorney general. You can join in the hearing and have your own attorney, if you wish. No attorney's fees are available.

Private lawsuit: You can bring a lawsuit only with a right-to-sue letter.

MONTANA

Statute: Montana Code Ann. §§49-1-101 to 49-2-601

State agency: Montana Human Rights Division
Department of Labor and Industry
Post Office Box 1728
1236 6th Avenue
Helena, MT 59624
(406) 444-2884

Exclusions: Nonprofit fraternal, charitable or religious groups

Time limits: 180 days. However, if you are using a valid company or union grievance procedure, this time can be extended by the amount of time spent using the grievance procedure, up to an additional 120 days.

Exhaustion: Yes. You can get a right-to-sue letter if the Commission makes a finding that there is no reasonable cause to believe that discrimination has occurred.

Monetary damages: Compensatory damages can be awarded both by the Commission and in a private lawsuit. No punitive damages can be awarded under state law.

Administrative procedure: If there is a finding of reasonable cause, your claim will be certified for an administrative hearing. At this hearing, you can have an attorney. No attorney's fees are available from the Commission, but you can petition the state court for a rehearing solely on the issue of attorney's fees. Attorney's fees are routinely granted in this manner.

Private lawsuit: You can bring a lawsuit only after the Commission has made a finding of no reasonable cause.

NEBRASKA

Statute: Nebraska Rev. Stats. §48-1101 to 1126

State agency: Nebraska Equal Employment Opportunity Commission
301 Centennial Mall South, 5th Floor
P.O. Box 94934
Lincoln, NE 68509
(402) 471-2024

Exclusions: Employers with fewer than 15 employees, the United States, Indian tribes, religious organizations and private membership clubs, domestic employment, those employed by their parent, spouse or child

Time limits: 180 days

Exhaustion: Unclear. You should probably file your complaint with the Commission first, to be safe.

Monetary damages: No compensatory or punitive damages can be awarded under state law.

Administrative procedure: The Commission has no enforcement power. Thus, even if the Commission finds that you have been harassed, it cannot enforce an order unless your employer agrees. If your employer does not cooperate, you must sue your employer in state court.

Private lawsuit: See Exhaustion.

NEVADA

Statute: Nev. Rev. Stats. Ann. §613.310 to .430

State agency: Nevada Equal Rights Commission
1515 East Tropicana, Suite 590
Las Vegas, NV 89158
(702) 486-7161

Exclusions: Employers with fewer than 15 employees, private membership clubs, the United States, Indian tribes

Time limits: 180 days

Exhaustion: Yes. If the Commission finds that there is probable cause to believe that you have been harassed, you can bring a private lawsuit.

Monetary damages: No compensatory or punitive damages are available under state law.

Administrative procedure: There is no administrative hearing, and the Commission has no enforcement power. After investigation and conciliation efforts, if the Commission finds that there is probable cause to believe that discrimination has occurred, it will advise you to go to the EEOC or to state court.

Private lawsuit: You may bring a lawsuit only after the Commission makes a finding of probable cause.

NEW HAMPSHIRE

Statute: N.H. Rev. Stats. Ann. §354-A:1 to A:14

State agency: New Hampshire Human Rights Commission
163 Loudon Road
Concord, NH 03301
(603) 271-2767

Exclusions: Employers of fewer than six employees, fraternal, charitable or religious organizations, domestic employment, those employed by their parent, spouse or child

Time limits: 180 days

Exhaustion: No

Monetary damages: No compensatory or punitive damages can be awarded under state law.

Administrative procedure: The Commission will hold a hearing. The complaint will be presented by an attorney for the Commission, but you can have your own attorney if you wish. Attorney's fees are available.

Private lawsuit: You may bring a lawsuit directly in state court.

NEW JERSEY

Statute: N.J. Stats. Ann. §10:5-1 to 38.

State agency: New Jersey Division on Civil Rights
31 Clinton Street
Newark, NJ 07102
(201) 648-2700

Exclusions: Domestic employment, those employed by their parent, spouse or child

Time limits: None indicated. Call the state agency for more information.

Exhaustion: No

Monetary damages: Compensatory and punitive damages can be awarded, both by the Division and in a private lawsuit, according to a recently enacted law. Check with the Division about how this law is being interpreted.

Administrative procedure: The Division will hold an administrative hearing. The complaint will be presented by an appointed attorney.

Private lawsuit: You may bring a lawsuit directly in state court. Attorney's fees are available.

NEW MEXICO

Statute: N.M. Stats. Ann. §28-1-1 to 15

State agency: New Mexico Human Rights Commission
Aspen Plaza
1596 Pacheco Street
Santa Fe, NM 87502
(505) 827-6838

Exclusions: Employers with fewer than four employees

Time limits: 180 days

Exhaustion: Yes. If the Commission has not settled the complaint or held a hearing within 180 days, you can request a letter of no determination, which will allow you to bring a private lawsuit.

Monetary damages: The Commission cannot award compensatory or punitive damages. State law is unclear as to whether compensatory damages can be awarded in a private lawsuit.

Administrative procedure: The Commission will hold an administrative hearing. You must get your own attorney for this hearing. Attorney's fees are available.

Private lawsuit: You can bring a lawsuit directly in state court only after the Commission has issued a letter of non-determination or held its hearing.

NEW YORK

Statute: N.Y. Executive Law §§290 to 301

State agency: New York State Division of Human Rights
55 West 125 Street, 13th Floor
New York, NY 10027
(212) 870-8566

Exclusions: Employers with fewer than four employees, domestic employment

Time limits: None is indicated in the state law. Call the agency to find out when you should file.

Exhaustion: No

Monetary damages: Compensatory damages can be awarded both by the Division and in a private lawsuit, but punitive damages can be awarded only in a private lawsuit.

Administrative procedure: There is an administrative hearing, and the state will provide you with an attorney.

Private lawsuit: You can bring a lawsuit directly in state court.

NORTH CAROLINA (has two state agencies)
Statute: Gen. Stats. of N.C. §143-422.1 to .3

For state and county employees and employees of the University of North Carolina:
State agency: North Carolina Office of Administrative Hearings
Post Office Drawer 27447
Raleigh, NC 27611
(919) 733-0431

Exclusions: Private employers

Time limits: 180 days

Exhaustion: Yes

Monetary damages: No compensatory or punitive damages can be awarded under state law.

Administrative procedure: There will be an administrative hearing, at which you must provide your own attorney. Attorney's fees are available.

Private lawsuit: You cannot bring a private lawsuit.

For private employees:
State agency: North Carolina Human Relations Commission*
21 West Jones Street
Raleigh, NC 27603
(919) 733-7996

Exclusions: Employers with fewer than 15 employees

Time limits: 180 days

Exhaustion: Yes

Monetary damages: No compensatory or punitive damages can be awarded under state law.

Administrative procedure: The Commission has no enforcement power. If your employer will not cooperate, the Commission will defer the claim to the EEOC.

Private lawsuit: You cannot bring a private lawsuit.

NORTH DAKOTA
Statute: N.D. Century Code Ann. §14-02, 4-01 to 21

State agency: North Dakota Department of Labor
State Capitol Building
600 East Boulevard
Bismarck, ND 58505
(701) 224-2660

Exclusions: Appointed staff of elected officials, domestic employment, those employed by their parent, spouse or child

Time limits: 300 days

Exhaustion: No

Monetary damages: No compensatory or punitive damages can be awarded under state law.

Administrative procedure: There is no administrative hearing. After investigation and conciliation, if the Department finds that there is cause to believe harassment has occurred, you will be given the right to sue in state court.

Private lawsuit: You can bring a lawsuit directly in state court.

OHIO

Statute: Page's Ohio Rev. Code Ann. §4112.01 to 99

State agency: Ohio Civil Rights Commission
220 Parsons Avenue
Columbus, OH 43215
(614) 466-5928

Exclusions: Employers with fewer than four employees, domestic employment

Time limits: Six months

Exhaustion: No

Monetary damages: Compensatory and punitive damages can be awarded in a private lawsuit. No compensatory or punitive damages can be awarded by the Commission.

Administrative procedure: The Commission will hold a hearing, at which the Attorney General will present the complaint. You may also have your own attorney, if you wish.

Private lawsuit: You may bring a lawsuit directly in state court.

OKLAHOMA

Statute: 25 Oklahoma Stats. §§1101 to 1802

State agency: Oklahoma Human Rights Commission
2101 North Lincoln Boulevard, Room 480
Oklahoma City, OK 73105
(405) 521-2360

Exclusions: Employers with fewer than 15 employees, domestic employment, those employed by their parent, spouse or child, bona-fide nonprofit private membership clubs, Indian tribes

Time limits: 180 days

Exhaustion: Yes. If the Commission has not completed its administrative process in 180 days, you can request a right-to-sue letter.

Monetary damages: No compensatory or punitive damages can be awarded under state law.

Administrative procedure: The Commission will hold a hearing, at which the complaint will be presented by Commission staff. You may also have your own attorney, if you wish. Attorney's fees are available. The Commission's order has no legal effect without a corresponding order from the state court. The Commission must bring an action for review by the state court to get such an order.

Private lawsuit: You can bring a private lawsuit only with a right-to-sue letter.

OREGON

Statute: Or. Rev. Stats. §659.010 to .990

State agency: Oregon Bureau of Labor and Industry
Civil Rights Division
P.O. Box 800
Portland, OR 97207
(503) 229-6601

Exclusions: Domestic employment, those employed by their parent, spouse or child

Time limits: One year

Exhaustion: No

Monetary damages: Compensatory damages can be awarded by the Division. State Law is unclear as to whether compensatory damages can be awarded in a private lawsuit. No punitive damages are available under state law.

Administrative procedure: The Division will hold a hearing, and a Division attorney will present the complaint. You may also have your own attorney, if you wish. Attorney's fees are available.

Private lawsuit: You may file a lawsuit directly in state court. You must bring this suit within one year of the harassment, if you don't file a complaint with the Division.

PENNSYLVANIA

Statute: 43 Penn. Stats. Ann. §§951 to 962.2

State agency: Pennsylvania Human Rights Commission
2971 East North 7th Street
Harrisburg, PA 17110
(717) 787-4412

Exclusions: Employers with fewer than four employees, agricultural workers, domestic employment, those employed by their parent, spouse or child

Time limits: 180 days

Exhaustion: No

Monetary damages: Compensatory damages can be awarded in a private lawsuit, but not by the Commission. No punitive damages can be awarded under state law.

Administrative procedure: The Commission will hold a hearing, at which you can have an attorney. However, only limited attorney's fees are available from the Commission.

Private lawsuit: You can bring a lawsuit directly in state court.

RHODE ISLAND

Statute: Gen. Laws of R.I. §28-5-1 to 40

State agency: Rhode Island Commission for Human Rights
10 Abbott Park Place
Providence, RI 02903
(401) 277-2661

Exclusions: Employers with fewer than four employees, domestic employment, those employed by their parent, spouse or child

Time limits: One year

Exhaustion: Yes. After 120 days, you can request a right-to-sue letter.

Monetary damages: Compensatory damages can be awarded both by the Commission and in a private lawsuit. Punitive damages can be awarded only in a private lawsuit.

Administrative procedure: The Commission will hold a hearing, at which you must be represented by your own attorney. Attorney's fees are available.

Private lawsuit: You can bring a private lawsuit only with a right-to-sue letter.

SOUTH CAROLINA

Statute: Code of S.C. title 1, §1-13-10 to 110

State agency: South Carolina Human Affairs Commission
P.O. Box 4490
Columbia, SC 29240
(803) 253-6336

Exclusions: Employers with fewer than 15 employees, bona-fide private membership clubs, Indian tribes, appointed staff of elected officials

Time limits: 180 days

Exhaustion: Yes. If the Commission doesn't bring a civil lawsuit within 180 days, you can get a right-to-sue letter.

Monetary damages: No compensatory or punitive damages can be awarded under state law.

Administrative procedure: There is no administrative hearing. If the Commission makes a finding of probable cause, it can bring a lawsuit against your employer. If the Commission doesn't bring suit within 180 days, you can bring a private lawsuit.

Private lawsuit: You may bring a private lawsuit only with a right-to-sue letter.

SOUTH DAKOTA

Statute: S.D. Codified Laws, Chapter 20-13
State agency: South Dakota Division of Human Rights
500 East Capitol Street
Pierre, SD 57501
(605) 773-4493
Exclusions: None
Time limits: 180 days
Exhaustion: Yes. A right-to-sue letter is available after 60 days.
Monetary damages: Compensatory and punitive damages can be
awarded in a private lawsuit, but not by the Division.
Administrative procedure: If the division finds probable cause to believe
that discrimination has occurred, there will be an administrative
hearing. You must get an attorney for this hearing, but no attorney's
fees are available.
Private lawsuit: You may bring a private lawsuit only with a right-to-sue
letter. Attorney's fees are available.

TENNESSEE

Statute: Tenn. Code Ann. §4-21-101 to 408
State agency: Tennessee Human Rights Commission
226 Capitol Boulevard, Suite 602
Nashville, TN 37219
(615) 741-5825
Exclusions: Employers with fewer than eight employees
Time limits: 180 days
Exhaustion: No
Monetary damages: Compensatory and punitive damages can be
awarded, both by the Commission and in a private lawsuit.
Administrative procedure: You are entitled to an attorney at the
administrative hearing. You can choose your own attorney, or have
one appointed for you. Attorney's fees are available.
Private lawsuit: You can file a lawsuit directly in state court within one
year. If you file a complaint with the Commission, you can withdraw
it at any time to file your own lawsuit.

TEXAS

Statute: Tex. Stats. Ann., Article 5221(k) §§1.01 to 10.05
State agency: Texas Commission on Human Rights
8100 Cameron Road, #525
P.O. Box 13493
Austin, TX 78753
(512) 837-8534
Exclusions: Employers with fewer than 15 employees, appointed staff of
elected officials.
Time limits: 180 days
Exhaustion: Yes. After 180 days, you can bring a private lawsuit.

Monetary damages: No compensatory or punitive damages are available under state law.

Administrative procedure: If the evidence supports the complaint, the Commission will recommend a finding of harassment to an administrative panel. If two of the three members of this panel agree that harassment has taken place, conciliation will be attempted. If conciliation efforts fail, the Commission can decide to file suit in the state court to enforce its finding. You can join this lawsuit, with or without an attorney. The case for the complaint will be presented by Commission staff. Attorney's fees are available.

Private lawsuit: You must first file a complaint with the Commission. Once 180 days have passed, you then have a right to sue in state court. You can also sue in state court if the Commission determines that the complaint has no merit—that there is no reason to believe that harassment has occurred. Finally, if the Commission decides that harassment has taken place, but doesn't bring a suit in state court to enforce this finding, you may bring your own lawsuit to do so.

UTAH

Statute: Utah Code Ann. §34-35-1 to 7.1

State agency: Utah Industrial Commission, Anti-Discrimination Division
160 East 300 South
Salt Lake City, UT 84111
(801) 530-6801

Exclusions: Employers with fewer than 15 employees, religious organizations

Time limits: Must file within 180 days

Exhaustion: Yes

Monetary damages: No compensatory or punitive damages are available under state law.

Administrative procedure: You may have an attorney at the administrative hearing. Attorney's fees are available.

Private lawsuit: You cannot bring a private action.

VERMONT

Statute: 21 Vermont Stats. Ann. §495

State agency: Vermont Attorney General's Office
Civil Rights Division
109 State Street
Montpelier, VT 05609
(802) 828-3171

Exclusions: None

Time limits: Unclear. A federal district court recently held that there is a three-year statute of limitations. However, you may have as long as six years to file.

Exhaustion: No

Monetary damages: Compensatory and punitive damages can be awarded in a private lawsuit only.

Administrative procedure: There is no administrative hearing. If, after investigation and conciliation efforts, no solution has been reached, you must litigate in state court.

Private lawsuit: You may bring a lawsuit directly in state court.

VIRGINIA

Although there is a state law prohibiting harassment of state employees only, there is no state agency.

WASHINGTON

Statute: Rev. Code of Wash. Ann. §49.60.010 to .330

State agency: Washington State Human Rights Commission
Evergreen Plaza Building, Suite 402
711 South Capitol Way
Olympia, WA 98504
(206) 753-6770

Exclusions: Employers with fewer than eight employees, nonprofit religious organizations, domestic employment, those employed by their parent, spouse or child

Time limits: Six months

Exhaustion: No

Monetary damages: The Commission can award up to $1,000 in compensatory damages, but no punitive damages. Unlimited compensatory and punitive damages can be awarded in a private lawsuit.

Administrative procedure: There will be an administrative hearing, at which the Commission will represent the complaint. If you wish to have your own attorney, you may do so. Attorney's fees are available.

Private lawsuit: You may bring a lawsuit directly in state court.

WEST VIRGINIA

Statute: W. Va. Code §5-11-1 to 19

State agency: West Virginia Human Rights Commission
1321 Plaza East, Room 106
Charleston, WV 25301
(304) 348-2616

Exclusions: Employers with fewer than 12 employees, domestic employment, those employed by their parent, spouse or child

Time limits: 180 days

Exhaustion: No

Monetary damages: Compensatory damages are limited to $2,500 from the Commission but are unlimited in state court. No punitive damages can be awarded under state law.

Administrative procedure: At the administrative hearing, the attorney general will present the complaint. You can have your own attorney, if you wish. If you do retain an attorney, attorney's fees are available from the Commission.

Private lawsuit: You can bring a lawsuit directly in state court.

WISCONSIN

Statute: Wis. Stats. Ann. §11.31 to 39
State agency: Wisconsin Equal Rights Division
Department of Industry, Labor and Human Relations
P.O. Box 8928
201 East Washington Avenue
Madison, Wl 53708
(608) 267-9678
Exclusions: Those employed by their parent, spouse or child
Time limits: 300 days
Exhaustion: Yes
Monetary damages: No compensatory or punitive damages can be awarded under state law.
Administrative procedure: You may have an attorney at the administrative hearing. Attorney's fees are available.
Private lawsuit: You cannot bring a private lawsuit.

WYOMING

Statute: Wyoming Stats. Ann. §27-9-101 to 108
State agency: Wyoming Fair Employment Commission
Herschler Building
2nd East
Cheyenne, WY 82002
(307) 777-7261
Exclusions: Employers with fewer than two employees, religious organizations
Time limits: 90 days
Exhaustion: Yes. You can get a right-to-sue letter if the Commission decides that its investigation will take more than 200 days.
Monetary damages: Compensatory damages can be awarded in a private lawsuit, but not by the Commission. Punitive damages cannot be awarded under state law.
Administrative procedure: You may have an attorney at the administrative hearing if you wish; however, no attorney's fees are available.
Private lawsuit: You can bring a private lawsuit only with a right-to-sue letter.

The same factual situation that is the basis for a sexual harassment claim under the Civil Rights Act or state FEP statutes may also serve as the ground for a tort action. Although not every case merits a claim of assault and battery or intentional infliction of emotional distress, these kinds of suits may compensate the victim of sexual harassment with substantial money damages—unlike Title VII of the Civil Rights Act, which limits the amount of money that may be collected.

One kind of tort action is called *assault and battery*. If the plaintiff brings an assault claim, she must prove that her harasser caused her to fear harmful or offensive physical contact. Both verbal and physical harassment may constitute assault. *Battery* is conduct that results in any harmful or offensive touching of another. Claims for assault and battery are frequently alleged in sexual harassment cases; usually both claims are brought together. Examples of conduct that may rise to the level of a claim for assault and battery include grabbing, brushing against, and fondling the woman, as well as outright sexual assault and rape.

Another tort commonly alleged in sexual harassment cases is called *intentional infliction of emotional distress*. To prove intentional infliction of emotional distress, a plaintiff must show that the conduct of her harasser was so shocking in character, or so extreme in degree, that a person of normal sensibilities would consider the action outrageous. This claim arises in most sexual harassment cases, because unwelcome physical conduct as well as the creation of a hostile work environment may be considered outrageous, and is often left to the jury to decide.

Employers may be liable for other tort actions when they handle employee hiring or sexual harassment complaints carelessly. For example, an employer may be sued for defamation if it makes or condones false statements about an employee that tend to damage the employee's reputation. Defamation is either oral (*slander*) or written (*libel*). An employer could be sued, for example, for telling someone that an employee was fired for sexual harassment if the charge later turns out to be false.

Negligent hiring and retention claims also arise in the context of sexual harassment lawsuits. If an employer fails to take reasonable care before hiring an employee (for instance, by not performing appropriate reference and background checks), and that employee later causes damage to other employees, the employer may be liable for negligent hiring. Similarly, if an employer retains an employee with a demonstrated propensity for misconduct, it may be liable for negligent retention.

Finally, an employer may be liable for the tort of invasion of privacy if private and embarrassing details about the harasser or the victim are unnecessarily and publicly disclosed.

Summary of Significant Legal Cases

The following cases, summarized in chronological order, were selected to show the evolution of the legal and financial liabilities for sexual harassment. The list is not meant to be exhaustive, but merely to show trends over the years; many sexual harassment cases are not listed here.

Monge v. Beebe Rubber Co., 114 N.H. 130, 316 A.2d 549 (1974)

An employer's termination of an employment contract was found to be a breach of contract when the termination was motivated by malice because a female employee refused the sexual advances of her foreman. The case was decided under state contract law rather than Title VII and did not use the words *sexual harassment.*

Miller v. Bank of America, 600 F.2d 211 (9th Cir. 1979)

In one of the first appellate cases, the Bank of America was found liable for a supervisor's sexual harassment, even though his behavior violated company policy and the bank was unaware of the sexual harassment. This liability was based on the concept of *respondeat superior* and was decided under Title VII of the Civil Rights Act.

Bundy v. Jackson, 641 F.2d 934 (D.C. Cir. 1981)

The court found that sexual insults and demeaning propositions constituted sexual harassment and were a form of sex discrimination, regardless of whether the plaintiff lost any tangible job benefits—such as wages or a promotion—as a result.

Wright v. Methodist Youth Services, Inc., 511 F. Supp. 307 (N.D. Ill. 1981)

In this case, a court found, for the first time, that the termination of a man because he rejected sexual advances made by his male supervisor was a violation of Title VII. The judge reasoned that a similarly situated woman would not have had sexual demands made of her.

Rogers v. Loews L'Enfant Plaza Hotel, 526 F. Supp. 523 (D.D.C. 1981)

The plaintiff was sexually harassed by her immediate supervisor while working at a hotel restaurant. The court found that she was entitled to general and punitive damages under state tort law theories of intrusion, assault and battery, and intentional infliction of emotional distress.

NLRB v. Downslope Industries, Inc., 676 F.2d 1114 (6th Cir. 1982)

Under the National Labor Relations Act, the court found that freedom from sexual harassment is a "working condition" for which employees may organize to protect themselves.

Davis v. United States Steel Corp., 779 F.2d 209 (4th Cir. 1986)

The inaction of a supervisor who observed an employee engaging in sexual harassment was found to be sufficient to make the company liable under the doctrine of *respondeat superior*. A supervisor has the responsibility to take the necessary corrective action.

Meritor Savings Bank v. Vinson, 477 U.S. 57 (1986)

This was the first U.S. Supreme Court case to find that sexual harassment is a form of sex discrimination under Title VII of the 1964 Civil Rights Act. The Court concluded that a claim of "hostile environment" sexual harassment is actionable under Title VII. Although the decision noted that employers cannot always be held liable for sexual harassment by management personnel, in this case, the Court found that a grievance procedure and policy against discrimination, coupled with the employee's failure to use that procedure, did not immunize the employer from liability. The Court also allowed the introduction of evidence about the plaintiff's "provocative" clothing and behavior.

Delgado v. Lehman, 665 F. Supp. 460, 468 (E.D. Va. 1987)

This is a significant case because of its holding that "[s]exual harassment need not take the form of overt sexual advances or suggestions, but may consist of such things as verbal abuse of women if it [is] sufficiently patterned to comprise a condition and is apparently caused by the sex of the harassed employee." In this case, a supervisor who was trying to protect his turf viewed women as threats. He went out of his way to demean the plaintiff and other women.

Hall v. Gus Construction Co., 842 F.2d 1010 (8th Cir. 1988)

The court held that the employer was liable for co-worker sexual harassment on the theory that the supervisor was the employer's agent. The foreman, as the agent of the company, had both actual and constructive knowledge of the harassment and failed to take appropriate action to stop the behavior.

Broderick v. Ruder, 685 F. Supp. 1269 (D.D.C. 1988)

In this precedent-setting case, an attorney who worked in an environment that was sexually offensive was found to be a victim of hostile work environment sexual harassment. She was forced to work in a department where managers offered promotions and other preferential treatment to those who submitted to sexual advances. Broderick was deprived of promotions and job opportunities; when she and other women voiced their displeasure, management responded with hostility and Broderick's job assignments were changed. The U.S. Securities and Exchange Commission was found liable in this situation because it failed to take action against supervisors when it had both actual and constructive knowledge of their conduct.

Shrout v. Black Clawson Co., 689 F. Supp. 774 (S.D. Ohio 1988)

The court held the employer liable for a supervisor's quid pro quo sexual harassment, under the doctrine of *respondeat superior*. The supervisor made sexual remarks, offensively touched the woman employee, refused to give her annual performance appraisals and salary reviews, and told her, "[T]hings don't have to be this way" when she complained to him. She endured such behavior for four years before filing charges with the EEOC. She was awarded $75,000 in compensatory damages and $50,000 in punitive damages because of the employer's failure to take action when it knew or should have known of the harassment. An expert witness testified that an "open door policy" was not sufficient to immunize the employer from liability and that it was reasonable to assume that lower level women employees would hesitate to contact the company president with complaints of sexual harassment.

Paroline v. Unisys Corp., 867 F.2d 185 (4th Cir. 1989)

The Fourth Circuit ruled that "reasonable minds could differ as to whether Unisys'[s] response was reasonably calculated to end the harassment." The plaintiff offered evidence that previous reprimands of the harassing supervisor failed to deter him from continuing the behavior and the court agreed.

Steele v. Offshore Shipbuilding, Inc., 867 F.2d 1311 (11th Cir. 1989)

In this case, the Eleventh Circuit held that an employer was not liable under the doctrine of *respondeat superior* because it took appropriate corrective action once it was informed of the sexual harassment. The court went on to find that the individual's actions constituted hostile environment sexual harassment and not quid pro quo sexual harassment, because he did not demand sexual favors for job benefits.

Waltman v. International Paper Co., 875 F.2d 468 (5th Cir. 1989)

This court found that a publicized sexual harassment policy and complaint procedure were insufficient to immunize the employer from liability because the employer told the plaintiff that she should expect such behavior when working with men. She was also told by human resources staff that they could not investigate her claims without revealing her identity and that any investigation would be detrimental to her. The court found that the employer's action was not reasonably calculated to end the harassment.

Ellison v. Brady, 924 F.2d 872 (9th Cir. 1991)

In *Ellison*, the Ninth Circuit became the first federal appeals court to rule that, in determining whether the hostile work environment affected the employee's psychological well-being, Title VII requires a "reasonable woman" standard. This standard may be more sensitive than the usual legal standard—that of a reasonable man—because a reasonable man might be less offended by sexually suggestive material than a reasonable woman would be. The court also decided that when an individual is harassed by a co-worker, it violates the law for the employer to relocate the employee who was harassed rather than the harasser.

Robinson v. Jacksonville Shipyards, 760 F. Supp. 1486 (M.D. Fla. 1991)

In this Florida case, the judge also ruled upon the effect of actions on a "reasonable woman." Here, the court found, calendars and posters featuring nude or scantily dressed women created an atmosphere of sexual harassment that unlawfully stereotyped women as sex objects. The court held: "A pre-existing atmosphere that deters women from entering or continuing in a profession or job is no less destructive to and offensive to workplace equality than a sign declaring 'men only.' " The court also ordered affirmative relief in the form of policy changes, training, and education. The case is now on appeal, and one of the issues raised is whether First Amendment free speech rights preclude the prohibition of visual sexual harassment.

Franklin v. Gwinnett County Public Schools, 112 S. Ct. 1028 (1992)

This was the first Supreme Court case to consider the issue of sexual harassment in schools. A high school student was harassed by her sports coach and teacher. The school conducted an investigation into her allegations. The teacher resigned, on the condition that all matters pending against him be dropped, and the school complied with his request. Reversing the lower court decision, the Supreme Court ruled, for the first time, that monetary damages are available against schools in Title IX cases. (Title IX prohibits sex discrimination in educational institutions that receive federal funds.)

Future Trends in Sexual Harassment Law

Several trends point the way for the future of sexual harassment law. The first relates to sexual harassment in housing. The Rutgers Women's Law Clinic has taken the lead in investigating cases in which a landlord sexually harassed a tenant or required sexual favors in exchange for the provision of housing. Sexual harassment in housing constitutes sex discrimination in violation of both Title VII and Title VIII, the Fair Housing Act of the 1968 Civil Rights Act. Regina Cahan, author of *Home Is No Haven: An Analysis of Sexual Harassment in Housing*, stresses that "[w]hen sexual harassment occurs at work . . . the woman may remove herself from the offensive environment. When the harassment occurs in a woman's home, it is a complete invasion of her life." (Siegel 1992). The Women's Rights Litigation Clinic at Rutgers School of Law-Newark has prepared a pamphlet, "Stop Sexual Harassment in Housing," available in English and Spanish. (This organization is described in chapter 5.)

Another trend is exemplified by a sexual harassment case recently filed against Stroh's Brewery in Minnesota. In addition to a workplace rife with pin-ups and other sexually degrading material, one of the main allegations is that the company's media campaign contributes to the hostile work environment because the advertising uses the sexuality of women to sell beer.

New also are state laws requiring companies of a certain size to post notices on the illegality of sexual harassment and on the procedure for filing a complaint with the state's human rights commission. Maine is the first state to adopt such a requirement. California and several other states are considering laws that will also mandate sexual harassment training in the workplace.

Sexual Harassment Statistics

EEOC Claims Filed

According to an EEOC spokesperson, the agency's limited statistics on the number of claims filed are not published, but are kept only as a matter of internal records. The agency began collecting these statistics in 1987. The number of claims filed with the EEOC since that year are as follows:

1988	5,499
1989	5,623
1990	6,127
1991	6,883
1992	7,407

The number of sexual harassment suits filed by the EEOC from 1987 to 1992 are as follows:

1987	45
1988	41
1989	50
1990	50

For updated information, contact the Office of Communications and Legislative Affairs, The Equal Employment Opportunity Commission, 1801 L Street NW, Washington, DC 20507.

Surveys on the Incidence of Sexual Harassment

Numerous studies have been conducted on the incidence of sexual harassment over the years. These studies have found widely varying results—from 15 to 80 percent of the respondents reported experiencing sexual harassment. Freada Klein, Ph.D., a sexual harassment expert and researcher, believes that these disparate results happen for three reasons:

1. The studies used different definitions of the term *sexual harassment,* or failed to define the term at all.
2. There were differences in how the respondents were selected. Respondents who "self-select" in response to a query in a magazine or newsletter, for example, may have attitudes different from those who are randomly selected.
3. The study results failed to show whether respondents were asked if they had experienced sexual harassment over a specific period of time. Asking whether a respondent has ever experienced sexual harassment may lead to a very different result than if respondents are asked if they have experienced harassment within the past year.

The reader, therefore, should be cautious in drawing conclusions from any particular survey without determining the methodology employed. Following are the major findings from four of the more extensive studies: the U.S. Merit System Protection Board study; the Gutek/L.A. study; the Defense Department Study; and the *Harvard Business Review/Redbook* study. In addition, summary results from a number of other studies on specific issues are presented.

The U.S. Merit System Protection Board Study

A May 1980 (released in 1981) U.S. Merit System Protection Board (USMSPB) survey of over 23,000 men and women federal

FIGURE 4-1
Overall Incidence Rate of Sexual Harassment
(Percentage of Federal Employees Who Experienced Sexual Harassment
between May 1978 and May 1980, by Severity of Harassment)

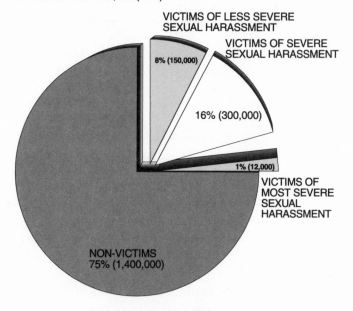

TOTAL FEDERAL WORKFORCE: 1,862,000
TOTAL VICTIMS: 462,000 (25%)

VICTIMS OF LESS SEVERE
SEXUAL HARASSMENT

VICTIMS OF SEVERE
SEXUAL HARASSMENT

8% (150,000)

16% (300,000)

1% (12,000)

VICTIMS OF
MOST SEVERE
SEXUAL
HARASSMENT

NON-VICTIMS
75% (1,400,000)

Note: These figures indicate the number of people harassed, classified by their most severe experience. Since many people reported they had had more than one experience, the number of harassment incidents is considerably larger.

Source: From a study conducted by the United States Merit Systems Protection Board, *Sexual Harassment of Federal Workers: Is It a Problem?* (Washington, DC: United States Government Printing Office, 1981).

executives branch employees (with a return rate of 85 percent) found that 42 percent of all female employees and 15 percent of all male employees reported being sexually harassed. The most ambiguous forms of sexual harassment—"sexual comments" and "suggestive looks"—were reported most often. (USMSPB 1981)

A 1987 follow-up study to the earlier MSPB study—of approximately 13,000 federal employees—found that 42 percent of all women and 14 percent of all men reported that they experienced some form of uninvited and unwanted sexual attention. The most frequently experienced type of uninvited sexual attention was "unwanted sexual teasing, jokes, remarks, or questions." (USMSPB 1987) Figures 4-1 and 4-2 provide the details of some of the results of the 1980 MSPB study.

FIGURE 4-2

Incidence Rate of Sexual Harassment among Women and Men
(Percentage of Female and Male Federal Employees Who Experienced Sexual Harassment between May 1978 and May 1980, by Severity of Harassment)

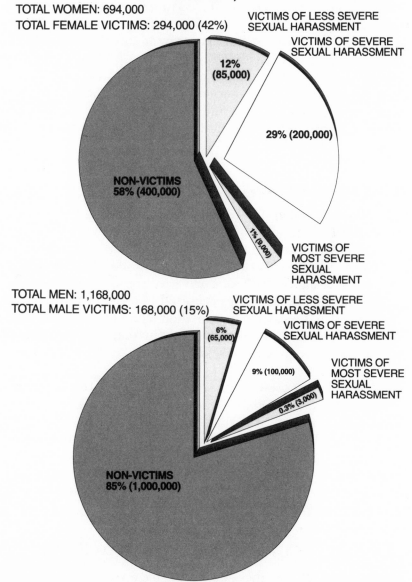

TOTAL WOMEN: 694,000
TOTAL FEMALE VICTIMS: 294,000 (42%)

VICTIMS OF LESS SEVERE SEXUAL HARASSMENT
VICTIMS OF SEVERE SEXUAL HARASSMENT

12% (85,000)

29% (200,000)

NON-VICTIMS 58% (400,000)

1% (9,000)

VICTIMS OF MOST SEVERE SEXUAL HARASSMENT

TOTAL MEN: 1,168,000
TOTAL MALE VICTIMS: 168,000 (15%)

VICTIMS OF LESS SEVERE SEXUAL HARASSMENT
VICTIMS OF SEVERE SEXUAL HARASSMENT

6% (65,000)

VICTIMS OF MOST SEVERE SEXUAL HARASSMENT

9% (100,000)

0.3% (3,000)

NON-VICTIMS 85% (1,000,000)

Note: These figures indicate the number of people harassed, classified by their most severe experience. Since many people reported they had had more than one experience, the number of harassment incidents is considerably larger.

Source: From a study conducted by the United States Merit Systems Protection Board, *Sexual Harassment of Federal Workers: Is It a Problem?* (Washington, DC: United States Government Printing Office, 1981).

The two MSPB studies also covered how employees define sexual harassment; employee responses to sexual harassment, including what actions employees think are the most effective in dealing with the issue and how they handled the problem; agency action to reduce sexual harassment; and how much sexual harassment costs the government. A discussion of the legal imperative to prevent sexual harassment and a review of the case law, as well as recommendations, are also presented. The 1980 report also detailed victims by age, marital status, racial and ethnic background, geographic location, annual salary, job classification, and other details. Similarly, the sex, age, marital status, ethnic background, and other details about the harasser were studied.

The Gutek/L.A. Study

In 1978, a number of workers, selected by random sampling from the Los Angeles telephone directories, were interviewed by telephone. Although this survey may be somewhat out of date, it is included here because it is one of the few random, scientifically designed studies. Forty-seven percent of the females and 46 percent of the males reported that they had experienced remarks of a sexual nature on their current jobs. Eleven percent of the women and 6 percent of the men reported that they had received requests for sexual activity on their present job. (Gutek 1985)

Table 4-1 represents Gutek's findings on the incidence of sexual harassment. Other factors Gutek studied include the nature and frequency of sexual harassment, the characteristics of harassers and the reactions of victims, workers' reports of sexual overtures, women's and men's attitudes about sexuality in the workplace, how differing environments influence sexuality, explanations for sexuality in the workplace, and unequal sex ratios and sex role spillovers.

The *Harvard Business Review*/*Redbook* Study

Among the most pertinent data available on sexual harassment in private employment is that found in an article by Eliza Collins and Timothy Blodgett, "Sexual Harassment . . . Some See It . . . Some Won't," in the March-April 1981 issue of the *Harvard Business Review*. The article reported on a survey that the *Review*

TABLE 4-1

Experiences of Social-Sexual Behaviors

	Males (N = 405)	Females (N = 827)
Ever experienced on current job		
Complimentary comments	46.0%	50.1%
Insulting comments	12.6	12.2
Complimentary looks, gestures	47.3	51.6
Insulting looks, gestures	12.3	9.1
Nonsexual touching	73.5	68.9
Sexual touching	20.9	15.3
Expected socializing	2.7	2.8
Expected sexual activity	1.0	1.8
Ever experienced on any job		
Complimentary comments	60.7%	68.1%
Insulting comments	19.3	23.3
Complimentary looks, gestures	56.3	66.6
Insulting looks, gestures	19.3	20.3
Nonsexual touching	78.0	74.4
Sexual touching	33.3	33.1
Expected socializing	8.4	12.0
Expected sexual activity	3.5	7.7
Ever experienced and labeled it sexual harassment		
Complimentary comments	10.4%	18.9%
Insulting comments	12.1	19.8
Complimentary looks, gestures	8.1	16.2
Insulting looks, gestures	9.6	15.4
Nonsexual touching	3.5	3.6
Sexual touching	12.3	24.2
Expected socializing	7.4	10.9
Expected sexual activity	3.2	7.6
Have you ever experienced sexual harassment?	37.3%	53.1%

Source: Reprinted from Barbara A. Gutek, *Sex and the Workplace: The Impact of Sexual Behavior and Harassment on Women, Men, and Organizations* (San Francisco: Jossey-Bass Inc., 1985).

conducted jointly with *Redbook* magazine. Questionnaires were mailed to 7,408 *Harvard Business Review* subscribers in the United States. Obviously, with such a mailing list, no claim can be made that the sample was random or unbiased. The sample also was skewed to ensure a large number of responses from females by including "virtually every female subscriber." Thirty-two percent of the questionnaires went to women and 44 percent of the responses came from women. The overall response rate was 24.9 percent. Clearly, the responses came from those most interested in the subject, and women tended to be more interested than men. A separate report on the survey was published by *Redbook* (Safran 1981).

The *Review* article reported that most people agreed on what sexual harassment was, but men and women seemed to disagree strongly on how frequently it occurred. Half of the women felt the amount of sexual harassment at work was greatly exaggerated, whereas two-thirds of the men felt that way. Two-thirds of high-level executives also felt harassment at work was exaggerated. The *Review* reported that top management appeared to be isolated from harassment situations, and that middle management was less aware of problems than lower levels of management.

Considering the obvious bias in the survey method, it is interesting to note that only 10 percent reported that they had ever heard of a situation such as: "Mr. X has asked me to have sex with him. I refused, but now I learn that he's given me a poor evaluation." (Collins and Blodgett 1981, 78)

Among the survey's major findings was the respondents' opinion that a supervisor's behavior was more serious and threatening than that of co-workers. Sexual harassment was seen as a power issue.

The study indicated that most respondents felt the EEOC guidelines were reasonable in theory, but some expressed the feeling that they would be difficult to implement because they were too vague. Respondents felt it would be impractical to take action on what to many women apparently were the most obnoxious and most pervasive forms of harassment, innuendo and jokes, but 68 percent of the male managers believed the EEOC guidelines would not be difficult to implement.

Some of the results of the *Harvard Business Review/Redbook* study detailing respondents' reports of the incidence of sexual harassment are presented in tables 4-2 and 4-3.

The Defense Department Study

In this 1988 report, mandated by then-Secretary of Defense Frank Carlucci in response to a recommendation of the Task Force on Women in the Military, survey responses were received from about 20,250 active-duty members of the four military services and the Coast Guard. The report consists of two confidential mail surveys of scientifically selected samples of active-duty military personnel conducted in 1988 and 1989. The much larger 1988 survey targeted about 38,000 personnel in the active services. The survey was designed to focus on: (1) the frequency of sexual harassment among the active-duty military; (2) the context,

TABLE 4-2
Views on Extreme Behavior by Percent of Total Respondents (1,846 *)

	Not harassment	Possibly harassment	Sexual harassment	Don't know	Heard of or observed in company	Not heard of or observed in company
A. "I can't seem to go in and out of my boss's office without being patted or pinched."	1%	8%	90%	1%	14%	83%
B. "Mr. X has told me that it would be good for my career if we went out together. I guess that means it would be bad for my career if I said no."	2	17	79	2	12	85
C. "Mr. X has asked me to have sex with him. I refused, but now I learn that he's given me a poor evaluation."	1	20	78	1	10	87
D. "I have been having an affair with the head of my division. Now I've told him I want to break it off, but he says I will lose out on the promotion I've been expecting."	4	7	87	2	7	90

* In some cases throughout the exhibits not all people answered all questions

Source: From Eliza G. C. Collins and Timothy B. Blodgett, "Sexual Harassment: Some See It...Some Won't," *Harvard Business Review* (March-April 1981).

TABLE 4-3
Views on Less Extreme Behavior according to Supervisor/Co-Worker Split Sample

	Not harassment	Possibly harassment	Sexual harassment	Don't know	Heard of or observed in company	Not heard of or observed in company
A. "Whenever I go into the office, my supervisor (a man I work with) eyes me up and down, making me feel uncomfortable."	20% 26	60% 54	16% 15	4% 4	61% 71	37% 27
B. "My supervisor (A man I work with) starts each day with a sexual remark. He insists it's an innocent social comment."	5 10	46 49	44 37	4 4	35 45	63 53
C. "Often in meetings my supervisor (a man I work with) continually glances at me."	62 65	26 26	1 2	10 6	50 61	47 36
D. "Every time we meet my supervisor (a man I work with) kisses me on the cheek."	4 17	43 47	46 20	7 10	11 18	86 79
E. "My supervisor (A man I work with) asked me out on a date. Although I refused, he continues to ask me."	10 33	39 41	48 20	4 5	26 42	71 56
F. "My supervisor (A man I work with) puts his hand on my arm when making a point."	43 46	44 42	3 4	10 9	59 63	36 33

Source: From Eliza G. C. Collins and Timothy B. Blodgett, "Sexual Harassment: Some See It...Some Won't," *Harvard Business Review* (March-April 1981).

location, and circumstances under which sexual harassment occurs; and (3) the effectiveness of current programs designed to prevent, reduce, and eliminate sexual harassment.

In 1981, the Department of Defense (DOD) formally established its policy, stating that "sexual harassment is unacceptable conduct and will not be condoned or tolerated in any way." Each of the services and the Coast Guard reissued that statement and established policies emphasizing the prevention of sexual harassment through extensive education and training. Survey questions covered the incidence and experiences of sexual harassment, actions taken to reduce sexual harassment, and the attitudes of leaders. Consistent with the department's policy, the language of the report calls reported experience of uninvited and unwanted sexual talk and behavior, as perceived by respondents, *sexual harassment*.

The percentage of active-duty military personnel experiencing at least one form of sexual harassment at least once while at work in the year prior to the survey was estimated to be about 22 percent of the respondents. Female personnel (64 percent) were almost four times as likely as male personnel (17 percent) to experience some form of sexual harassment. (See figure 4-3.)

The two most severe forms of sexual harassment reported were pressure for sexual favors and actual or attempted rape or sexual assault. Fifteen percent of the female and 2 percent of the male respondents reported pressure for sexual favors. Five percent of the female and 1 percent of the male respondents reported actual or attempted rape or sexual assault.

Although verbal types of sexual harassment occur more frequently than other forms of sexual harassment, just 4 percent of respondents (female: 9 percent; male: 3 percent) experienced *only* verbal forms. The type of sexual harassment reported in the year prior to the survey by the *majority* of all *victims* (who are 64 percent of female personnel and 17 percent of male personnel) was sexual teasing, jokes, remarks, or questions (female victims: 82 percent; male victims: 74 percent).

Female victims (88 percent) were more likely than male victims (73 percent) to report experiencing two or more of the ten forms of sexual harassment listed on the questionnaire. Female victims generally experienced sexual harassment more frequently than male victims, although frequency of occurrence varied by type of sexual harassment. See table 4-4 for results on the types of behavior experienced as sexual harassment in the DOD study.

FIGURE 4-3

Percentage Experiencing Sexual Harassment from Someone at Work
in the Last Year

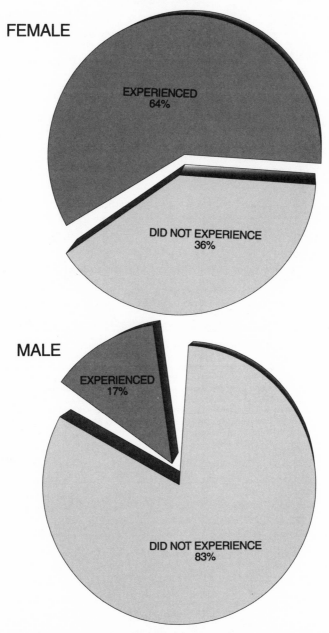

FEMALE

EXPERIENCED
64%

DID NOT EXPERIENCE
36%

MALE

EXPERIENCED
17%

DID NOT EXPERIENCE
83%

Source: From a study conducted by the Department of Defense, written by the Department of Defense Manpower Data Center, *Sexual Harassment in the Military: 1988* (Washington, DC: The Department of Defense, 1988). Available from the Assistant Secretary of Defense (Public Affairs) Room 2E777, The Pentagon, Washington, DC 20301-1400.

TABLE 4-4

All Types of Sexual Harassment Received from Someone at Work during the Year Prior to the (DOD) Survey, by Gender

	All Services	
Responses	Female	Male
Type of Sexual Harassment:		
Actual or Attempted Rape or Sexual Assault	5%	1%
Pressure for Sexual Favors	15	2
Touching, Cornering	38	9
Looks. Gestures	44	10
Letters, Calls	14	3
Pressure for Dates	26	3
Teasing, Jokes	52	13
Whistles, Calls	38	5
Attempts To Get Participation*	7	2
Other Attention	5	1
None Experienced	36	83

The data in this table are weighted. Weighted data have been statistically adjusted to represent the active military population. Weighted statistics are estimates, within some error, of characteristics of the active military population. The weighting scheme used slightly underestimates the total Active Force.

Percentages are rounded to the nearest whole number. Percentages of 0 may indicate less than 0.5, but not actually 0. Percentages will not sum to 100 because respondents could select more than one answer.

*Attempts to get [respondent's] participation in any other kinds of sexually oriented activity."

Reference: Section II, Question 2: "Have you received any of the following kinds of *uninvited and unwanted* sexual attention *during the last 12 months* from someone where you work in the active-duty military?" (Abbreviated response options are given above under "Type of Sexual Harassment.")

Source: From a study conducted by the Department of Defense, written by the Department of Defense Manpower Data Center, *Sexual Harassment in the Military: 1988* (Washington, DC: The Department of Defense, 1988). Available from the Assistant Secretary of Defense (Public Affairs) Room 2E777, The Pentagon, Washington, DC 20301-1400.

Miscellaneous Additional Studies of the Incidence of Sexual Harassment

A 1975 survey of 155 women in Ithaca, New York, by Working Women's Institute found that 70 percent of the respondents had experienced some unwanted sexual advances. (Siegel 1992)

In 1976, *Redbook* magazine published a questionnaire on sexual harassment to which over 9,000 women responded. Eighty-eight percent of the respondents reported having experienced unwanted sexual attentions on the job. (Safran 1976)

Of the more than 1,300 employers responding to Business and Legal Report's (BLR's) 1992 sexual harassment survey, 42 percent received a complaint during the past year, and most of the complaints resulted in disciplinary action against the wrongdoer. (Business & Legal Reports 1992) Manufacturing employers were a bit more likely to have received a complaint than nonmanufacturing or nonbusiness employers (44 percent in manufacturing, as compared with 42 percent in both nonmanufacturing and nonbusiness firms), and they also seemed more disposed to administer discipline (66 percent in manufacturing, as compared with 59 percent in nonmanufacturing and 54 percent in nonbusiness organizations).

Employers with more than 500 employees were most likely to have received a complaint (56 percent), while organizations with fewer than 100 employees were least likely to have received one (21 percent). Approximately three of every ten employers that received a complaint found no basis for it, a finding that remained fairly consistent regardless of size or industrial category. Fewer than one in eight respondents experienced the filing of a formal complaint with the government, but this still added up to over 100 formal charges for this population.

A survey by *Working Woman* magazine in December 1988, conducted by sexual harassment expert Freada Klein and Klein Associates, Inc., surveyed Fortune 500 manufacturing and service companies. Directors of personnel, human resources managers, and equal opportunity officers who represented 3.3 million employees at 160 large corporations responded in depth to the 49-question survey. The survey reported a huge gap between the incidence of sexual harassment and the rate of complaint filing. Almost 90 percent of the companies surveyed received at least one complaint in the past 12 months and 25 percent received 6 or more. Experts involved in the survey agreed, though, that the numbers seem unbelievably low, leading them to speculate that most workers do not report sexual harassment complaints. The survey found that companies received only 1.4 complaints per 1,000 women. This compares to 42 percent of women in the USMSPB study over a two-year period and 14 percent of the men, as well as to Freada Klein's own studies, which showed that at least 15 percent of female employees have been sexually harassed in the last 12 months.

A 1992 follow-up survey by *Working Woman* of 9,000 readers, as well as a simultaneous survey following up the 1988 survey of Fortune 500 companies, revealed that more than 60 percent of the readers said they personally had been harassed and more than a third knew a co-worker who had been harassed. However, as only one out of four women reported the harassment and most companies received fewer than five complaints a month, the writers concluded that the vast majority of women who are harassed still do not feel they can safely report a problem. Only one out of five women believed that most complaints were given justice, while more than 70 percent of personnel managers think they were.

In a review of all of the available studies, the National Council for Research on Women concluded that at least one out of every two women will experience sexual harassment at some point during her academic or working life. (Siegel 1992)

A self-selected survey of the readers of *Glamour* magazine in 1981 found that 85 percent believed that they had experienced some sort of sexual harassment on the job.

Reviewing the results from several different measures of prevalence, Gutek (1985) suggested that up to 53 percent of women had been harassed sometime in their working lives.

A random telephone survey of 400 people in the Chicago area found that nearly a third of the women and a fifth of the men reported being sexually harassed at work. The study was conducted by the Medill School of Journalism and Northwestern University. (Webb 1992)

The Incidence of Sexual Harassment among Particular Groups and Professions

Military

Two-thirds of women in the military say they have been sexually harassed. (Department of Defense 1990)

Blue Collar Workers

A telephone-interview study of 139 unskilled female auto workers revealed that 36 percent of the interviewees had experienced sexual harassment. In a small survey of coal miners, 53 percent of the women had been propositioned by the boss and 76 by co-workers; 17 percent had been physically attacked. Researcher Peggy Crull found that traditional women's work is more likely to be characterized by one extreme, the threat of losing a job for failing to comply with sexual demands; the other extreme, a sexually demeaning work environment, is the more typical mode of harassment for women working in formerly all-male settings. (Crull 1984)

In "Blue-Collar Blues: The Sexual Harassment of Women Autoworkers," Gruber and Bjorn note that, in contrast to women in clerical work, for example, women auto workers are likely to be highly visible and viewed as "outsiders." (Gruber and Bjorn 1982, 272) Gruber and Bjorn also point out that male auto workers are apt to feel threatened by the "invasion" of women into the auto plant and by the fact that these women have similar jobs and earn similar wages. "In situations where objective work conditions do not result in the subordination of women, it is quite likely that sexual harassment will occur as men attempt to regain an upper hand." (Gruber and Bjorn 1982, 272) In other words, when status differences between men and women are blurred, other means of creating differences between the sexes and maintaining male dominance become salient. (Gruber and Bjorn 1982, 290)

Professional Workers

The American Medical Women's Association (AMWA) issued a study in 1991 entitled "Gender Bias against and Sexual Harassment of AMWA Members in Massachusetts," documenting that within a one-year period, 54 percent of respondents encountered some form of sex discrimination. In addition, approximately one-fourth experienced sexual harassment (27 percent). Unwanted sexual attention not viewed as sexual harassment was experienced by more than twice as many respondents (55 percent). (Lenhart 1991)

In "Women in Non-Traditional Occupations: Comparisons Between Women Engineers and Dentists in Michigan," Kaisa Kauppinen-Toropainen of the Center for the Education of Women, University of Michigan, documented that 14 percent of the engineers surveyed reported experiencing unwanted pressure for sexual favors at work. Twenty-two percent mentioned sexually suggestive posters, pictures, or other materials of a sexual nature in the workplace. (Siegel 1992)

Several studies have documented sexual harassment of women in the legal profession. A *National Law Journal*/West Publishing Survey in 1989 found that 60 percent of 900 female associates and partners in the country's top 250 law firms experienced sexual harassment. (National Law Journal 1989 [ABA 1992]) Thirteen women reported rape or attempted rape. In "The State of the Legal Profession," a 1990 survey by the ABA Young Lawyers Division, the researchers found that 85 percent of 3,000 female lawyers reported having experienced or observed one type of harassment, and 45 percent had experienced or observed five types, during the last two years. (American Bar Association Commission on Women in the Profession 1992)

In the field of journalism, a survey of women reporters and editors in Washington, DC, conducted by Katherine McAdams, an assistant professor of journalism at the University of Maryland, found that 80 percent of the 102 journalists who responded to the questionnaire said that sexual harassment on the job is a problem. Sixty percent of those said that they had been subjected to it personally. (Hoffman 1992)

At the United Nations, a survey of 875 women and men in both professional and general service (clerical) categories found that half of the women as well as 31 percent of the men respondents reported that they had at some time either personally experienced sexual pressures or were aware that such pressures existed within the organization. The most specific situation in which such unprofessional conduct was reported was in the matter of promotion (62 percent), followed by recruitment (13 percent); obtaining a permanent contract (11 percent); and transfer and going on missions (7 percent each). (Kelber 1977)

The 1992 *Working Woman* Magazine Survey concluded that "the higher a woman is in the corporate hierarchy, the more likely she is to be harassed," and "that's probably why Working Woman readers reported higher rates of harassment (60 percent) than respondents to other surveys, whose rates hover between 25 and 40 percent." (Sadroff 1992)

Younger Women Workers

Young women are particularly vulnerable to sexual harassment from male superiors in the workplace. In the 1980 Merit System Protection Board random survey of women of all ages and educational backgrounds, women aged 16 to 19 reported the highest incidence of sexual harassment of any group. According to a 1992 *Working Woman* survey, almost 30 percent of the incidents reported occurred among women aged 18 to 24 years old. Considering the small size of this age group in the work force, this percentage is disproportionate.

Women of Color

According to the National Council for Research on Women (Siegel 1992), although there is historical and social science research documenting white men's violence against women of color and same-race violence, there has been little reliable research about the dynamics between racism and sexual harassment. Several studies are currently underway to assess the incidence rates for women of color, including one being conducted by Dr. Michele Paludi. (See chapter 3 for a brief biography of Paludi.)

In Schools and Colleges

In their 1984 survey of sexual harassment, Dzeich and Weiner concluded that 20 to 30 percent of female college students experience sexual harassment. Yet they also found that the academic institutions in their study averaged only four complaints each during the 1982–1983 academic year. (Dzeich and Weiner 1984)

Paludi, in her work, *Academic and Workplace Sexual Harassment* (1990), summarizes the research on the incidence of sexual harassment in academic institutions. (See table 4-5.)

A presentation of the 1985 American Psychological Association reports the results of a mail survey of graduate student members of APA's Division of Clinical Psychology and Division of

TABLE 4-5
Summary of Research on the Incidence of Sexual Harassment

Adams, Kottke, and Padgitt (1983)

13% of women students surveyed, reported they had avoided taking a class or working with certain professors because of the risk of being subjected to sexual advances; 17% received verbal sexual advances, 13.6% received sexual invitations; 6.4% had been subjected to physical advances; 2% received direct sexual assault

Chronicle of Higher Education Report of Harvard University (1983)

15% of the graduate students and 12% of the undergraduate students who had been sexually harassed by their professors changed their major or educational program because of the harassment

Wilson and Kraus (1983)

8.9% of the female undergraduates in their study had been pinched, touched, or patted to the point of personal discomfort

Bailey and Richards (1985)

12.7% of 246 graduate women surveyed reported that they had been sexually harassed; 21% had not enrolled in a course to avoid such behavior; 11.3% tried to report the behavior, 2.6% dropped a course because of it; 15.9% reported being directly assaulted

Bond (1988)

75% of 229 faculty experienced jokes with sexual themes during their graduate training; 68.9% were subjected to sexist comments demeaning to women; 57.8% of the women reported experiencing sexist remarks about their clothing, body, or sexual activities; 12.2% had unwanted intercourse, breast, or genital stimulation

Gutek (1985)

53.1% of private sector workers surveyed reported being fired, not being promoted, not given raises, all because of refusal to comply with requests for sexual relationships

Source: Reprinted from *Academic and Workplace Sexual Harassment* by Michele A. Paludi and Richard B. Barickman by permission of the State University of New York Press. Copyright © 1991 by State University of New York.

Counseling. Of 246 women responding, 12.7 percent of graduate women surveyed reported that they had been sexually harassed; 21 percent did not enroll in a course to avoid such behavior; 11.3 percent tried to report the behavior; 2.6 percent dropped a course because of it; 15.9 percent reported being directly assaulted. (Siegel 1992)

Sexual harassment and teens is an area that has not been extensively studied. Nan Stein of Wellesley College is currently involved in such a study through *Seventeen* magazine, which will be published in 1993. According to Strauss, in response to a sexual harassment questionnaire distributed to student leaders from 13 school districts at a Minnesota State Sex Equity Student Leadership conference:

> 80 percent of the students said they were aware of sexual harassment in their schools
>
> 75 percent said they were aware of sexual harassment between students
>
> 50 percent said they were aware of sexual harassment between students and staff
>
> 26 percent said sexual harassment "goes on all the time"
>
> 50 percent said "it happens to a fair number of people"
>
> 6 percent said "it doesn't happen" (Strauss 1992, 3)

A study conducted by a Minnesota secondary vocational school surveyed 250 students from four school districts. Approximately 50 percent of the teenage girls reported having been verbally and physically harassed at school; another 30 percent stated that they had been harassed at work. (Strauss 1992)

Psychological and Physical Effects of Harassment

Researchers have attempted to document the psychological and physical effects of harassment on victims. Gutek (1985) reports that 38 percent of the women in her Los Angeles study said the incident affected their feelings about their jobs and 28 percent said it affected how they related to other people at work. In general, Gutek found that the harassment had a greater effect on work than it did on the woman's private life, although about 15 percent of the women reported that the incident affected their health or their relationships with other men.

The women in the Gutek/L.A. survey were also asked how they felt right after the incident. The two strongest reactions were disgust and anger: over two-fifths of the women said they felt disgust and about one-third said they were angry. Fewer women (under 15 percent) reported feeling anxious or hurt, and fewer than 10 percent said they felt very depressed, sad, or guilty. It may be significant, however, that they were reporting reactions to events that occurred over a year ago. Some initial hurt, Gutek speculates, may have turned to anger over time. In addition, many of the strong emotions the women felt at the time of the harassment may have been forgotten a year later.

Although many victims of sexual harassment publicly appear to brush it off, the effects of stress as a result of harassment are significant. The American Psychiatric Association recognizes sexual harassment as a "severe stressor." (American Psychiatric Association 1987) As part of a growing list of identifiable effects, summarized by Siegel (1992), the researchers found anxiety attacks, headaches, sleep disturbance, disordered eating, gastrointestinal disorders, nausea, weight loss or gain, and crying spells. Fear, anger, anxiety, depression, self-questioning, and self-blaming are among the most common effects women describe.

Data from surveys of corporate employees indicate that employees who feel they have experienced sexual harassment, when compared to nonharassed employees, are substantially less positive about their employment (Klein 1991). Common responses include

Less job satisfaction

Lower rating of the immediate supervisor

Less favorable view of company communication

Diminished confidence in the senior management team

Reduced organizational commitment

Increased likelihood to leave the company

Federal working women in the USMSPB (1981) survey reported that unwanted sexual attention affected their lives.

Thirty-six percent said it affected their feelings about work, 33 percent reported an impact on their emotional or physical condition, 15 percent said it affected their ability to work with others, 11 percent said it affected the quantity of their work, and 10 percent reported an effect on the quality of their work. (USMSPB 1981, 81)

Conversely, the Department of Defense Study (Department of Defense 1988, 30) found that the majority (85 percent of women, 94 percent of men) reported that they neither received nor needed either counseling or medical assistance. However, 11 percent of the women and 3 percent of the men reported that although they received neither, counseling would have been helpful. The survey does not reveal why more of these victims did not seek or feel a need for medical assistance or counseling from a trained professional.

Paludi (1991) reports on the "Sexual Harassment Trauma Syndrome" (formulated by Shullman in 1989), which has been applied to the effects of harassment on the physical, emotional, interpersonal, and career aspects of women's lives. Research has indicated that, depending on the severity of the harassment, between 21 percent and 82 percent of all women report that their emotional or physical condition, or both, deteriorated as a result. Furthermore, like victims of rape who go to court, harassment victims may experience a second victimization when they attempt to deal with the situation through legal or institutional means. Stereotypes about sexual harassment and women's victimization blame women for the harassment (MacKinnon 1979). These stereotypes center around the myths that sexual harassment is a form of seduction, that women secretly want to be sexually harassed, and that women do not tell the truth. (Paludi 1991)

Finally, readers who responded to the *Working Woman* (1992) survey reported such ill effects as being fired or forced to quit their jobs (25 percent), seriously undermined self-confidence (27 percent), impaired health (12 percent) and long-term career damage (13 percent). (Klein 1988)

Characteristics of the Harasser

Gutek (1985) studied the characteristics of both male and female harassers and found that the men who make advances toward women are very different from the women who make advances

TABLE 4-6
Profile of Initiators

How Long Associated with Initiator?

	Less than 1 day	Less than 2 months	2–6 months	Over 6 months	Total (N)
Female Recipients	5.8	20.0	24.2	50.0	100% (310)
Male Recipients	5.6	23.8	25.2	45.5	100% (143)

Initiator Behaves This Way toward Others

	Yes	No	Total (N)
Female Recipients	71.0	29.0	100% (259)
Male Recipients	52.3	47.7	100% (109)

Initiator Is a Supervisor

	Yes	No	Total (N)
Female Recipients	44.8	56.3	100% (306)
Male Recipients	5.5	94.5	100% (139)

Initiator Age

	Under 30	30–39	40–49	Over 50	Total (N)
Female Recipients	19.0	31.8	26.0	23.1	100% (311)
Male Recipients	56.6	34.4	9.0	0.0	100% (145)

Initiator Married

	Yes	No	Total (N)
Female Recipients	65.4	34.6	100% (288)
Male Recipients	28.4	71.6	100% (131)

Attractiveness of Initiator

	Above average	Not above average	Total (N)
Female Recipients	41.8	58.2	100% (306)
Male Recipients	71.6	28.4	100% (141)

Source: Reprinted from Barbara A. Gutek, *Sex and the Workplace: The Impact of Sexual Behavior and Harassment on Women, Men, and Organizations* (San Francisco: Jossey-Bass Inc., 1985).

toward men. (See table 4-6.) The "average" man who made advances was very much like the "average" man in the survey, with the exception that the initiator tended to behave the same way toward other women workers. Not so with the average woman. The men described a female initiator as young, attractive, not married, and not a supervisor. Gutek doubted that these women were in a position to harass anyone.

In a statement of the Ad Hoc Group for Public Information on Sexual Harassment, written by experts who gathered in Washington to provide public information on sexual harassment during the October 1991 Senate Judiciary hearings, Fitzgerald (reported in Siegel 1992, 27) reported that

> data from the major studies of victims . . . have suggested that most harassers are older than their victims (although some are younger); married (although some are single); and of the same race as their victims. Some harass many women (43 percent of U.S. Merit Systems Protection Board victims believed that their harassers had also harassed others), whereas others harass only once. Further, harassers are found in all types of occupations, at all organizational levels, among college professors as well as the business and professional world, and among individuals who live otherwise exemplary lives.

How Victims Respond

According to Klein (1988), most women who are sexually harassed do nothing. "Few incidents are reported to employers; the formal complaint rate across all companies is 1.4 per thousand women employees per year." This is a small percentage compared to the surveys reporting the incidence of sexual harassment. "In most organizations, at least 90 percent of sexual harassment victims are unwilling to come forward for two reasons: fear of retaliation and fear of loss of privacy." (Klein 1991) Several surveys have supported Klein's opinions, including the survey of federal employees, which found that only 5 percent of those who had experienced sexual harassment filed formal complaints or requested investigations. (USMSPB 1987)

During the 1991 Senate Judiciary hearings, while considering the allegations that Clarence Thomas harassed Anita Hill, many senators focused on the question of why Hill did not report Thomas at the time the incidents allegedly occurred. According to sexual harassment experts quoted in Siegel (1992), Anita Hill's failure to complain ten years earlier is common behavior for victims.

Based on her surveys of victims, Barbara Gutek found three common reasons why victims do not formally complain. Fifty percent of the women she surveyed reported that they did not believe anything would come of it. Another 50 percent also reported that they were afraid they would be blamed. Finally, victims reported that they were concerned about the harasser and did not want to hurt him. According to Gutek, women excuse the harasser with statements such as "he's going through a bad time." (Gutek 1985) In the 1988 *Working Woman* survey, victims cited fear of retaliation as the chief reason for not reporting incidents of harassment. (Klein 1988)

Do Women Invite Harassment?

Only a few studies have openly addressed the issue of whether women invite harassment, and they have conflicting results. For example, 78 percent of the women and 86 percent of the men in the *Harvard Business Review/Redbook* study agreed or partly agreed with the statement: "Women can and often do use their sexual attractiveness to their own advantage" (Collins and Blodgett 1981, 90). The article suggested that many believe women invite sexual harassment by their dress and actions.

However, *Redbook*, reporting on the same study, found that male and female views differed. Only a third of the male respondents, compared to half of the women, defined the following statement as sexual harassment: "Whenever I go to see Mr. X, I wear a tight skirt. It seems to help my career." Parenthetically, it might be noted that in the earlier *Redbook* survey, conducted in 1976, 30 percent of the 9,000 female respondents reported using their sexual attractiveness to their own advantage. (Safran 1981, 7) Of those who responded to the 1981 survey, two-thirds of the male respondents and three-fourths of the female executives did not believe that a woman could avoid being the target of unwanted approaches if she dressed and behaved "properly."

Paradoxically, there is some evidence that the more a woman is attuned to sex discrimination in the workplace, the *less* likely she is to encounter sexual harassment. In a study of 220 female lawyers from a midwest city, researchers found that the respondents fell into two categories, careerist and feminist. They defined *careerists* as women who believe that sexism no longer exists and that the law is an open, equally competitive arena. *Feminists* in this study view the legal profession as an uneven playing field, with women having lesser status. The authors found that 27 percent of the careerists were subjected to unwanted sexual advances, compared to only 12 percent of feminists. (American Bar Association Commission on Women in the Profession 1992)

Gutek (1985) found that a common stereotype is that some women are willing to use their sexuality to advance and thus gain an unfair advantage over men competing for the same job. She found, however, "virtually no evidence that women benefit in this way." She also found comparable stereotypes about men—that they "sleep their way to the top or get jobs to find wives—exceedingly rare." She did find that a majority of both sexes agreed with the statement that if a man or woman was propositioned at work, he or she could have done something to prevent it. She found different results, however, from women who experienced negative consequences of sexual harassment; they were less likely than other women to believe that women cause overtures or propositions. "Whereas 71 percent of women who had not experienced any negative consequences of sexual harassment agreed that women cause or could prevent propositions, 60 percent of female victims agreed with the statement." (Gutek 1985, 103)

Paludi (1990) found that "[t]here is ample evidence that women experience an enormous amount of guilt and self-blame surrounding harassment, just as they do over rape and incest." She suggests that one reason for this self-blame may be that women are—contrary to some popular theories—reluctant to view themselves as victims and would rather assume that they did something to cause the harassment. Such self-blame, Paludi concludes, ironically, gives victims a feeling that they have some degree of power over their experience.

Trainers who conduct sexual harassment workshops for students, businesses, and government report that one of the most often asked questions is: "Don't women provoke men by wearing sexy clothes?" Provocative dress, however, is in the eye of the beholder. Dzeitch and Weiner (1984, 66) point out that part of the problem for women is that "some people have trouble distinguishing seductive attire from that which simply emphasizes beauty and self-esteem":

The sexual message of clothing is in the eye of the beholder, and women have suffered great misunderstanding from the opposite sex. A 1980 study at the University of California at Los Angeles found that of 432 blacks, whites, and Hispanics between the age of 14 and 18, none viewed a male's open shirt, tight pants, tight swim trunks, or jewelry as indications that he was seeking sex. But males generally assumed that low-cut tops, shorts, tight jeans, or braless-ness meant that a female was encouraging a sexual reaction. Females, however, contended that such dress simply indicated they were trying to be in style.

The authors concluded that sexual harassment is not caused by what women wear or excused by a man's misreading the messages of attire:

"Provocative dress" has nothing to do with sexual harassment. Whether women wear high collars, dresses that flatten their breasts, skirts that hide their ankles, or veils that cover their faces, they are forced to endure sexual harassment. It did not begin with tube tops and short shorts, and it will not cease as long as society insists on believing that men cannot restrain their sexual impulses and that women, by their dress, invite sexual advances.

Differences in Perceptions between Men and Women about Harassment

One of the most interesting results of the study of the difference in perceptions between men and women about sexual harassment is the "gender gap" identified by Gutek (1985). She found that, in general, men are flattered by sexual advances at work, while women are insulted. Furthermore, she found that neither men nor women were aware of this difference.

Gutek reported different attitudes of the 178 men and 221 women toward whether social-sexual behavior at work was harassment. Reporting on the 1978 telephone survey, she found that higher percentages of women believed each of eight categories of behavior was harassment. (See table 4-7.)

The *Harvard Business Review* reported that most people agreed on what sexual harassment was, but men and women seemed to disagree strongly on how frequently it occurred. Half of the women felt the amount of sexual harassment at work was greatly exaggerated, whereas two-thirds of the men felt that way.

TABLE 4-7
What Is Sexual Harassment?

	Males	Females
Is sexual harassment		
Complimentary comments	21.9%	33.5%
Insulting comments	70.3	85.5
Complimentary looks, gestures	18.9	28.9
Insulting looks, gestures	61.6	80.3
Nonsexual touching	6.6	7.3
Sexual touching	58.6	84.3
Expected socializing	91.1	95.8
Expected sexual activity	94.5	98.0

Source: Reprinted from Barbara A. Gutek, *Sex and the Workplace: The Impact of Sexual Behavior and Harassment on Women, Men, and Organizations* (San Francisco: Jossey-Bass Inc., 1985).

Redbook, reporting on the same survey, found that male executives did not see sexual horseplay and subtle advances as clearcut harassment. Men in the Merit Systems Protection Board study had a tendency to think that victims were "somewhat responsible for bringing sexual harassment on themselves."

The Costs to Employers of Harassment

The Merit Systems Protection Board report concluded that sexual harassment had cost the federal government $189 million for the two-year period ending in May 1980. The losses included estimates of lost productivity and increased turnover. The 1988 update estimated costs of $267 million during the study period. The 1980 figures represent the costs of replacing employees who left their jobs ($36.7 million); paying sick leave to employees who missed work ($26.1 million); and reduced individual and work group productivity ($204.5 million). (USMSPB 1981)

The 1988 *Working Woman* survey (Klein 1988) found that the total annual cost of sexual harassment per Fortune 500 company for both men and women to be $6,719,593 (excluding some costs, such as litigation). These costs included loss in productivity, turnover, and extra leave taken by victims. The study also found the cost of sexual harassment to be $282.53 per employee per year for a typical Fortune 500 service or manufacturing firm of 23,784 employees, and that a corporation of that size could begin meaningful prevention efforts for $200,000 (a cost of $8.41 per employee).

Reporting on the *Harvard Business Review* survey, *Redbook* indicated that two out of three executives believed unwanted sexual behavior was bad for business. It could hurt efficiency and lead to turnover of trained and valuable employees. (Safran 1981, 49)

Employers' Response to Harassment

According to the 1992 *Working Woman* survey, most Fortune 500 executives believe their own companies are doing a good job in the area of preventing and dealing with sexual harassment. Eighty-one percent report having training programs on sexual harassment, compared with only 60 percent in the 1988 survey—although only half of *Working Woman* readers work for a company with these procedures.

The U.S. Merit Systems Protection Board's 1988 survey reported that there is no clear correlation between any agency's estimates of its training efforts on the issue of sexual harassment and the reported incidence of harassment in that agency. According to each agency's own estimate, on the average, a federal employee received a total of one to two hours of training on sexual harassment during the period from 1980 to 1986. All agencies had (at that time) issued policy statements or other written guidance on sexual harassment.

The American Bar Association Commission on Women in the Profession (1992) reported on a survey by the American Management Association, which found that the top disciplinary actions taken against harassers were formal reprimand, probation or suspension, transfer of the harasser to a new position, counseling, and mediation with both parties. The same survey found that 52 percent of AMA's 524 member companies have dealt with sexual harassment allegations in the last five years: 60 percent of the sexual harassment claims resulted in disciplinary action against the harasser, and only 17 percent were dismissed without action.

Seventy-three percent of the respondents in the *Harvard Business Review/Redbook* study reported that they favored organizations establishing a policy against harassment, but only 29 percent worked in companies with such a policy. However, some employers were seriously concerned with the issue: one reported that three store managers had been fired in the past three years for sexual harassment.

Impact of Hill/Thomas on Harassment

Sadroff (1992) reported that, in the nine months since Anita Hill's testimony, inquiries sent to the EEOC rose 150 percent, and actual charges filed rose 23 percent. She also reported that *Working Woman* readers were far more likely than human-resource executives to believe Hill over Thomas (59 percent to 38 percent). Women with more education, higher incomes, and in professional or managerial positions were most likely to reject Thomas's story, as were women who had been harassed. Women who had been harassed were also more sympathetic about the time lapse than women who had never been harassed (63 percent versus 39 percent). In addition, more than half of working women who had been sexually harassed said they could understand why Hill would continue to work for a man who treated her the way Thomas did. Two-thirds of the executives agreed that it was not unusual for a professional woman to continue to work with a man who had harassed her.

Almost half the *Working Woman* readers believed that publicity about the case has reduced the "comfort level" between women and men in the workplace. In addition, in 1992, more than half the readers intended to vote against their senator if he or she voted for Thomas's confirmation. In fact, the situation has been credited with the election of several women to the Senate in 1992, including Carol Mosely Braun, an Illinois Democrat who won in the primary over Alan J. Dixon, a senator who had voted to confirm Thomas. She is the first black woman elected to the Senate. As expressed by Eleanor Holmes Norton: "The greatest surprise of Anita Hill is that she managed to encourage other women even though she did not get justice for herself." (Sadroff 1992) Similarly, Solomon (1992), found that 81 percent of Fortune 500 companies now provide employees with sexual harassment training as a result of Anita Hill's testimony, compared to 60 percent in 1988.

Several surveys conducted since the hearings have shown an increase in the number of people who now believe that Hill, not Thomas, was telling the truth. For example, a *Wall Street Journal-*NBC poll taken in September 1992 found that 44 percent of those surveyed believed Hill, up from 24 percent just after the hearings in 1991. Belief in Thomas's testimony dropped from 47 percent to 34 percent (Cass 1992).

References

American Bar Association Commission on Women in the Profession, "Sexual Harassment After Anita Hill," *Perspectives* 1, no. 2 (Spring 1992): 1.

American Bar Association Commission on Women in the Profession, "Sexual Harassment Surveys Detail the Extent of the Problem," *Perspectives* 1, no. 2 (Spring 1992): 2.

American Psychiatric Association, *Diagnostic and Statistical Manual of Mental Disorders*. 3d ed. 11 (Washington, DC: American Psychiatric Association, 1987).

Business & Legal Reports, Inc., "What To Do about Personnel Problems," *Business & Legal Reports, Michigan Edition* 2, no. 214 (July 1992): 1–3.

Cass, Connie (A.P.) "Hill: Sexism Taints Courts," *Rocky Mountain News*, 13 October 1992, at 23A, col. 1.

Collins, Eliza G. C. and Timothy B. Blodgett, "Sexual Harassment: Some See It . . . Some Won't," *Harvard Business Review* 59, no. 2 (March-April, 1981): 76–95.

Conte, Alba, *Sexual Harassment in the Workplace: Law and Practice* (New York: John Wiley & Sons, 1990).

Crull, Peggy, "Contrasting Sexual Harassment in Female- and Male-Dominated Occupations." In Karen Sacks and Dorothy Remy, eds., *My Troubles Are Going To Have Trouble with Me: Everyday Trials and Triumphs of Women Workers* (New Brunswick, NJ: Rutgers University Press, 1984): 218–228.

————, "Stress Effects of Sexual Harassment on the Job: Implications for Counseling," *American Journal of Orthopsychiatry* 52 (1982): 539–544.

Department of Defense Manpower Data Center, *Sexual Harassment in the Military: 1988* (Washington, DC: Department of Defense, 1990). Available from The Assistant Secretary of Defense (Public Affairs), Room 2E777, The Pentagon, Washington, DC 20301-1400.

Dzeich, Billie Wright, and Linda Weiner, *The Lecherous Professor: Sexual Harassment on Campus* (Boston: Beacon Press, 1984).

Eskenazi, Martin, and David Gallen, *Sexual Harassment: Know Your Rights!* (New York: Carroll & Graf, 1992).

Gruber, James E., and Lars Bjorn, "Blue-Collar Blues: The Sexual Harassment of Women Autoworkers," *Work and Occupations* 9, no. 3 (1982): 271–298.

Gutek, Barbara, *Sex and the Workplace* (San Francisco: Jossey-Bass, 1985).

Hoffman, Lisa (*Chicago Tribune*), "Reporters Find Sexual Harassment an Impediment," *Denver Post*, 23 June 1992, at 16, col. 2.

Kelber, Mim, "The UN's Dirty Little Secret," *Ms.* (November 1977): 51, 79.

Klein, Freada, *The 1988 Working Woman Sexual Harassment Survey Executive Report* (Cambridge, MA: Klein Associates, 1988).

Klein, Freada, *Testimony Before the Committee on Education and Labor*, House of Representatives, Hearings on H.R. 1, The Civil Rights Act of 1991 (1991).

Lenhart, Sharyn A., Freada Klein, Patricia Falcao, Elizabeth Phelan, and Kevin Smith, "Gender Bias Against and Sexual Harassment of AMWA Members in Massachusetts," *JAMWA Journal* 46, no. 4 (July/August 1991): 121–125.

MacKinnon, Catharine A., *Sexual Harassment of Working Women* (New Haven, CT and London: Yale University Press, 1979).

National Law Journal, "Women in Large Firms: A High Price for Admission?" (December 11, 1989): 82. Reprinted in American Bar Association, *Lawyers and Balanced Lives: A Guide to Drafting and Implementing Sexual Harassment Policies for Lawyers* (Chicago: American Bar Association, 1992).

Omilian, Susan M., *Sexual Harassment in Employment* (Wilmette, IL: Callaghan, 1987).

Paludi, Michele A., ed., *Ivory Power: Sexual Harassment on Campus* (Albany, NY: State University of New York Press, 1990).

Paludi, Michele, and Richard B. Barickman, *Academic and Workplace Sexual Harassment: A Resource Manual* (Albany, NY: State University of New York Press, 1991).

Petrocelli, William, and Barbara Kate Repa, *Sexual Harassment on the Job: What It Is and How To Stop It* (Berkeley, CA: Nolo Press, 1992).

Sadroff, Ronni, "Sexual Harassment: The Inside Story," *Working Woman* (June 1992): 47–51.

Safran, Claire, "Sexual Harassment: The View from the Top; The Joint *Redbook-Harvard Business Review* Report," *Redbook* (March 1981):46–51.

Safran, Claire, "What Men Do to Women on the Job: A Shocking Look at Sexual Harassment," *Redbook* (November 1976): 149, 217–223.

Siegel, Deborah L., *Sexual Harassment: Research & Resources* (New York: National Council for Research on Women, 1992).

Solomon, Alisa, "One Year After Anita Hill . . . Has America's Crash Course in Preventing Sexual Harassment Made a Difference?," *Glamour* (November 1992): 238, 239, 309–311.

Strauss, Susan, *Sexual Harassment and Teens: A Program for Positive Change* (Minneapolis, MN: Free Spirit, 1992).

United States Merit Systems Protection Board, *Sexual Harassment in the Federal Workplace: Is It a Problem?* (Washington, DC: Government Printing Office, 1981).

———, *Sexual Harassment in the Federal Government: An Update.* (Washington, DC: Government Printing Office, 1988).

Wagner, Ellen J., *Sexual Harassment in the Workplace: How to Prevent, Investigate and Resolve Problems in Your Organization* (New York: American Management Association, 1992).

Webb, Susan, "Chicago Area Survey," *The Webb Report* (August 1992).

The Women's Legal Defense Fund, *Sex Discrimination in the Workplace*, 3d ed. (Washington, DC: Women's Legal Defense Fund, 1988).

5

Directory of Organizations

AFL-CIO: Union Privilege
1444 I Street, NW, 8th Floor
Washington, DC 20005
(202) 336-5460

Union Privilege is a nonprofit organization that provides various benefits to union members, including legal assistance and insurance. Membership is automatic for AFL-CIO local union members; the cost of membership in local unions varies. The organization offers a nationwide legal services plan free to most members of AFL-CIO. Initial consultation and follow-up are also free, and other attorney's fees are discounted 30 percent. Many AFL-CIO locals also have their own legal services plans.

Alexander Hamilton Institute
197 West Spring Valley Avenue
Maywood, NJ 07607
(800) 879-2441

The Alexander Hamilton Institute is a private company specializing in human resource management issues. Although the institute sometimes conducts seminars on personnel issues, including sexual harassment, it serves primarily as a publishing company, producing a wide variety of personnel topics with a legal emphasis.

PUBLICATIONS: Two newsletters, *Personnel Alert,* and *Managers Legal Bulletin,* which include articles on employment issues such as sexual harassment; a booklet for managers, *What Every Manager Must Know to Prevent Sexual Harassment*; a wide variety of other materials on personnel training issues.

American Arbitration Association
140 West 51st Street
New York, NY 10020-1203
(212) 484-4000

This national nonprofit organization offers mediation and arbitration services through local offices across the country for individual employees, unions, management, all levels of governments, attorneys, and other individuals and groups. The AAA also provides fact-finding teams for neutral investigation of workplace disputes, including sexual harassment. Services are provided to both members and nonmembers for a wide variety of fees, depending on the service provided. Membership also varies depending on the type required. Dues for individual memberships are $100.

PUBLICATIONS: None specially covering the issue of sexual harassment; a wide variety of publications on arbitration, labor negotiation and employment, and related legal issues.

American Association of University Women
1111 16th Street, NW
Washington, DC 20036
(202) 785-7744

A national organization of women university graduates dedicated, in part, to furthering the education of women. Through its Legal Advocacy Fund, the association supports sexual harassment cases brought by university women students, faculty, and staff against institutions of higher education. The Education Fund sponsors research on the issue of women's education and discrimination against women in educational settings. At-large membership is $35. Individual branch memberships through local organizations are $26.

PUBLICATIONS: *How Schools Shortchange Girls,* a study of major findings on girls and education, including sexual discrimination issues; a variety of other publications relating to education of girls and women.

American Bar Association (ABA)
750 North Lakeshore Drive
Chicago, IL 60611
(312) 988-5555

This national organization for attorneys provides a number of educational, lobbying, and information services for and about attorneys. The association provides a booklet listing local lawyer referral services by state and county. (Many state bar associations also give legal referrals.) Dues for membership vary, from $35 to $225, depending on the number of years a lawyer has been in practice. The directory can be ordered by nonmembers from the order department of the ABA.

PUBLICATIONS: *Directory of Lawyers Referral Services*; many other publications relating to the law and lawyers.

American Bar Association
Commission on Women in the Profession
750 North Lakeshore Drive
Chicago, IL 60611
(312) 988-5555

Founded in 1987, the commission has four primary objectives: to assess the status of women in the legal profession; identify barriers that prevent women lawyers from full participation in the work, responsibilities, and rewards of the profession; develop educational programs and materials to address discrimination against women lawyers; and make recommendations to the ABA for action to address problems identified by the commission. The 12-member commission is comprised of lawyers and judges from around the country and includes representatives from private practice, public sector, academia, and the judiciary. First Lady Hillary Clinton was a recent chair of the commission.

The commission develops programs, policies, and publications to advance and assist women lawyers. In addition, the commission educates the profession about work and family issues that affect all lawyers. In 1990, the commission published a manual designed to help lawyers design workplace policies for balanced lives; one section of that manual addressed issues relating to sexual harassment, and that portion has since been published separately. In addition, the commission serves as a clearinghouse for individual complaints of sexual harassment by providing information and referrals. The commission also presents well-attended programs on sexual harassment and other issues related to discrimination against women at national ABA meetings and provides material on the issue to state and local bar associations. Users of the commission's services do not have to be members of the ABA.

Since its inception in 1987, the commission has been committed to eradicating sexual harassment in the workplace. On this issue, the commission continues to hold programs and workshops, write articles, give speeches and presentations to bar associations, law schools, and conferences, and provide information and resources to the media and legal community.

PUBLICATIONS: *A Guide to Drafting and Implementing Sexual Harassment Policies,* containing an overview of the issues as well as examples of recommended policies and procedures; *Lawyers and Balanced Lives: A Guide to Drafting and Implementing Workplace Policies,* containing an overview of the issues as well as policies on parental leave, alternative work schedules, and sexual harassment; *Perspectives,* a newsletter on issues relating to women in the profession, which sometimes includes articles on sexual harassment and other discrimination against women lawyers.

American Civil Liberties Union (ACLU)
Women's Rights Project
132 West 43rd Street
New York, NY 10036
(212) 944-9800

The ACLU is an organization dedicated to the preservation and protection of individual civil liberties and civil rights. Most states have at least one state office that provides legal assistance and referrals. The national Women's Rights Project litigates and provides litigation assistance in class action and precedent-setting cases challenging sex discrimination in employment, education, and other gender discrimination issues. According to the national office, requests for assistance should first be made to a state or local ACLU office.

PUBLICATIONS: None specifically related to sexual harassment; a number of publications on general civil rights issues.

American Federation of State, County and Municipal Employees (AFSCME)
1625 L Street, NW
Washington, DC 20036
(202) 429-5090

A national labor union with over one million members who work in state, county, and municipal government; this union provides a variety of support and educational services to members. The second largest union affiliated with the AFL-CIO, AFSCME is the nation's fastest-growing union. It provides training workshops for members on the issue of sexual harassment and on-site workshops for employees. The national union also assists with collective bargaining and helps suggest language on sexual harassment to include in labor agreements. The union contends that full-time women workers still earn, on the average, less than two-thirds of what men earn and that at least half of this gap is due to systematic underpayment in jobs that are filled primarily by women. AFSCME works to obtain pay equity, which it defines as eliminating discrimination in pay for female-dominated jobs. An affiliate organization called PEOPLE (Public Employees Organized to Promote Legislative Equality) works for laws to improve public service and elect politicians responsive to the needs of public employees and health care and social service employees. Dues vary depending on the local union.

PUBLICATIONS: A booklet, *Stopping Sexual Harassment, An AFSCME Guide,* which provides basic information for workers who believe that they have been harassed.

American Federation of Teachers (AFT)
Human Rights Department
555 New Jersey Avenue, NW
Washington, DC 20001
(202) 879-4400

The Federation represents the concerns of 796,000 teachers and related professionals. The AFT is an affiliate of the AFL-CIO international union. Organized into local chapters, the union holds a national conference each year to consider educational issues. As a part of its resolution stating the organization's policies on the issue of sexual harassment, the group supports legislative and regulatory changes to ensure that no one will be denied unemployment compensation because of a sexual harassment claim, as well as offering a separate resolution supporting training and education on student-to-student sexual harassment. Dues vary depending on the local branch.

PUBLICATIONS: A variety of materials on various educational issues, including a pamphlet, *Sexual Harassment: Unprofessional, Unacceptable, Unlawful.*

American Psychological Association
750 1st Street, NE
Washington, DC 20002
(202) 336-5500

This national organization of professional psychologists provides referrals to state and local associations that will furnish names of specialists who deal with the psychological problems associated with sexual harassment.

PUBLICATIONS: A pamphlet, *How To Choose a Psychotherapist*; plans include a forthcoming title on sexual harassment.

American Society for Training and Development
1640 King Street
Alexandria, VA 22313
(703) 683-8100

This national organization of professional workplace trainers supplies information and referral services on sexual harassment training. Dues for membership are $150 per year. Members include practitioners, managers, administrators, and researchers working in the field of training and human resource development. ASTD's Information Center is a member inquiry service that assists human resource practitioners in identifying resources for program development, professional development, or both. Information is available on sexual harassment awareness seminars, videos, books, and journal articles. Fees for services are different for nonmembers than for members.

PUBLICATIONS: None specially published by ASTD; provides information referrals to publications produced by other organizations.

Anderson-davis
14309 Layton Drive
Aurora, Colorado 80015
(303) 699-7074

Anderson-davis is an educational services and consulting firm specializing in the areas of sexual harassment, employment discrimination, effective speaking, and conflict resolution. The group focuses on helping companies reduce their liabilities for employment discrimination and conflict and build effective communications in the workplace. Anderson-davis provides training programs and management briefings, policy and complaint procedure analysis, and training for in-house trainers and human resource professionals. It also produces videotapes, trainers' manuals, and participant workbooks, primarily in the area of sexual harassment.

PUBLICATIONS: A variety of videotapes and manuals relating to sexual harassment, all distributed by BNA, Inc. (see listing for Bureau of National Affairs).

Asian-American Legal Defense and Education Fund (AALDEF)
99 Hudson Street, 12th Floor
New York, NY 10013
(212) 966-5932

Founded in 1974, AALDEF is a nonprofit group devoted to the protection of the legal rights of Asian-Americans through impact litigation, legal advocacy, community education, and law student training. AALDEF provides legal advice and attorney referrals for Asians and Asian-Americans on a wide variety of employment and other issues. It also conducts legal rights workshops and provides information on any new legal developments concerning the Asian-American community. AALDEF has worked in the areas of immigration, labor, Japanese-American redress, anti-Asian violence, and voting rights, as well as discrimination in employment. Dues for this nonprofit organization range from basic ($50) to patron ($1,000).

PUBLICATIONS: A newsletter, *Outlook*, which may occasionally include articles on employment discrimination relating to the Asian-American community.

Association for Union Democracy
Women's Project
500 State Street, 2d Floor
Brooklyn, NY 11217
(718) 855-6650

Open to union members of any and all unions for dues of $15 yearly, the Association for Union Democracy provides nationwide attorney referrals, legal advice, counseling, and organizational assistance for women in unions. AUD is a pro-union civil liberties group helping all union members develop democracy within their unions. The Women's Project helps women with problems on the job and within their unions. The project also offers training, workshops, and educational programs on sexual harassment for members and nonmembers alike.

PUBLICATIONS: None specifically on the subject of sexual harassment; *Union Democracy Review* and *$50 + Club News,* both newsletters which may contain occasional articles on sexual harassment and related discrimination issues.

Bureau of National Affairs (BNA) Communications
9439 Key West Avenue
Rockville, MD 20850
(800) 233-6067

A private company that specializes in books, special reports, audio-video materials, and training programs on a wide variety of legal issues, including sexual harassment.

PUBLICATIONS: Videos include *A Costly Proposition, Intent vs. Impact, Myth v. Fact,* and *Preventing Sexual Harassment,* all of which serve as training videos to prevent sexual harassment problems; a wide variety of books and manuals on employment-related issues and sexual harassment. Call for current list.

Business & Legal Reports, Inc. (BLR)
39 Academy Street
Madison, CT 06443
(203) 245-7448

BLR is a national publisher of regulatory compliance and employee training information. As such, it publishes approximately 200 different books, newsletters, and videos serving professionals involved in human resources, safety and health, environmental, and transportation management, with the goal of interpreting the many complex federal and state laws pertaining to the operation of American businesses. The company's stated mission is "to help companies to problem solve in a *pro*active, rather than *re*active, fashion."

PUBLICATIONS: Over 200, including a monthly newsletter, *Human Resources Manager's Legal Reporter*, which includes articles on sexual harassment; the book *How To Hire the People You Need without Discriminating*; and the training guidebook, *What Every Employer Should Be Doing about Sexual Harassment. What To Do about Personnel Problems in [Your State]*, is a comprehensive offering of two-volume sets for each of 29 states. Volumes are updated six times annually and subscribers also receive two monthly newsletters, including news on sexual harassment issues. Pamphlets include *How To Recognize and Prevent Sexual Harassment in the Workplace* and *Preventing Sexual Harassment in the Workplace*. Videotapes include *Preventing Sexual Harassment in the Workplace*. Call or write for a current list.

Business and Professional Women/USA (BPW/USA)
2012 Massachusetts Avenue, NW
Washington, DC 20036
(202) 293-1100

Founded in 1919 by the United States War Department, as a vehicle to bring working women together to help with the war effort during World War I, the organization continued after the war with the goal of promoting full participation, equity, and economic self-sufficiency for working women. BPW/USA members in 3,000 local organizations nationwide promote the advancement of working women through career development, networking, educational scholarships, and legislative advocacy. Currently, the national membership organization includes over 3,000 local chapters. The national organization publishes a position paper on sexual harassment. Dues for members-at-large are $50. Local dues vary.

Related organizations include the BPW Foundation, a nonprofit education and research organization that has awarded more than $5 million in scholarships, loans, and fellowships to some 7,000 women. The foundation also awards research grants to scholars studying women and work and provides assistance to women entering nontraditional career fields. The foundation also sponsors education and training for members on such topics as starting a business, leadership development, career strategies, work and family issues, and work force 2000.

Another related organization is the BPW Political Action Committee. BPW/PAC represents the collective power of individuals who support BPW's national legislative agenda. One plank of the agenda is to eliminate all forms of violence and abuse against women; another is to secure pay equity, equal treatment, and economic equality in all areas of employment for all women. The political action committee provides contributions and endorsements to women and pro-women national candidates who support BPW's legislative priorities. BPW/PAC is supported by voluntary contributions from BPW members. Membership benefits include networking opportunities, a reference library dedicated to working women's issues, a legislative hotline, and annual conventions and meetings with workshops and training, including a recent workshop on sexual harassment.

PUBLICATIONS: *A Crime of Power, Not Passion, Sexual Harassment in the Workplace*, a position paper on sexual harassment; a national magazine, *National Business Woman*, which may include articles on discrimination against women; a number of other publications and reports relating to women and work, including *You Can't Get There From Here: Working Women and the Glass Ceiling*.

Center for Women in Government
State University of Albany, Draper Hall 310
135 Western Avenue
Albany, NY 12222
(518) 442-3900

Founded in 1978, the Center for Women in Government works to identify and remove barriers to employment equity for women in public service and to develop women's leadership in the public policy arena. The center's program includes research, training, technical assistance, and policy education. The center provides sexual harassment training for New York state employees. It also serves workers nationwide through training, videos, digests of important sexual harassment cases and laws, and pamphlets on sexual harassment.

PUBLICATIONS: *Sexual Harassment—It's No Game*, a video-based training package designed for the public sector, along with a two-to-three-hour written curriculum on the same subject; *Managing Sexual Harassment Problems: A Guidebook for Problem-Solvers*, a description of the types of sexual harassment cases and strategies for dealing with them; *Sexual Harassment: A Digest of Landmark and Other Significant Legal Cases*, a booklet describing legal avenues and summarizing key court decisions.

Center for Women Policy Studies (CWPS)
2000 P Street, NW, Suite 508
Washington, DC 20036
(202) 872-1770

CWPS is an independent, privately funded, policy research and advocacy institution. Founded in 1972, the center has concentrated on complex, cutting-edge women's issues throughout its 20-year history. The center's central premises are: that all issues affecting women are interrelated;

that sex and race bias throughout society must be addressed simultaneously; and that analyses of the status and needs of women must recognize their diversity—by race and ethnicity, by economic status, by disability, by sexual identity, and by age. The center's programs combine advocacy, research, policy development, and public education to advance the agenda for women's equality and empowerment. CWPS programs address educational equity, economic opportunity for low-income women, work and family policies, women and AIDS, reproductive rights and health, and violence against women. The center provides written materials on sexual harassment.

PUBLICATIONS: An extensive list of publications (write or call for current catalogue); writings on sexual harassment include *In Case of Sexual Harassment . . . A Guide for Women Students,* a manual; *Sexual Harassment Action Packet,* a packet of materials including policy statements and action strategies for addressing sexual harassment on campus; *Peer Harassment: Hassles for Women on Campus, a Report.*

Coalition of Labor Union Women (CLUW)
15 Union Square
New York, NY 10003
(212) 242-0700

CLUW is America's only national organization for union women. Not a union itself, CLUW strives to make organized labor—and the public in general—more sensitive to the needs of working women and their families. CLUW has 75 chapters across the country and over 20,000 members representing more than 60 unions. The organization's goals include those of organizing the unorganized, promoting affirmative action in the workplace, stimulating political action and legislation on women's issues, and increasing the participation of women in their unions. CLUW provides a referral service to other organizations, if necessary. CLUW also refers union members with complaints of sexual harassment to the appropriate person within the local union. A resource center with clippings, training materials, and a video library is available for members at CLUW offices. A hotline for individuals who have sexual harassment complaints, which provides counseling and referrals, is also offered. On the hotline, CLUW receives one or two calls per week relating to sexual harassment. The group also provides education on sexual harassment, organizes conferences and workshops, testifies and lobbies for legislation, supports strikes and boycotts, and publishes a newsletter and other written materials for union women. Finally, CLUW provides sample contract language, resolutions, and policies on sexual harassment, as well as legal referrals for individual members.

PUBLICATIONS: *The 9 to 5 Guide to Combatting Sexual Harassment,* published together with *9 to 5;* a leaflet, *Sexual Harassment, It's Not Funny, It's*

Not Flattery and It's Not Your Fault, and a palm card of the same title; a newsletter, *CLUW News,* which sometimes includes articles on sexual harassment and other discrimination issues.

College and University Personnel Association
1233 20th Street, NW
Washington, DC 20036
(202) 429-0311

With a national membership of over 1,700 colleges and universities and other related organizations, CUPA serves more than 5,200 human resource administrators working in higher education. CUPA promotes the effective development and management of the personnel profession. It offers professional development programs and specialized workshops on personnel topics, and provides publications, benefits, and legislative information services to help administrators stay current with developments in human resources. CUPA publishes a book and video on sexual harassment.

PUBLICATIONS: A book describing definitions, legal developments, and policy recommendations relating to sexual harassment and the university, *Sexual Harassment: Issues and Answers,* and a companion videotape of the same title.

Commerce Clearing House
4025 West Peterson Avenue
Chicago, IL 60646
(312) 583-8500

A private publishing company that offers material on many legal issues. It publishes a training manual on sexual harassment for managers and supervisors and offers other publications on related personnel issues. Call or write for a current catalogue.

PUBLICATIONS: *Sexual Harassment Manual for Managers and Supervisors,* a training manual; *Equal Employment Opportunity Manual for Managers and Supervisors,* a guide to EEO concepts and procedures; *Explanation of the Civil Rights Act of 1991,* a guide to the new law; several other titles on legal issues in employment.

Communications Workers of America (CWA)
501 3d Street
Washington, DC 20001
(202) 434-1100

Calling itself "A Union for the Information Age," CWA, the largest telecommunications union in the world, represents 650,000 workers in private and public sector employment in the United States and Canada.

More than 1,200 chartered CWA local unions are affiliated. Founded at meetings in Chicago and New Orleans in 1938, CWA has gradually broadened its base from the telephone industry to other industries. CWA members are employed in telecommunications, printing and news media, public service health care, cable television, general manufacturing, electronics, gas and electric utilities, and other fields. CWA holds collective bargaining agreements for large employers such as AT&T and GTE. CWA considers sexual harassment offensive and dehumanizing and will not tolerate it in any form in any workplace. The CWA Sexual Harassment Policy adopted by the International Executive Board states that CWA will not condone any form of sexual harassment. Virtually all CWA contracts contain a nondiscrimination clause, prohibiting discrimination on the basis of gender, and take the position that sexual harassment is discrimination on the basis of gender. The union provides internal training for union members and staff as well as written materials on sexual harassment. Dues vary depending on the local branch.

PUBLICATIONS: *Sexual Harassment on the Job,* a booklet covering the basics of sexual harassment.

Coronet MTI Film and Video
108 Wilmot Road
Deerfield, IL 60015
(800) 621-2131

Coronet is a private company that produces and distributes training videotapes on sexual harassment for businesses and schools. The product list is constantly changing. Call or write for a current list.

PUBLICATIONS: Videotapes relating to the issue of sexual harassment include *So Like You,* a program that looks at the same situation from two points of view; *Race and Sex Discrimination in the Workplace: What You Need to Know,* a general look at discrimination in hiring and the workplace; *Sex Bias in the Workplace,* dramatizing a situation in which a man is promoted instead of a more able woman; *A Discussion of Sex Bias in the Workplace,* a discussion with sex bias experts from a variety of fields.

Equal Employment Opportunity Commission (EEOC)
1801 L Street, NW
Washington, DC 20507
(800) 669-4000

The EEOC is the federal agency charged with administering and enforcing the nation's equal employment opportunity laws. To contact the nearest EEOC office, call (800) 669-4000. You will be directed to the appropriate office. For information regarding EEOC procedures and regulations, call (800) 669-EEOC. All information is printed in both English and Spanish.

PUBLICATIONS: Many different publications on equal opportunity issues, including a fact sheet on sexual harassment, *Facts About Sexual Harassment,* which includes information about how to file a charge; annual report detailing the activities of the agency on many fronts, including sexual harassment claims.

Equal Rights Advocates (ERA)
1663 Mission Street, Suite 550
San Francisco, CA 94103
(415) 621-0672 (general information)
(415) 621-0505 (advice and counseling hotline)

One of the country's oldest and most active women's law centers, ERA is dedicated to the empowerment of women through the establishment of their economic, social, and political equality. Beginning in 1974 as a firm specializing in issues of sex-based discrimination, ERA has evolved into a legal organization with a multifaceted approach to women's legal issues. Although court cases are a primary function, ERA also works to empower women to help themselves through practical advice and public education. ERA seeks to forge alliances with community groups and build effective issue-oriented coalitions, while emphasizing public education and media statements to inform public opinion. This group of attorneys and other parties interested in equal rights for women sponsors legal action, as well as offering legal advice and counseling—in both English and Spanish—to women who are the object of discrimination. Some of the group's major cases have included, for example, helping workers obtain pregnancy-related disability benefits, and representing an assembly line worker who suffered a heart attack as a result of sexual harassment. ERA provides referrals to attorneys and women's groups nationwide for victims of sexual harassment. Memberships vary from a student/low-income membership at $15 per year to an advocate membership of $1,000.

PUBLICATIONS: Various pamphlets on women's issues, as well as *The Equal Rights Advocate,* a newsletter that sometimes addresses issues of sexual harassment; *The Affirmative Action Handbook: How To Start and Defend Affirmative Action Programs,* a joint publication of Equal Rights Advocates and the San Francisco Lawyers' Committee for Urban Affairs.

Federally Employed Women (FEW)
1400 I Street, NW, Suite 424
Washington, DC 20005
(202) 898-0994

Formed in 1968, FEW is a national nonprofit membership organization of federally employed women, with chapters throughout the United States. According to the bylaws, FEW shall be "operated exclusively for the charitable and educational purposes of taking action to end sex discrimination and toward the advancement of women in employment in the federal government." FEW provides education and training for career development; it also lobbies on legislation of interest to the group such as the Equal Rights Amendment, health care, and violence against women. The group provides written materials on how federal workers can stop sexual harassment, find and select an EEO attorney, and go to court. Dues vary, depending on the type of membership.

PUBLICATIONS: A booklet, *Combating Sexual Harassment: A Federal Worker's Guide*; *News and Views*, a newsletter that sometimes contains articles relating to sexual harassment.

Fund for the Feminist Majority
1600 Wilson Boulevard
Arlington, VA 22209
(703) 522-2214 (general information)
(703) 522-2501 (sexual harassment hotline)

The Feminist Majority was founded by former National Organization for Women president Eleanor Smeal with the goal of involving more women in "areas of power," including politics, business, and government. The organization's ongoing "Feminization of Power" campaign, a nationwide effort, seeks "to inspire unprecedented numbers of feminists to seek leadership positions, to promote a National Feminist Agenda, and to heighten awareness and visibility of the feminist majority." The organization consists of two separate groups, the Fund for the Feminist Majority and the Feminist Majority Foundation.

The Fund for the Feminist Majority (FFM) is a lobbying and political advocacy group. The Feminist Majority Foundation is the organization's research and education arm, which, in addition to developing educational materials and activities, pursues projects on the use of initiatives and referenda for women's rights and contraceptive research and development. FFM is a nonprofit organization dedicated to increasing the percentage of feminist women in elected office as well as advancing the National Feminist Agenda. The fund also supports education, lobbying, and public relations on these issues. The group's hotline recommends resources and organizations that deal with the subject of sexual harassment.

PUBLICATIONS: *Training Resources on Sexual Harassment*, a list of resources on the subject of sexual harassment; *Organizational Resources*, a list of organizations that deal with the subject; *The Feminist Majority Report*, a quarterly newsletter; *The Feminization of Power*, photographs and biographies of women in political office and public life in the United States and abroad who "made a feminist difference."

Haines Associates
708 South Washington Square
Philadelphia, PA 19106
(215) 922-1617

A private consulting firm that provides consulting and training on equal employment and discrimination issues. It conducts seminars for human resource managers and provides private consulting. A manual for managers and supervisors on sexual harassment is also offered.

PUBLICATIONS: A variety, including *Sexual Harassment,* a manual for supervisors and employees.

Institute for Women and Work
School of Industrial and Labor Relations
Cornell University
15 East 26th Street, 4th Floor
New York, NY 10010
(212) 340-2800

The institute is a division of the New York State School of Industrial-Labor Relations at Cornell University. As such, it serves as an intellectual, research, and education center with the stated purpose of providing a "forum to examine and evaluate the economic, political, social and educational issues that connect women and their work." The institute focuses on women's status in the workplace and the economic status of women. It offers seminars and training on the wage gap, family, discrimination, and work and publishes a bibliography of sexual harassment resource materials. Occasional training seminars on sexual harassment are also offered, primarily for union members. For a fee, the institute will conduct and collect research on the issue of sexual harassment in specific industries.

PUBLICATIONS: *Sexual Harassment Bibliography,* a collection of written resources on the subject; *Research Surveys on Sexual Harassment in the Workplace,* a list of surveys on the issue.

Mexican American Legal Defense and Education Fund
1430 K Street, NW
Washington, DC 20005
(202) 628-4074

With offices in Chicago, Los Angeles, San Antonio, and San Francisco, this organization provides a lawyer referral service for Mexican-Americans as well as sponsoring some litigation on civil rights issues and advocacy. The group is devoted to promoting the rights and educational opportunities of Mexican-Americans. It provides attorney referrals for workers or students seeking to bring sexual harassment claims.

PUBLICATIONS: *MALDEF News,* a quarterly newsletter detailing the work of the organization.

NAACP Legal Defense and Education Fund, Inc.
99 Hudson Street
New York, NY 10013
(212) 219-1900

The NAACP works to advance the rights of African-Americans. Legal counseling, as well as referrals for workers or students seeking to bring sexual harassment claims, is offered.

PUBLICATIONS: Various publications relating to fund-raising and capital punishment, none specifically on the issue of sexual harassment.

National Association for Women in Education (NAWE)
1325 18th Street, NW, Suite 210
Washington, DC 20036
(202) 659-9330

One of the oldest organizations for women in education, NAWE provides support and career development for women who work in higher education. The association's stated mission is to provide "educational opportunities and professional support for all women—not just younger women, minorities, the disadvantaged and the disabled, but those in the mainstream as well—throughout their careers." This nonprofit group conducts two conferences a year for members and also sponsors a conference for women student leaders. Other programs provide assistance in professional development, scholarly research, and legislative advocacy.

PUBLICATIONS: *Initiatives,* a trade journal, which may include articles about sexual harassment on college campuses.

National Association of Working Women, 9 to 5
614 Superior Avenue, NW
Cleveland, OH 44113
(216) 566-9308 (general information)
(800) 522-0925 (job problem hotline)

One day in the early 1970s, when Karen Nussbaum was a clerk-typist at Harvard University, a young man walked into her office, stood in front of her, looked directly at her and asked, "Isn't anyone here?" At that moment, Nussbaum realized what her working life lacked: respect. She went on to help form 9 to 5, a national nonprofit membership organization dedicated to respect for American office workers, with local chapters throughout the country. (This group served as a source of material for the popular movie of the same name.) A toll-free, confidential telephone hotline, staffed by trained job counselors, provides information and referrals on how to deal with sexual harassment and other problems on the job. During the special confirmation hearings for Clarence Thomas, 9 to 5 received more than 14,000 calls in 5 business days from working women looking for help with sexual harassment on the job. Discrimination and harassment top the list of job problems on the hotline. The group publishes books and reports on sexual harassment, available at a discount to members. Members also receive legal referrals to attorneys specializing in sexual harassment. A newsletter published five times a year sometimes provides articles on the subject of sexual harassment. The group assists employers across the country with training and workshops on the issue. Some 9 to 5 local chapters offer sexual harassment support groups and referrals to training resources. National dues are $25.

PUBLICATIONS: A book, *The 9 to 5 Guide to Combatting Sexual Harassment*; two pamphlets, *Sexual Harassment, What Every Working Woman Needs to Know from 9 to 5*; *Is Your Organization Able to Deal with Sexual Harassment? Skills for Managers from 9 to 5*; *9 to 5 Newsline*, a newsletter published five times a year, which sometimes includes articles on sexual harassment.

National Conference of State Legislatures Women's Network
1607 250th Avenue
Corwith, IA 50430
(515) 583-2156

An affiliate of the National Conference of State Legislatures, the Women's Network is composed of women state legislators from around the country. Their purpose is to increase the power of women within their own legislatures relating to women's issues and family issues and also to increase the power of women within the national conference. Issues of concern to the network have included maternal and child health, public/private partnerships in child day care, family and medical leave, and shattering the "glass ceiling" in both the public and private sectors. Other issues related to gender discrimination in state legislatures and elsewhere have also been emphasized by this group.

PUBLICATIONS: A newsletter, published three times a year, that may occasionally address issues of sexual harassment and sex discrimination. Periodically this organization publishes policy briefs on various issues of interest to women legislators.

National Council for Research on Women (NCRW)
Sexual Harassment Information Project
47-49 East 65th Street
New York, NY 10021
(212) 570-5001

In 1981, representatives from 28 university-based centers, policy organizations, and educational coalitions met to share resources and form a working alliance that bridged distinctions among scholarship, policy, and action programs. Funded by private foundations and companies, the council functions to facilitate collaborative research, communications, and cooperative exchanges; to promote visibility for feminist research; and serve as a clearinghouse for research. This coalition now includes 70 centers and organizations that support and conduct feminist research, policy analysis, and educational programs. Among the council's projects are a work-in-progress database, an annual meeting, a quarterly newsletter, a national network of women's caucuses, a variety of directories on research and women's issues, and Beyond Parent Tracks, a national seminar series on work and family issues. The center publishes a comprehensive guide to research and resources on sexual harassment, including lists of key researchers and expert witnesses on sexual harassment. NCRW was an early co-sponsor of one of the largest outreach efforts to date on the issue of sexual harassment: *Women Tell the Truth: A Conference on Parity, Power and Sexual Harassment,* a sold-out meeting held in the spring of 1992 at Hunter College in New York, which drew 2,000 activists, academics, artists, working women, students, and professionals and included Anita Hill as the keynote speaker.

PUBLICATIONS: *Sexual Harassment: Research and Resources* (launched immediately following the Senate Judiciary hearings on Clarence Thomas's Supreme Court nomination) lists research and resources available on sexual harassment, including legal definitions, a bibliography, and a list of experts and conferences; *Women's Research Network News,* a newsletter that sometimes includes articles on conferences, research, and other information on sexual harassment.

National Education Association (NEA)
Human and Civil Rights Department
1201 16th Street, NW
Washington, DC 20036
(202) 833-4000

A national membership organization for teachers. The NEA seeks to advance the career development of teachers and works on a variety of education issues. The group provides training, videos, and brochures on sexual harassment, available to union members only.

PUBLICATIONS: *Sexual Harassment,* a brochure and training packet on the subject.

National Employment Lawyers Association
535 Pacific Avenue
San Francisco, CA 94133
(415) 397-6335

The National Employment Lawyers Association was founded in 1985 to provide assistance to lawyers in protecting the rights of employees. It now serves as a network of plaintiffs' attorneys who specialize in employment law. The association exists primarily to serve the needs of its members, including education and training, but it also promotes federal and state legislation on the issue of employment. Dues are $150 per year.

PUBLICATIONS: *Pleading and Practice*, a loose-leaf service with litigation guides on employment issues, including sexual harassment; *The Employee Advocate*, a newsletter on legal issues relating to employment law, including sexual harassment.

National Organization for Women Legal Defense and Education Fund (NOW LDEF)
99 Hudson Street, 12th Floor
New York, NY 10013
(212) 925-6635

For the past 20 years, attorneys at NOW LDEF—a national, nonprofit, public interest advocacy organization, funded by grants and private donations—have worked to promote education on women's rights and to fight legal battles for women whose rights have been denied. The fund works in the workplace, the schools, and the legal system itself to ensure that "equality becomes reality for all." The fund has worked with major corporations, small businesses, and the courts and government officials to eliminate sexual harassment and discrimination from the workplace, combining public education and litigation. A legal resource kit on sexual harassment that is specifically geared toward attorneys, plus other publications on sexual harassment, are offered. Legal referrals are available through the mail.

Some of the cases on sexual harassment NOW LDEF has worked on include *Coffman v. MNK Trucking*, a case that challenged sexual harassment and retaliation, including coercion and prostitution at work, and which settled favorable for the plaintiff; *Price Waterhouse v. Thomkins*, in which the U.S. Supreme Court ruled that, in employment discrimination cases, evidence of sex stereotyping constitutes evidence of sex discrimination; *Robinson v. Jacksonville Shipyards*, in which a federal district court judge in Florida ruled that workplace display of pictures of nude and partially nude women, combined with verbal assaults, constitutes sexual harassment on the job and that sex stereotyping is involved in sexual harassment; and *Newsday v. Long Island Typographical Union*, in which the U.S. Court of Appeals for the Second Circuit ruled that an explicit, well-defined public policy against sexual harassment in the workplace justifies the overruling of a federal court labor arbitrator's reinstatement of a terminated sexual harasser.

PUBLICATIONS: *Sexual Harassment in the Schools Resource Kit*, a list of articles, books, cases, and other resources on this subject; *LDEF: In Brief,* a newsletter that sometimes includes articles on sexual harassment; *Legal Resource Kit: Employment—Sex Discrimination and Sexual Harassment,* one of 15 kits drafted by NOW LDEWF to answer the most frequently asked questions, with an overview of federal guidelines on sexual harassment and a legal summary; *Eliminating Workplace Sexual Harassment: Guidelines for Management,* a guide for corporations seeking to write, implement, or improve their sexual harassment policies.

National Resource Center for Consumers of Legal Services
PO Box 340
Gloucester, VA 23061
(804) 693-9330

A nonprofit organization, this resource center is organized to assist groups of all sorts in establishing plans for legal services that are high in quality and low in cost. The center provides education, research, and information on this issue. Membership is open to any person or organization interested in legal services delivery and includes legal service plans, their sponsoring organizations, bar associations, and interested individuals. Dues are scaled according to ability to pay and degree of involvement. The center provides nationwide legal referrals to attorneys experienced in sexual harassment cases. It also publishes materials on how to choose a lawyer.

PUBLICATIONS: A variety on legal services plans, as well as a pamphlet, *Choosing and Using a Lawyer.*

National Women's Law Center
1616 P Street, NW, Suite 100
Washington, DC 20036
(202) 328-5160

This national nonprofit organization focuses on policy areas important to women, including sexual harassment. The center serves as a national resource for those committed to advancing the status of women through the law and conducts research on and provides testimony on sexual harassment and other issues, as well as funding litigation in women's rights areas. Founded in 1972, areas of interest related to protecting women's rights include fighting to lift women and their families out of poverty and into self-sufficiency, working for equal access in education and employment, and supporting women's reproductive rights and access to health care. The center has a special focus on women who are most disadvantaged, particularly low-income women and women of color. The center is funded by private donations.

PUBLICATIONS: *Fact Sheet on Sexual Harassment,* addressing the basic questions and answers on the subject.

National Women's Political Caucus
c/o The Capitol Hill Women's Political Caucus
PO Box 599, Longworth Building
Washington, DC 20515
(202) 986-0994

Founded in 1971 to encourage women's participation in the political process, the caucus is dedicated to the growth of women in politics. The District of Columbia chapter has produced a model sexual harassment policy for congressional members, and an honor roll of members of Congress who have adopted sexual harassment policies. The group also conducts a seminar for staff members who work on Capitol Hill, as well as participating in the orientation of new congress members. Originally, to receive the support of the caucus, women candidates must have supported choice in abortion rights, the Equal Rights Amendment, and federal funding for child care. The criteria are now expanding and changing from these original goals.

PUBLICATIONS: A model sexual harassment policy for congress members; an honor roll of members of Congress who have adopted sexual harassment policies.

Pacific Resource Development Group
145 NW 85th Street, Suite 104
Seattle, WA 98117
(800) 767-3062
(206) 782-7015

Pacific Resource is a private company devoted to education and training on the subject of sexual harassment, headed by trainer and consultant Susan Webb. The group produces employee handbooks and videotape training packages on sexual harassment, a monthly newsletter, and training manuals for managers. Workshops presented by the group have been offered to more than 60,000 employees in more than 1,500 companies and organizations nationwide. The group also provides a train-the-trainer program, for companies that want their own personnel to conduct sessions, and training for investigators to facilitate in-house complaint resolution.

PUBLICATIONS: *Sexual Harassment . . . Shades of Gray: Guidelines for Managers, Supervisors & Employees,* a handbook explaining the basic principles of sexual harassment, definitions, prevention, and training; a videotape training package, *Sexual Harassment: Shades of Gray*; a monthly newsletter on sexual harassment, *The Webb Report*; a series of booklets on sexual harassment; a *Resource Manual,* a *Training Manual,* and an *Investigator's Manual.*

Society for Human Resource Management (SHRM)
606 North Washington Street
Alexandria, VA 22314
(703) 548-3440

SHRM is a membership organization for human resource managers, with over 80,000 members from around the world. The organization provides its membership with government and media representation, education and information services, conferences and seminars, and publications that assist human resource practitioners. The organization publishes a variety of written information for members, including advice on developing sexual harassment policy, as well as a library and computer database on personnel issues. SHRM also produces an interactive video training program on sexual harassment. There are more than 400 local chapters. Dues are $160 annually, with additional chapter dues.

PUBLICATIONS: *Preventing Sexual Harassment in the Workplace,* a video training program that also includes instructor guides and participant workbooks; *HR Magazine* and *HR News,* a newsletter, both of which may contain articles on sexual harassment and related discrimination issues; *HR Legal Report,* a quarterly newsletter providing in-depth analysis of current legal issues for human resource professionals, which also contains occasional discussions of sexual harassment and discrimination.

State of New York Division for Women
Governor's Task Force on Sexual Harassment
State Capitol, 2d Floor
Albany, NY 12224
(518) 474-3612

The task force was created by Governor Cuomo's Executive Order in March 1992, with a mandate to determine the extent to which sexual harassment continues to exist in New York State public and private sector workplaces and to make recommendations for assuring effective redress for victims, enhancing public understanding of sexual harassment, and eradicating it from the workplace. Specifically, the task force is to assess the scope and efficacy of existing law, regulations, and other remedies for sexual harassment; examine the economic and social costs of sexual harassment; study public beliefs, attitudes, stereotypes, and policies about sexual harassment; and make recommendations for alleviation of sexual harassment. The task force will hold public hearings and regional meetings across the state to provide forums for members of the public to share their thoughts, experiences, and insights and will present a comprehensive report to the governor in 1993.

PUBLICATIONS: A pamphlet, *Sexual Harassment,* which outlines basics about the issue, published in English, Spanish, and Chinese.

Tele-Lawyer
19671 Beach Boulevard, Suite 207
Huntington Beach, CA 92648
(800) 835-3529

This private company provides legal advice over the telephone at a reasonable per-minute charge. Staff lawyers will also review documents, such as employment contracts, and do legal research on issues, including sexual harassment. Founded by Huntington Beach lawyer Michael Cane in 1990, he and five other attorneys work the phones twelve hours a day, five days a week. For a cost of three dollars per minute, charged to the caller's phone bill or credit card, the lawyers answer questions about a variety of subjects, including, for example, how to file an EEOC claim or a small-claims court lawsuit; how to handle a speeding ticket; and what to do with a threatening letter from the Internal Revenue Service.

United Auto Workers Union (UAW)
Women's Department
800 East Jefferson
Detroit, MI 48214
(313) 926-5212

Under the UAW umbrella, different groups have come together, from auto workers to state workers to nursing home workers. The goal of the women's department is to help bring women into active participation in their local unions, to encourage women to run in union elections, to give women skills for bargaining, and to develop leadership and education. Although the women's department is still conducting some workshops on sexual harassment, it is currently developing revised written and video training materials and new workshops for UAW and other union members.

PUBLICATIONS: Currently revising materials to be used for training and in workshops.

U.S. Department of Labor, Women's Bureau
200 Constitution Avenue, NW
Room S3311
Washington, DC 20210
(202) 523-6665

The Women's Bureau division of the U.S. Department of Labor focuses on a variety of issues relating to women and work. Currently, the bureau provides a detailed list of sexual harassment resources, including organizations, training materials, court cases, and articles.

PUBLICATIONS: *Sexual Harassment Resources,* a list of materials relating to sexual harassment.

Wider Opportunities for Women (WOW)
1325 G Street, NW
Washington, DC 20005
(202) 638-3143

This national, nonprofit organization focuses primarily on women in nontraditional employment. The group offers a booklet on sexual harassment and provides consulting services for employers on the issue of sexual harassment.

PUBLICATIONS: *Sexual Harassment Solutions,* a booklet that profiles a successful policy on sexual harassment and includes a fact sheet on sexual harassment.

Women Employed Institute
22 West Monroe, Suite 1400
Chicago, IL 60603
(312) 782-3902

This membership organization provides career development, networking, and support for Chicago working women. The group provides telephone counseling on sexual harassment in the Chicago area and offers referrals to local attorneys. The institute has produced a fact sheet on sexual harassment and provides sexual harassment prevention training for area employers.

PUBLICATIONS: *Women Employed News,* a newsletter that sometimes addresses the issue of sexual harassment; *Sexual Harassment,* a fact sheet on the issue.

Women's Alliance for Job Equity (WAJE)
1422 Chestnut Street, Suite 1100
Philadelphia, PA 19102
(215) 561-1873

WAJE provides direct services to individuals experiencing sexual harassment on the job, as well as sexual harassment prevention training for employers. The alliance also presents public education workshops on sexual harassment prevention. The group provides regular job problem meetings, peer support programs, and legal referrals for WAJE members, who are primarily women working in nonmanagement jobs. WAJE also offers an on-site training program for local employers. WAJE receives about 1,000 calls a year; 40 percent are from women who say they have been sexually harassed. Dues range from $10 per year for a contributor to $100 a year for a supporter.

PUBLICATIONS: A newsletter, *Wage-Earner Notes,* which frequently includes articles on sexual harassment; a videotape and companion training manual, *Sexual Harassment Prevention.*

Women's Law Project
125 South 9th Street, Suite 401
Philadelphia, Pa 19107
(215) 928-9801

The Women's Law Project is a nonprofit, feminist, legal advocacy organization that was founded in 1974. The project works to abolish discrimination and injustice and to advance the legal and economic status of women and their families. During the past 18 years, the project has worked in the fields of health, reproductive freedom, employment, domestic relations, housing, insurance credit, and education. Through lawsuits, education, and working with government, the project hopes to break new ground on these legal issues. It provides a telephone counseling service as well as information on sexual harassment and how to find a lawyer.

PUBLICATIONS: None specifically on sexual harassment; a variety on other issues relating to women and the law.

Women's Legal Defense Fund
1875 Connecticut Avenue, NW, Suite 710
Washington, DC 20009
(202) 986-2600

The Women's Legal Defense Fund works for "policies that reflect the realities women face in their everyday lives": policies that provide equal opportunity, reproductive freedom, quality health care, and economic security. Founded in 1971 to increase opportunities for women, the Women's Legal Defense Fund works in Congress, the courts, the administrative branch of government, the states, at the grass-roots level, and with the media to advance public policy for women. Dues vary from a single membership, $50–90, to the Capital Club, $5,000. The fund sponsors public education, written information, advocacy, and target litigation on sexual harassment.

PUBLICATIONS: A poster entitled *Sexual Harassment in Your Workplace: Your Legal Rights*; a newsletter, *WLDF News,* which frequently includes articles on sexual harassment and related discrimination issues; *Sexual Harassment in the Workplace,* a fact sheet on the issue.

Women's Rights Litigation Clinic
Rutgers School of Law-Newark
15 Washington Street
Newark, NJ 07102-3192
(201) 648-5637

Founded as a temporary, student-initiated undertaking in 1972 and institutionalized as a permanent enterprise in 1973, with Nadine Taub as the director, the clinic has focused on litigation and legal counseling relating to women's rights. Open to both second- and third-year students, the Women's Rights Litigation Clinic offers a legal practice experience to students. These students, working with attorney-instructors, have achieved a number of important victories, particularly in the areas of gender equality and reproductive rights. It has received requests for assistance from individuals and organizations throughout the country, and inquiries regarding its activities from Europe and Australia. The clinic litigated the landmark case of *Tomkins v. Public Service Electric & Gas Co.*, in which the court found sexual harassment to be an impermissible form of sex discrimination in employment. It filed an *amicus curiae* (friend of the court) brief in *T.L. v. Toys R Us*, a case extending the definition of hostile environment in which the Appellate Division of New Jersey adopted the standard of a "reasonable victim," rather than a "reasonable perpetrator"; and filed another amicus brief in *Thoreson v. Penthouse Ltd.*, in which the clinic sought to uphold a lower court award to an employee of *Penthouse* magazine of $60,000 in compensatory damages for demands by her boss that she sleep with two of the men he did business with. Students also field a high volume of calls from women, counseling them on claims of sexual harassment and other work-related issues. The clinic may be the first in the country to focus on sexual harassment in housing with community education and outreach, including a brochure on the subject in English and Spanish, meetings with tenant organizations, and a presentation to the New Jersey Commission on Sex Discrimination, as well as its representation of a woman in court who had been harassed by her landlord. The center is funded by grants, private donations, and recovery of fees from lawsuits, as well as receiving some funding from the Rutgers Law School.

PUBLICATIONS: *Stop Sexual Harassment in Housing*, a flyer on the issue and what to do about it, published in English and Spanish.

6

Selected Print Resources

AN ATTEMPT HAS BEEN MADE IN THIS SECTION, as in other chapters of this book, to present all points of view on the issue of sexual harassment. Few articles, however, and no entire books, take the position that sexual harassment should be viewed as a personal, rather than a legal, problem; question the extent of government regulation in this area; warn about the risk of false charges; or represent the point of view of the alleged harasser. An attempt, therefore, has been made to present representative samples of books questioning the feminist position on sex roles or sex discrimination in the section entitled "Related Gender Issues." In addition, because the whole question of sexual harassment has come to the forefront only in the last 20 years, the number of books and monographs available on this issue is necessarily limited. Since the issue has changed and evolved so rapidly, many works are already outdated. Some of these are still listed in this chapter because they present a particular point of view or because they are of historical significance. Before relying upon facts or legal precedent in any particular work, however, check the date it was published.

Bibliographies

Crocker, Phyllis L. **"Annotated Bibliography on Sexual Harassment in Education."** *Women's Rights Law Reporter* 7, no. 2 (Winter 1982): 91–106.

Prepared as a part of the Sexual Harassment in Education Project of the NOW Legal Defense and Education Fund, this bibliography includes 131 items, consisting of papers and report; articles; books, legal cases, and papers; organizational publications; works in progress; and resources. The major focus of the bibliography is on higher education, although a few entries deal with secondary and vocational education and with sexual harassment in therapy. Articles reflecting a hostile or frivolous viewpoint are listed "because they illuminate some of the unstated but deeply held beliefs with which organizers and litigators have to contend." The annotations list contact persons, making the work useful for locating obscure material. Unfortunately, with a 1982 publication date, the list obviously does not include some more recent material.

Gartland, Patricia, and Winfred Bevilacqua. **"Sexual Harassment: Recent Research and Useful Resources."** *Journal of the National Association for Women Deans, Administrators, & Counselors* 46, no. 2 (Winter 1983): 47–50.

This select, partially annotated list of 37 items includes books and handbooks, resource agencies, audiovisual materials, and a dozen journal articles that reflect the range of literature available in 1983 on sexual harassment. Approximately half of the list covers harassment in higher education. The list focuses on handbooks published by professional associations and resource agencies.

Jacobs, Daniel J. **"Sexual Harassment and Related Issues: A Selective Bibliography."** *Record of the Association of the Bar of the City of New York* 46, no. 8 (December 1991): 930–939.

This extensive list of 167 entries focuses on the most recent articles on legal issues arising in sexual harassment cases. Its coverage is mainly of legal periodicals, although it includes a few general publications, some books, and some government publications. The listings are not annotated.

McCaghy, M. Dawn. **Sexual Harassment: A Guide to Resources.** Boston: G. K. Hall, 1985. 181p. Index. ISBN 0-8161-8669-3.

McCaghy, a former reference librarian at Bowling Green State University who also holds a bachelor's degree in sociology, compiled this comprehensive bibliography, which includes sources to mid-1983. A few 1984 references appear. The extensive subject categories include the feminist perspective, general overview, the legal perspective, and the management response, among others. Each source listing provides a balanced discussion of its contents. Training and audiovisual materials are also listed and summarized. The work includes a comprehensive author-title index and a separate subject index. An excellent reference work, the book's only drawback is that it is now out-of-date in this fast-changing field, but it is included here because it is the only hardback, readily available bibliography on the subject of sexual harassment.

NOW Legal Defense and Education Fund. **Sexual Harassment in the Schools Resource Kit.** New York: NOW Legal Defense and Education Fund, 1992. 5p.

This short list of entries relating to sexual harassment in schools focuses on secondary education, although some listings relate to colleges and universities. Prepared by the Project of Equal Education Rights of the NOW Legal Defense and Education Fund, the entries include news articles, magazine articles, scholarly publications, books, pamphlets, surveys, and resource organizations. An annotation of the major Supreme Court cases is also included. Because the whole question of sexual harassment and young people is a new issue, this bibliography is especially valuable because it compiles the few sources that are available. Each listing is annotated.

Anthologies

Mahoney, M. R., et al. **"Gender, Race, and the Politics of Supreme Court Appointments: The Import of the Anita Hill/Clarence Thomas Hearings."** *Southern California Law Review* 65 (March 1992): 1279–1582.

In this 300-page symposium, scholars from a number of different disciplines leap into the Hill/Thomas debate with a score of articles. English and classics professors, for example, discuss the backdrop of the drama in terms of myth and storytelling; historians address the historical context; and political scientists consider the political maneuvering behind the hearings. Also reprinted is an address by Anita Hill before the National Forum for Women in State Legislatures. A sample of the titles reveals some of the content: "Cringing at Myths of Black Sexuality," "October Tragedy," and "Roman Oratory, Pornography, and the Silencing of Anita Hill." None of the contributors to this collection pulls any punches; all appear to be squarely in Anita Hill's camp or, at the least, critical of the way the Senate handled the proceedings. Nevertheless, the writing is colorful and passionate, providing ample evidence of how deeply affected many people were by this uniquely American drama.

Morrison, Toni, ed. **Racing Justice, Engendering Power: Essays on Anita Hill, Clarence Thomas, and the Construction of Social Reality.** New York: Pantheon Books, 1992. 475p. ISBN 0-679-74145-3.

This volume attempts to frame the entire Clarence Thomas/Anita Hill controversy within the broader context of race and gender. Toni Morrison contributes an introduction and brings together 18 provocative and original essays, all but one written specifically for this book, by prominent academicians—black and white, male and female. These writings address not only the racial and sexual but also the historical, political, cultural, legal, psychological, and linguistic aspects of a single revelatory moment in American history. The diverse contributors include, for example, A. Leon Higginbotham, Jr., a judicial colleague of Clarence Thomas; and Carol M. Swain, an assistant professor of politics and public affairs at Princeton University's Woodrow Wilson School. As Toni Morrison emphasizes in the introduction: "For insight into the complicated and complicating events that the confirmation of Clarence Thomas became, one needs perspective, not attitude; context, not anecdotes; analysis, not postures. For any kind of lasting illumination the focus must be on the history routinely ignored or played down or unknown." This complex, thoughtful, and challenging book does just that. While noting that what happened was upsetting and serious, Morrison concludes that

> regardless of political alliances, something positive and liberating has already surfaced. In matters of race and gender, it is now possible and necessary, as it seemed never to have been before, to speak about these matters without the barriers, the silences, the embarrassing gaps in discourse. It is clear to the most reductionist intellect that black people think differently from one another, it is also clear that the time for undiscriminating racial unity has passed. A conversation, a serious exchange between black men and women, has begun in a new arena, and the contestants defy the mold. Nor is it as easy as it used to be to split along racial lines, as the alliances and coalitions between white and black women, and the conflicts among black women, and among black men, during the intense debates regarding Anita Hill's testimony against Clarence Thomas's appointment prove.

National Association of College and University Attorneys. **Sexual Harassment on Campus: A Legal Compendium.** Washington, DC: National Association of College and University Attorneys, 1988. 201p.

This compendium pulls together in one source some of the leading law review and journal articles on sexual harassment in higher education. It also includes the sexual harassment policies and procedures from several universities and organizations and provides guidance for administrators on the drafting of sexual harassment policies. The work includes a selected bibliography and outlines major court cases. It also contains an analysis of leading Supreme Court cases and a selection of articles from the *Journal of the National Association for Women Deans, Administrators & Counselors* on such subjects as implementing a sexual harassment program at a large university. A useful source for identifying avenues for further research on sexual harassment and colleges.

Paludi, Michele A., ed. **Ivory Power: Sexual Harassment on Campus.** Albany, NY: State University of New York Press, 1990. 298p. Index, bibliography. ISBN 0-7914-0457-9 (cloth); 0-7914-0458-7 (paper).

Paludi, a research psychologist and director of the research collective on sexual harassment at Hunter College, edited this collection of scholarly papers on the issue, which starts from the premise that the most reliable data indicate that 30 percent of women students are sexually harassed by at least one instructor in college. (When definitions of *sexual harassment* include gender harassment—sexist comments and behavior—the incidence is 70 percent.) This collection covers the myths and realities of sexual harassment on campus; definitions and measurement; methods of studying the problem; the impact of harassment on cognitive, physical, and emotional well-being; studies of the men who become harassers; and how administrators should handle complaints. Extensive appendixes detail sample references on the subject, including audiovisual materials, workshop ideas, and training materials. One unique feature of the book is its emphasis on the experience of graduate women and women faculty and administrators. The collection takes a sociological perspective to the question of understanding and eliminating sexual harassment, while also addressing the interface of racism and sexism on college campuses and the legal issues involved in academic sexual harassment cases. An important work on the study of sexism and the study of women's professional advancement—or lack thereof.

Paul, Ellen Frankel, Lloyd R. Cohen, Linda C. Majka, Alan Kors, Jean Bethke Elshtain, and Nicholas Davidson, **"Sexual Harassment or Harassment of Sexuality?"** *Society* 28, no. 4 (May/June 1991): 4–45.

In this journal symposium, several authors present articles questioning the basic idea of allowing sexual harassment claims to rise to the level of legal complaints. In an article entitled "Bared Buttocks and Federal Cases," for example, Ellen Frankel Paul, a professor of political science, argues that "for women to expect reverential treatment in the workplace is utopian"; complains that "[s]exual harassment is a notoriously ill-defined and almost infinitely expandable concept"; and insists that "[w]omen must develop a thick skin to survive and prosper in the workplace." Similarly, contributor Cohen, a law professor at Chicago-Kent School of Law, agrees that the definition of *sexual harassment* has become "more, rather than less, elusive with use" and expresses his concern that the threat of legal sanctions will drive men away from necessary and proper courtship rituals. "Even if it were possible theoretically to define a category of sexual harassment as evil, it may still not be sensible to impose legal sanctions on such behavior," he concludes, because the workplace represents, for a number of people in our mobile society, "by far the best avenue for finding and pursuing romantic interests." Alan Kors, a history professor at the University of Pennsylvania, laments the rise and strictures of sexual and racial harassment policies in the university, and worries that they will impinge upon the rights of free speech and academic freedom. Philosophy and political science professor Elshtain comments on the collision of attempts to restrict pornography and the rights of free speech. Finally, Nicholas Davidson, author of *The Failure of Feminism*, provides a critique of "Feminism and Sexual Harassment," arguing that the feminist position on the issue represents an unreconcilable conflict between the desire for equal treatment of the sexes and the supposed need for protection from sexual advances. "On the one hand, feminists have endlessly assured us, women are 'strong,' . . . just as tough as men. . . . On the other hand, if women are just as tough as men . . . why do they need the protection of special 'sexual harassment' laws? After all, could a woman not just say no?" Such contradictions, he argues, means that "women's liberation has, in a sense, produced women's oppression." In all, this lively series of articles provides a much-needed counterpoint to the scores of books and periodicals that simply assume—without much analysis—that legal redress for sexual harassment claims is a worthy ideal.

Sumrall, Amber Coverdale, and Dena Taylor, eds. **Sexual Harassment: Women Speak Out.** Freedom, CA: Crossing Press, 1992. 321p. ISBN 0-89594-544-4 and ISBN 0-89594-2.

This book, dedicated to Anita Hill, arose out of the anger of one of the co-owners of Crossing Press, Elaine Goldman Gill, after watching the Clarence Thomas confirmation hearings. The editors called—in newspapers, on radio stations, and on college campuses—for submissions from women detailing their own experiences. Hundreds of manuscripts arrived in response. The editors describe the accounts as: "painful, angry, humiliating, humorous and empowering." In their words:

> Women all over the country—in their homes, at work, in the laundromat, at the hairdressers, in classrooms—watched Anita Hill's testimony, and the repeated questions, insinuations, disbelief, and laughter from the senators. For countless numbers of women, the Hill-Thomas hearings opened the gates of denial, and long-repressed memories came tumbling out.

In this book, women write of their experiences and how they responded to them. Some women were depressed or had physical symptoms; some fought back; some denied the harassment; some found humorous or other ways to deal with the harasser. Presented alphabetically, the stories are interspersed with quotations from and cartoons by women. The book includes a resource section for women who have experienced harassment.

The responders are a varied and interesting lot. They range from a 68-year-old woman who was forced to leave several jobs because of harassment to a 45-year-old woman who recalls being fondled, when a 12-year-old, by an electrician working in her school. Women from a wide variety of careers, from writers to police officers, relate the harassment they suffered and the consequences to their lives. Though not by any means a scientific survey of women harassment victims, the book provides valuable samples of women's experience in this area and may serve as comfort to other women suffering the same fate. This is a unique book in the literature of sexual harassment because it allows women to express their pain, outrage, and eventual power in their own words. Yet some readers may be troubled by the book's ironclad feminist stance. As Andrea Dworkin, an authority on rape, writes in the introduction:

> [O]utside, the woman is public in male territory, a hands-on zone; her presence there is taken to be a declaration of availability—for sex and sexual insult. . . . The verbal assaults and some physical assaults are endemic in the environment. . . . None of us can stand up to all of it; we are incredulous as each new aggression occurs. We hurry to forget. It can't have happened, we say; or it happens all the time, we say—it is too rare to be credible or too common to matter. We won't be believed or no one will care: or both.

Books, Monographs, and Selected Articles

Sexual Harassment

Berns, Walter. **"Terms of Endearment: Legislating Love."** *Harper's* (October 1980): 14–20.

Berns, a resident scholar at the American Enterprise Institute, wrote this short piece just before the first EEOC guidelines on sexual harassment were to become final. Berns criticizes the guidelines for not defining sexual harassment and predicts that the requirement that the employer provide an environment free of "sexual contamination" will eventually lead to dress codes for women, lest they provoke men. Although he admits that the regulations relate to behavior in the workplace, Berns argues that

> many lovers who end up in the bedroom meet in the workplace. [The EEOC's] purpose is the prevention of sexual harassment, not the inhibiting of romance; but in its efforts to identify the one, the

commission will intrude upon the other. This will interfere with the easy and sometimes playful familiarity that characterizes the relationships of men and women.

He believes that the government should respect "the privacy of erotic relationships" and notes that "traditionally, love has been seen to be none of the government's business." A playful, witty critique of the early EEOC guidelines.

Black, Beryl. **Coping with Sexual Harassment.** New York: Rosen Publishing Group, 1987. 149p. Index, bibliography. ISBN 0-8239-0732-5.

This book is one of the few to discuss incidents of sexual harassment experienced by young people at work and ways of coping with this problem. Written in an engaging style, the book presents the story of a fictional teenager who is sexually harassed at her first job. Excerpts from her diary and her letters to an advice column, "Ted and Monica," tell her story. The fictional columnists reply to her and solicit letters from their readers. The readers' letters reveal their own views on the subject as well as their experiences with both male and female homosexual and heterosexual harassment at work and in school. "Ted and Monica" respond with advice from psychological experts and an exposition of the law and EEOC guidelines. Without writing down to the reader, the book manages to impart a great deal of information in an innovative format. A list of organizational resources and a short book list are included. The book emphasizes the serious consequences of sexual harassment; in fact, some readers may find a few of the scenarios exaggerated when several teens end up killing themselves or their harassers. Young people, however, will probably be drawn into the many stories presented as well as the diverse points of view.

Bouchard, Elizabeth. **Everything You Need To Know About Sexual Harassment.** Revised ed. New York: Rosen Publishing Group, 1992. 64p. Index, bibliography. ISBN 0-8239-1490-9.

One of a series of books for young people on social issues, this work presents clear and concise definitions of sexual harassment in education and employment and explains how victims can handle the problem and where to go for help. Bouchard, a Chicago writer and teacher, explains the topic in a format that uses fictionalized examples of sexual harassment, followed by questions and answers concerning the scenarios. In addition to these real-life situations, subjects covered include how to spot sexual harassment, why it happens, who it happens to, avoiding sexual harassment, choices for action, and how to cope. Particularly helpful is the glossary explaining words that may be new to younger readers; the list of sources for help, such as the Equal Employment Opportunity Commission (EEOC) and various women's organizations; and a short list of suggestions for further reading. A balanced discussion of the Anita Hill/Clarence Thomas case is also included. Photographs of the dramatized situations help hold a reader's interest. In addition, large type and numerous topic headings make this book easy, yet accurate and helpful, reading. The advice on avoiding harassment is practical, such as keeping the relationship on a business level and saying "no" assertively right from the start. How to ask your harasser to stop, how to write him or her a letter, how to file an EEOC complaint, and when to seek legal advice are also treated with down-to-earth suggestions.

Brock, David. **"The Real Anita Hill."** *American Spectator* (March 1992): 18–30.

In this article—widely cited and discussed by supporters of Supreme Court Justice Clarence Thomas—David Brock provides fuel for the view that Anita Hill manufactured or exaggerated her charges against Thomas. After extensively investigating Hill's background and reviewing interviews with former colleagues, students, and professors, Brock concludes that Hill used the situation as an opportunity to further her own political ambitions and legal career, as well as to retaliate against Thomas because he had once passed her over for a promotion. Brock also contends that opponents of Thomas (including pro-choice groups) persuaded Hill to come forward in order to thwart the nomination. Some of Brock's allegations are so bizarre as to be unbelievable, such as those from two former law school students of Professor Hill's, who claimed that they found pubic hair in papers she returned to them. These and other stories about Hill are offered to show that she, not Clarence Thomas, had strange ideas about sexual relationships and may be "a bit nutty, and a bit slutty." Brock also claims that Hill once lied about a minor traffic accident. Feminist defenders of Hill will undoubtedly dismiss this piece as unproven gossip or worse, but it is included here because it presents an opposing view to that expressed by the many women journalists and women's magazines who have declared Anita Hill a wronged feminist heroine.

Collins, Eliza G. C., and Timothy B. Blodgett. **"Sexual Harassment: Some See It . . . Some Won't."** *Harvard Business Review* 59, no. 2 (March-April 1981): 76–95.

This report summarizes the results from a joint survey, with *Redbook* magazine, of more than 1,800 business executives drawn from *Harvard Business Review* subscribers. The researchers designed questions to probe perceptions of what harassment is, how frequently it occurs, and how management responds. The text is well-written, and memorable quotations are interspersed with the survey results, which gives the study a more interesting style. The survey pinpointed differences in men's and women's perceptions, most notably with regard to how much harassment actually occurs, how top managers respond to various situations, and how they ought to respond. Opinions about EEOC guidelines and company policies were also solicited. At the time of this survey (1981), most respondents of both sexes favored company policies governing harassment, but few worked for companies that actually had such policies. A classic study, often cited as one of the few to address the thoughts and views of top executives rather than workers.

Conte, Alba. **Sexual Harassment in the Workplace: Law and Practice.** New York: John Wiley & Sons, 1990. 556p. Index. ISBN 0-471-50743-1.

This comprehensive legal treatise covers all facets of the law of sexual harassment. Conte surveys the options available to victims under various laws and guides their attorneys through administrative and judicial proceedings. The book provides a state-by-state breakdown of relevant common and statutory law and discusses the issues unique to the area of sexual harassment. Extensive discussions of most sexual harassment cases are included, along with sample legal forms for various phases of litigation. Written in a style that general readers can follow, the book probably offers too much legal detail and analysis for the lay researcher. Nevertheless, if specific legal citations, analysis, or practice pointers are required, this is the resource to use. Note, however, that the main book only includes pre-1990 cases; that volume is kept up to date with yearly supplements.

Dzeich, Billie Wright, and Linda Weiner. **The Lecherous Professor: Sexual Harassment on Campus.** Boston: Beacon Press, 1984. 219p. Index, bibliography. ISBN 0-8070-3100-3.

Of the 6 million women who enter college each year, these authors estimate that 1 million will experience some form of sexual harassment by male professors. With experience as both professors and administrators, Dzeich and Weiner provide the first book-length account of this issue and suggestions for solving it. The writers dismiss many myths, such as the idea that college women ask for sexual harassment by dressing provocatively or by using sex to advance their own academic careers. Their research reveals otherwise; they quote, for example, an ombudsman at a southern college: "We very seldom get the campus-queen type in our office. My guess is that they are less likely to be harassed than those who are average in appearance. I think professors avoid them for the same reason a lot of college men hesitate about asking them out. They don't know how to act with them, and they're afraid of being rejected." Similarly, the authors assert that "the assumption that a student's clothes are an invitation to teachers rather than male peers is wishful and muddled thinking by college professors."

Drawing on in-depth interviews with students, faculty members, deans, and department heads at colleges and universities across the country, the authors researched all aspects of this issue, including the characteristics of academia that contribute to harassment, what a typical harasser is like, the effects on both male and female students, and the professional dilemmas faced by women faculty members. The authors also define sexual harassment by analyzing the power differences between students and teachers. Finally, they detail positive steps that students, parents, administrators, and faculty can take to diminish the incidence of sexual harassment. Although the book provides the kind of in-depth material suitable for an academic researcher, the general reader will also find it useful because it is written in a readable style and contains many quotations from students, faculty, and administrators in a lively mix.

Eskenazi, Martin, and David Gallen. **Sexual Harassment: Know Your Rights!** New York: Carroll & Graf, 1992. 224p. Index, bibliography. ISBN 0-88184-816-6.

One of a crop of books that sprouted after the Clarence Thomas confirmation hearings, this work consists mainly of a collection of writings from other sources, including a reprint of a speech given by Anita Hill as part of a panel on sexual harassment and policy making at the National Forum for Women in State Legislatures convened by the Center for the American Woman and Politics in late 1991. Another contributor is attorney and sexual harassment pioneer Catharine MacKinnon, with a reprint from her 1979 book detailing the incidence of sexual harassment and the experience of women who have been sexually harassed. The book includes special sections on federal employees and educational institutions; the National Organization for Women Legal Resource Kit on the issue is also reprinted. The EEOC guidelines, a question-and-answer section written by the authors, a list of resources, a bibliography, and an index complete the book. Although it clearly answers the most basic questions about what sexual harassment is and what to do about it, and is laudable for its reasonable price ($9.95 in 1992), the book suffers from a somewhat jumbled composition of material from a wide variety of sources.

Estrich, Susan. **"Sex at Work."** *Stanford Law Review* 43 (April 1991): 813–862.

This major law review article by Susan Estrich, the Robert Kingsley Professor of Law and Political Science at the University of Southern California, traces the history of sexual harassment cases starting from the law on rape. As she states: "While the crime of rape is centuries old, the federal cause of action for sexual harassment is an invention of our times. . . . The very existence of such a cause of action is a triumph for feminist scholars and practitioners, as well as for victims of sexual harassment." Estrich is one of a handful of legal theorists who argue that the law is dominated by age-old male biases and attempt to shape the direction of the law in terms relevant to women. In this article she addresses "the most persuasive and painful evidence of the durability of sexism in the law's judgment of the sexual relations of men and women." Rather than providing a legal treatise on sexual harassment in this article, Estrich intends to "reveal the attitudes and understandings underlying legal doctrine in this area." In so doing, she seeks to change the future direction of the law. In her review of the cases, Estrich finds a pervasive and sexist attitude in the hundreds of cases she studied; this bias assumes that sexual behavior at work is normal and even desirable. She argues that this attitude leads to unacceptable problems of proof for women in sexual harassment cases. She recommends, for example, that the requirement that the woman prove advances are "unwelcome" be eliminated as "gratuitous and personally humiliating." She does not believe that courts should protect the right of a few to have "consensual" sex in the workplace (a right, she argues, most women, according to the studies, do not even want) at the cost of exposing the "overwhelming majority to oppression and indignity at work." She recommends that companies implement policies against sexual relationships among employees in the workplace, at least with those who work directly for them. Although some may find Estrich's proposals for legal reform radical, the depth of her scholarship and analysis is impressive.

Farley, Lin. **Sexual Shakedown: The Sexual Harassment of Women on the Job.** New York: McGraw Hill, 1978. 228p. Index. ISBN 0-07-019957-4.

Now out of print, this classic book was the first to be published on the issue of sexual harassment and is still widely available in libraries and private collections. The work grew out of the experience of Farley, a journalist, when she taught a class on women and work at Cornell in 1974. Because there was no research readily available to use as class material, Farley turned to the use of small "consciousness raising groups." Although the groups consisted of women from different backgrounds and ranged from affluent to poor, Farley found that "when we had finished, there was an unmistakable pattern to our employment. Something absent in all the literature, something I had never seen although I had observed it many times, was newly exposed. Each one of us had already quit or had been fired from a job at least once because we had been made too uncomfortable by the behavior of men." After naming the problems women faced on the job "sexual harassment," Farley set about finding out how widespread the problem was and what the issue meant. Writing from a feminist perspective, Farley emphasizes that "job segregation" by sex is to a large degree sustained by male sexual harassment. That same segregation, Farley believes, rolled back the momentum of affirmative action and created a female ghetto. Sexual harassment comes about because "assertions of male dominance are socially sanctioned." She concludes that job segregation is the primary mechanism in the capitalist society that maintains the superiority of men over women, because it enforces lower wages for women in the labor market and lower wages encourage women to marry. The book presents many individual women's stories and takes the position that much of the female turnover in jobs is because of sexual harassment, rather than the traditional stereotypes that women lack seriousness about work, become pregnant, or leave out of sheer flightiness. In conclusion, Farley finds that the only hope is for women to become equal partners in the work force. To do so, she suggests, women must organize, help each other file claims of sexual harassment, if necessary, and take assertiveness courses. Farley provides historic and economic analyses, discusses legal remedies, and examines union and employer reactions to the issue. The author's stance is unabashedly feminist; she views our society as "first, last, and foremost a patriarchy" in which the historic function of sexual harassment has been to keep women "in line." Nevertheless, her arguments are supported by case studies, interviews, and extensive research documented by nine pages of endnotes.

Gutek, Barbara A. **Sex and the Workplace.** San Francisco: Jossey-Bass, 1985. 216p. Index, bibliography. ISBN 0-87589-656-1.

Gutek, a professor of psychology, business administration, and executive management, and a key figure in sexual harassment research, publishes extensively on the dynamics of sexual harassment in the workplace. This book represents a review of a comprehensive program of research on sex at work and the interactions of women and men at work. The book is based on findings from several studies, primarily from a large random-sample survey of 1,257 working men and women in Los Angeles County. This study revealed generalized information on sexual behavior, including sexual harassment, which workers have such problems, how they react, and, most uniquely, the kinds of organizational conditions that foster such problems. The book includes an historical overview of the issues of sex at work, how sex segregation of work and pay differentials between men and women affect the psychological experiences of working women and men, the characteristics of harassers, and the reactions of victims of harassment. Also presented are the verbatim comments of men and women who reported sexual overtures from the other sex. One of Gutek's most often quoted and important findings is the giant gender gap in attitudes: men consistently say they are flattered by sexual overtures from women at work, while women consistently say that they are insulted by sexual propositions from men. An academician, Gutek never offers an opinion without citing the research that supports her view. One of her conclusions is that where men and women work together in equal numbers in the same jobs, there are virtually no social-sexual problems. By contrast, she finds, sexual harassment is much more prevalent where women or men are segregated in certain jobs. In general, Gutek concludes, women are hurt by sex in the workplace but men are not: "Contrary to popular belief, women do not use sex at work nearly as frequently as men do." An essential, well-researched work.

Klein, Freada. **The 1988 Working Woman Sexual Harassment Survey Executive Report.** Cambridge, MA: Klein Associates, 1988. 36p.

This report summarizes the results of a survey conducted at the behest of *Working Woman* magazine; a shorter report was published in that periodical. In March 1988, a 49-item questionnaire was sent to the heads of human resources of the Fortune 500 service and manufacturing companies. This writing summarizes the methodology of the survey and the results. One of the most important findings of this survey is that sexual harassment costs a typical Fortune 500 company $6.7 million per year (a cost of $282.53 per employee per year); these costs are comprised of turnover, absenteeism, reduced productivity, and use of internal complaint mechanisms. In contrast, the report emphasizes that preventive steps can be taken for $200,000. Another significant finding is that most incidents of sexual harassment are not reported to employers. The study also details the percentage of respondents with written policies and the effect of top management's commitment to end sexual harassment. The report includes recommendations for human resource professionals. This survey is one of the most often cited as providing reliable data on sexual harassment.

MacKinnon, Catharine A. **Sexual Harassment of Working Women.** New Haven, CT and London: Yale University Press, 1979. 312p. Index. ISBN 0-300-02298-0 (cloth); 0-300-02299-9 (paper).

Written by a well-known feminist scholar, this book is widely credited with being the first to articulate a legal basis for the thesis that sexual harassment is a form of sex discrimination and, therefore, illegal. Published before most of the legal precedent on the issue, the book addresses whether sexual harassment could be considered a violation of the equal protection clause of the Constitution, or discrimination in employment because of sex under Title VII of the Civil Rights Act of 1964 or other laws. The work also considers whether a woman who quits her job because of sexual harassment should be entitled to unemployment compensation and whether an employer is responsible for the actions of its employees who engage in sexual harassment. This book was one of the first to frame the problem in the context of the inferior position of women in the labor market, as well as to provide a factual account of the nature and extent of sexual harassment and to show how that harassment grows out of and reenforces the traditional social roles of men and women in our society. Because there were no systematic studies of sexual harassment at the time the book was written, MacKinnon was forced to rely on evidence from women's observations of their own lives. MacKinnon never waivers from her feminist stance. She states, for example, that "[o]ne thing wrong with sexual harassment (and with rape) is that it eroticizes women's submission. It acts out and depends on the powerlessness of women as a gender, *as women.*" Arguing that "an analysis of sexuality must not be severed and abstracted from analysis of gender," MacKinnon concludes that "[w]omen want to be equal and different, too," that is, we must accept that women in the workplace face different issues before we can correctly understand sexual harassment. Although the book is now out-of-date in this rapidly changing legal field, and its complex style may be difficult reading for the lay person, the book is impressive because it was the first to attempt a legal analysis of the issue of sexual harassment. The book fulfills the author's expressed goal: "to bring to the law something of the reality of women's lives."

Martindale, Melanie. **Sexual Harassment in the Military: 1988.** Arlington, VA: Defense Manpower Data Center, 1990. 56p.

This report summarizes the results of the first large-scale study of sexual harassment in the military. A wealth of data is presented, including the incidence of sexual harassment; the context, location, and circumstances under which sexual harassment occurs; and the effectiveness of current military programs to prevent and deal with harassment. The major finding is that 64 percent of the women and 17 percent of the men in military service had experienced sexual harassment in the year preceding the study. The respondents, however, were not asked directly and explicitly about "sexual harassment," but rather about specific, behaviorally described "uninvited and unwanted sexual attention" received at work. The report is a straightforward presentation of the data and survey results, complete with graphs and tables. The author does not take a position on the meaning of the results or make recommendations for future action.

Massachusetts Department of Education, Division of Curriculum and Instruction. **Who's Hurt and Who's Liable: Sexual Harassment in Massachusetts Schools: A Curriculum and Guide for School Personnel.** Quincy, MA: Massachusetts Department of Education, Bureau of Operational Support, 1986. 87p.

Developed by Nan Stein, who was a sex-equity/civil-rights specialist for the Massachusetts Department of Education, this curriculum was the first to be offered to secondary schools on the subject of sexual harassment. As such, it has been used as a model by schools all across the country. It provides information for all members of the school community: students, teachers, counselors, and administrators. The guide defines sexual harassment; explains the legal issues involved; describes administrative strategies; suggests student activities and classroom lessons; and includes other materials relating to the issue. The curriculum takes the position that sexual harassment in schools is a pervasive problem and an obstacle to equal educational opportunities.

McIntyre, Douglas I. **Sexual Harassment in Government.** Ann Arbor, MI: University Microfilms, 1984. 342p. Bibliography.

This Ph.D. thesis, originally submitted to the department of government at Florida State University, is a statistical survey on the issue of sexual harassment, based on a random sample of female employees of the state of Florida. Unlike many studies that have been conducted on the issue of sexual harassment, this one followed scientific, objective survey techniques. In addition, the thesis reviews national information on sexual harassment, including case law, other surveys, and the EEOC guidelines and considers recommendations for national policy, the obligations of employers, and suggestions for action by employers. The book is most useful as a model of how a sexual harassment survey should be conducted, because it includes extensive discussions of the methodology and the original survey material.

Meyer, Mary Coeli, Inge M. Berchtold, Jeannenne L. Oestreich and Frederick J. Collins. **Sexual Harassment.** New York and Princeton: Petrocelli Books, 1981. 200p. Bibliography. ISBN 0-89433-156-6.

This book, written from a management perspective, presents a good introduction to the scope of the problem. Sparked by the 1980 EEOC regulations that first suggested organizations could be legally responsible for sexual harassment, the book defines the problem and provides case studies, sample policy statements for organizations, suggested awareness training, tips on how employees can handle harassment, and lists of organizations, legal precedent, and other resources. Although now somewhat dated and apparently out of print, the book is still widely available in most libraries, and is one of the first comprehensive source books to address the problem. Women activists, however, may be put off by the management-oriented tone of the book, which presents as many examples of sexually harassed men as women (other experts have concluded that sexual harassment by women is rare), and continually emphasizes that the harassee has a responsibility to communicate clearly with the harasser. The book also rejects the feminist argument that sexual harassment is another example of a purposeful attempt to oppress women. The authors argue instead that it is a sometimes innocent and baffled response by men to confusing social evolution and technological change; that is, harassment is perpetrated by those who cannot adapt or respond to changing roles. The book remains one of the few works to acknowledge and emphasize the complexity of the issue, stressing that men and women may view the same situation differently, without pointing the finger at easy victims or villains.

Neville, Kathleen. **Corporate Attractions: An Inside Account of Sexual Harassment.** Washington, DC: Acropolis Books Ltd., 1990. 301p. Index. ISBN 0-87491-952-5 (cloth); 0-87491-953-3 (paper).

Kathleen Neville was an advertising sales executive and reporter with a Buffalo, New York, television station in 1981 when she was sexually harassed by her boss, who demanded sexual favors in return for continued employment. This book is an unflinching and engrossing account of the six-year legal battle that ensued when she was fired after she refused his advances. Twice victimized—once by her harasser and then by the legal system—a federal district court judge and an appellate court found that Neville had been sexually harassed but was fired for unrelated reasons, even though she had years of outstanding performance evaluations. Neville offers tips for other victims on reporting the initial harassment, communicating with the harasser and co-workers, and selecting a competent attorney, with the hope that others will be able to avoid her painful experience. She also details "New Rules for the Workplace" so that men and women workers can avoid harassment claims. The book exposes the physical, emotional, and financial costs of both the harassment and the lengthy legal process. Neville learned the hard way that she, not her harasser, ended up on trial. The account will make any victim think twice before pursuing a harassment claim.

Omilian, Susan M. **Sexual Harassment in Employment.** Wilmette, IL: Callaghan, 1987. 177p. Index. ISBN O-8366-0013-4.

Although aimed at attorneys representing a plaintiff or a defendant in a lawsuit based on sexual harassment, the clear language of this book—mostly free of legalese—makes it accessible to the lay person. This comprehensive report analyzes most of the court decisions that have considered the issue of sexual harassment and includes a consideration of questions yet to be answered (in 1987) by the courts. Omilian also discusses a long list of cases in which the victim could not prove a sexual harassment claim and includes tips for both sides in litigating a sexual harassment case. The book lacks a glossary of legal terms, which would have made it even more useful to a lay person, and the text may provide more detail than is needed by the average researcher. Still, the work offers a wealth of information about individual cases and legal analysis. Unfortunately, because it was published in 1987, this work misses some more recent sexual harassment cases that significantly changed the face of the law in this area.

Paludi, Michele A., and Richard B. Barickman. **Academic and Workplace Sexual Harassment: A Resource Manual.** Albany, NY: State University of New York Press, 1991. 215p. Index. ISBN O-7914-0829-9 (cloth); O-7914-8030-2 (paper).

Paludi is a research psychologist who has published a number of works on sexual harassment, developmental psychology, and women's issues. She directed the research collective on sexual harassment at Hunter College. Barickman helped establish the Hunter panel on sexual harassment; he has also written on the issue of sexual harassment and gender. Despite the title, this work focuses mainly on sexual harassment on campus, rather than in the workplace. Written from a feminist perspective, the book takes the position, for example, that there is no such thing as a consensual sexual relationship between a student and a faculty member, because of the disparity in power between the two groups. The authors provide extensive results from various studies, such as the incidence of sexual harassment claims and the psychological impact of harassment. The work is important and useful because of the depth of research offered. Written in an academic style, the book suffers from a lack of clear organization; the writers constantly interrupt the text in a confusing manner with tables and study results. In addition, much of the book consists of articles previously published in other journals, resulting in some repetition.

Petrocelli, William, and Barbara Kate Repa. **Sexual Harassment on the Job: What It Is and How To Stop It.** Berkeley, CA: Nolo Press, 1992. 198p. Index. ISBN 0-87337-1771-1.

This book is part of a series published by Nolo Press on "how-to" legal issues. The authors provide a clear guide to understanding the laws on sexual harassment, deciding whether an employee has a claim, the complaint process, and even such rarely covered matters as how to read legal citations and manage an attorney. Although the book does include sample sexual harassment policies and tips for employers on finding the right training consultant or materials, the focus of the book is on employees who believe they may have been harassed. Written in language easy for the lay person to understand, the book includes a useful list of resources as well as a state-by-state compendium of laws relating to harassment. An excellent guide through the legal thicket of laws and policies in this area, the book is well-designed and includes lively quotations from a variety of experts and commentators on the subject of sexual harassment. The authors take the position that sexual harassment is not about sex, but about power: "Sexual harassment is a male tactic to make a woman vulnerable in the work place. It often works."

Phelps, Timothy M., and Helen Winternitz. **Capitol Games.** New York: Hyperion, 1992. 458p. Index, bibliographical note. ISBN 1-56282-916-5.

Timothy Phelps, the *Newsday* Supreme Court reporter who broke the story about Anita Hill's allegations of sexual harassment against Clarence Thomas, and co-author, Helen Winternitz, an award-winning journalist and author, present a blow-by-blow description of events leading up to the hearing on Thomas's nomination and the behind-the-scenes maneuvering during and after the hearings. A classic piece of investigative reporting, *Capitol Games* answers questions not provided by the televised proceedings, including why another woman who had also accused Thomas of sexual harassment, Angela Wright, did not testify; the failure of Democratic senators to control the hearing process; and the backgrounds and disagreements of the legal and public relations teams who advised both Hill and Thomas. Insider accounts of how Thomas positioned himself as a black conservative, how he was selected, and how the radical right backed his cause provide fascinating background information on the newest Supreme Court Justice. Hill's legal career and family background are also scrutinized. The authors take no position on the issue of who was telling the truth during the hearings, but focus instead on providing readers with enough facts and information to make their own decisions. The book serves as a chronicle of the nomination spectacle that captivated the American public in the fall of 1991, as well as an engrossing account of the mix of race, sex, and politics that fueled the proceedings.

Siegel, Deborah L. **Sexual Harassment: Research & Resources.** New York: National Council for Research on Women, 1992. 56p. Bibliography. ISBN 1-880547-12-0.

This useful research guide continues an overview of the definitions, laws, surveys, and other research available relating to sexual harassment. Compiled after the Clarence Thomas hearings and the enactment of the 1991 Civil Rights Act, this report contains some of the most up-to-date references. Much of the text consists of quotations from sexual harassment experts who were interviewed especially for this publication; it therefore offers material not found in any other book on the subject. Extensive appendixes provide information on researchers and expert witnesses, organizations, conferences, and even guidelines for organizing forums on the issue. A selected bibliography and list of available videos are also offered. An excellent compilation.

Strauss, Susan. **Sexual Harassment and Teens: A Program for Positive Change.** Minneapolis, MN: Free Spirit, 1992. 149p. Index, bibliography. ISBN 0-915793-44-X.

This book, designed to sensitize students, faculty, and staff to the issue of sexual harassment of teens, includes a complete course for sexual harassment training designed for grades 7 through 12. Strauss is a trainer and organizational development specialist with a hospital in Minneapolis. She has also designed and directed educational programs on sexual harassment and assisted in developing school policies on the issue. The book also includes 40 reproducible forms and handouts, as well as a sexual harassment survey. The curriculum is designed to help adults identify and solve sexual harassment problems in any school, community organization, youth group, or other gatherings of young people. Case studies, activities, and a review of the laws and guidelines, as well as suggested policies, procedures, and a list of resources, are provided. Designed for educators, this book covers the basics needed to teach sexual harassment awareness to young people as well as providing an actual curriculum in a clear, concise format. The program was developed as a result of studies conducted in Minnesota schools, which revealed that 50 percent of teenaged girls reported having been verbally and physically harassed at school.

United States Merit Systems Protection Board. **Sexual Harassment in the Federal Workplace: Is It a Problem?** Washington, DC: Government Printing Office, 1981. 202p. Bibliography.

This study, mandated by Congress, was the first to be scientifically designed and to draw on a nationwide sample. Some 23,000 federal workers were sent questionnaires; over 20,000 responded. Replete with statistical data, tables, and graphs, this pivotal report examines the extent and impact of sexual harassment, its victims and perpetrators, awareness of the problem, and the perceived effectiveness of various remedies. The study found that harassment was widespread in the federal workplace: 42 percent of female employees and 15 percent of males reported harassment in the two-year period studied. Extensive details are presented on the characteristics of both victims and harassers, as well as the costs of harassment to the government and the effect on victims. Appendixes to the report include the research methodology, the survey questionnaire, official policy documents, and a survey of the literature. A 14-page annotated bibliography is included.

————. **Sexual Harassment in the Federal Government: An Update.** Washington, DC: Government Printing Office, 1988. 49p.

This report updates the more detailed 1981 offering of the same title. This time, a questionnaire was sent to a representative cross-section of approximately 13,000 federal employees, of whom 8,523 responded. The report found an increase in employees' inclination to define certain types of behavior as sexual harassment, but no decrease in the amount of harassment experienced. By the time of this study, all federal agencies reported having sexual harassment policies in place. The report includes an update of the material presented in the earlier volume, as well as new material on agency actions to reduce sexual harassment and a review of the case law. Recommendations for further government action are also offered.

Wagner, Ellen J. **Sexual Harassment in the Workplace: How To Prevent, Investigate, and Resolve Problems in Your Organization.** New York: American Management Association, 1992. 148p. Index. ISBN 0-8144-7787-9.

Wagner, an attorney and human resource consultant, here presents a useful guide for management, refreshingly free from legal jargon. The book includes a step-by-step approach to investigating a claim of sexual harassment within an organization. It also covers avoiding pitfalls such as defamation or wrongful discharge claims; deciding on appropriate discipline or counseling; instituting termination procedures; handling personnel files and reference requests; and preventing future claims. Included are sample policy statements and interview questions, training guides, a complete glossary of legal terms, and a straightforward explanation of legal precedent without legalese. The book includes one of the few discussions on the relatively new legal claim of "paramour preference" and explains how sexual favoritism can open the door to third-party claims of sexual discrimination.

Webb, Susan L. **Step Forward: Sexual Harassment in the Workplace.** New York: Mastermedia, 1991. 116p. ISBN 0-942381-51-2.

Susan Webb is a consultant and trainer specializing in the area of human relations. She frequently provides expert witness testimony and training on the subject of sexual harassment and conducts investigations into allegations of harassment and other interpersonal conflicts. This slim volume is an easy-to-follow manual telling what employees and management need to know about the issue. Filled with interactive quizzes, this book offers answers to the standard questions, including "What is sexual harassment?", "How can I be sure it's sexual harassment?", "Whose fault is it?", and "Don't women harass men too?" Included are suggestions for limiting liability, training guidelines, and an analysis of future trends. The book provides a number of quick lists, such as "a 6-step program for managers to stop sexual harassment," "the 10 factors for assessing an incident," and "how to conduct an investigation." The history of sexual harassment and the important cases on the issue are also discussed briefly. This is one of the few books to include a survey of sexual harassment studies from around the world—sure to be the next hot topic in this area. Published just after the Clarence Thomas confirmation hearings, the book mentions the controversy and comments upon the rise in the level of interest in the subject those hearings engendered. In a section about the future, Webb mentions that many who work in the human rights field believe that, in poor economic times, all forms of harassment and discrimination occur more frequently. A section on the costs of harassment summarizes some of the more dramatic awards.

Related Gender Issues

The American Association of University Women Educational Foundation. **How Schools Shortchange Girls.** Washington, DC: American Association of University Women Educational Foundation, 1992. 116p. ISBN 0-8106-2501-6.

Researched by the Wellesley College Center for Research on Women, in this significant report the AAUW presents a persuasive and startling examination of how girls are disadvantaged in America's schools, grades K–12. The book includes recommendations for educators and policymakers, as well as concrete strategies for change. Ironically, AAUW's first national study—undertaken in 1885—was initiated to dispel the commonly accepted myth that higher education was harmful to women's health. This latest report explodes the truth behind another myth, namely, that girls and boys receive equal education. The findings support the premise that Title IX of the 1972 Education Amendments, which prohibits discrimination in educational institutions receiving federal funds, has not solved the problem of equal education. The report is a synthesis of the available research on the subject of girls in schools and presents compelling evidence that girls are not receiving the same quality of education as boys. The research documents a wide range of findings; for example, that teachers are more likely to call on boys than on girls and that the curriculum lacks positive women role models. One of the recommendations of the report is that schools need policies against sex discrimination and sexual harassment to assure equal educational opportunities for girls.

Davidson, Nicholas. **The Failure of Feminism.** Buffalo, NY: Prometheus Books, 1988. 392p. Index, bibliography. ISBN 0-87975-408-4.

Nicholas Davidson, a writer with degrees in history from the University of Massachusetts at Amherst and the University of Chicago, presents this extensively annotated assault on feminism. He answers the question: "Has feminism failed?" with a resounding yes. Davidson argues that some of our most basic assumptions about gender originated in the scientific confusion of the last century and submits that we need a new recognition of the centrality of both masculinity and femininity to the human experience. If we fail "to achieve a workable gender balance," he argues, our civilization itself may not survive. "It is not enough to tolerate gender," writes Davidson, "we must celebrate it." After exploring the history of feminism, Davidson insists that the feminist perspective has led to ills such as a lack of spontaneity in sex and frigidity in women. Although he does not directly address the issue of sexual harassment, he argues that aggression in men is a force of nature, in both sex and other areas, that will never really change. Davidson's book is offered here for its thorough and widely read critique of the feminist perspective that "the human condition is a product of men's oppression of women. Women must resist this oppression by refusing to submit to sex on men's terms," and his conclusion that "[t]he belief that gender is a purely cultural construct is fast becoming a peculiar archaism." He draws on examples such as the Israeli kibbutzim to argue that, even there, the attempt to eliminate sex roles has failed. One puzzling note occurs in one of his final conclusions: that women (although apparently not men!) should have the choice of whether to work full or part time or to be full-time housekeepers. Many feminists would argue that this is what they have been working toward all along. A contentious book, sure to provoke discussion and thought.

Faludi, Susan. **Backlash: The Undeclared War against American Women.** New York: Crown, 1991. 552p. Index. ISBN 0-517-57698-8.

Faludi, a Pulitzer Prize-winning journalist, presents a witty and exhaustively researched indictment of the media, political, and legal establishments; she alleges that they have manufactured a backlash of public opinion in response to the gains women have made in the past 20 years. She submits a persuasive account of how such supposed phenomena as unmarried and unhappy women in their thirties, the rise in female infertility, and a return to the fashion of the 1950s are all attempts to keep women in their place and to, in effect, punish females for the few advances that have been achieved. Although the book's specifics on sexual harassment are few, she does discuss several major cases and detail the retaliation all of the women in her examples have suffered for daring to come forward with sexual harassment claims. More importantly, however, the book serves as one view of the context in which sexual harassments claims are brought, and validates the feminist position that perpetrators of sexual harassment are intentionally seeking to thwart the economic and professional progress of women. Already, this controversial book is a classic in the field of women's studies.

Farrell, Warren. **The Myth of Male Power.** New York: Simon & Schuster, 1993. 512p. Index, bibliography. ISBN 0-671-79349.

Farrell was the only man to have been elected three times to the board of the National Organization for Women. Described as "the Gloria Steinem of Men's Liberation" by the *Chicago Tribune*, he is also the author of *The Liberated Man* and the best-seller, *Why Men Are the Way They Are*, a professor, and a popular workshop leader. In this new work, which is sure to enrage some feminists, Dr. Farrell argues that male power is largely a myth because of the special obligations imposed on men, such as the expectation that men will support a family and be drafted. In this book, Farrell defines *power* as "control over one's own life" and concludes that the male obligation to earn more money than a woman before she will love him does not lead to power or control over the man's life. He asserts that neither sex, because of historical sex roles, has had control over their lives. The work is included in this listing because of Farrell's widely publicized thesis that a woman's fantasy of meeting and being taken care of by a successful man fuels much of the drive men have to succeed and their resulting insensitivity.

On the issue of harassment, Farrell contends that women expect to date, and even marry, men whom they meet at work; he believes that this expectation leads to confused signals in the workplace. As an example, he points to the many popular romance novels wherein the heroine initially resists the advances of her supervisor or boss but eventually submits and lives happily ever after. Men, he contends, are confused about how to interpret the mixed messages they receive at work, which may lead to claims of sexual harassment. When the issue of sexual harassment surfaced, he argues, we were told "men don't 'get it' " when, in fact, *neither* sex "gets" it. Men do not understand women's fears of harassment that stem from the passive role; women do not understand men's fears of sexual rejection that stem from the initiating role. Both sexes are so preoccupied with their own vulnerability that neither sex " 'gets' the other sex's vulnerability." Devoting an entire chapter to sexual harassment, Farrell asserts that

> [w]hen . . . women complained they were being sexually harassed, the government radically expanded its protection of women by expanding its prosecution of men. Simultaneously, construction sites with shaky scaffolding and coal mines with shaky ceilings were left uninspected—and the men left unprotected. In brief, men were left unprotected from premature death while women were protected from premature flirtation.

Allowing claims for sexual harassment, Farrell argues, is a double-edged sword for women, because "paying an equal wage to a woman who is a few hundred times more likely than a man to sue for harassments and hazards is not to an employer's advantage. *The overprotection of women and the underprotection of men, then, soon leads to discrimination against hiring women.*" The book is loaded with statistics and footnotes with which

Farrell proves his points. Although some of Farrell's positions and examples may be exaggerated or calculated to provoke, the book is one of the few to question the wisdom and effectiveness of government legislation against sexual harassment; it is thus an important contribution to the debate and a book guaranteed to inspire lively discussion.

Paglia, Camille. **Sex, Art, and American Culture.** New York: Vintage Books, 1992. 337p. Index. ISBN 0-697-74101-1 (paper).

In this follow-up to *Sexual Personae,* Paglia presents a book of essays on topics that range from Madonna to Anita Hill, date rape to MTV. She continues to provide quotable quotes for the media by denouncing feminism as Puritanism or describing a fraternity party as "Testosterone Flats," while emphasizing a woman's responsibility for date rape. On the issue of Anita Hill, she applauds the idea of sexual harassment guidelines, but frets that the hostile workplace category of sexual harassment claims means that "women are being returned to their old status of delicate flowers who must be protected from assault by male lechers. It is anti-feminist to ask for special treatment for women." Anita Hill, Paglia argues, is "no feminist heroine. . . . [I]f Anita Hill was thrown for a loop by sexual banter, that's her problem. If by the age of 26 and a graduate of Yale Law School she could find no convincing way to signal her displeasure and disinterest, that's her deficiency." Paglia's controversial views on date rape have raised the hackles of many feminists who believe that she is simply blaming the victim by insisting that women must be more cautious in dating situations. While the book may enflame many, it is sure to fuel debate on the issues Paglia considers.

————. **Sexual Personae.** London & New Haven, CT: Yale University Press, 1990. 718p. Index. ISBN 0-300-04396-1.

Paglia, an associate professor of humanities at Philadelphia College of the Performing Arts, burst upon the scene in 1990 with this scholarly book and received a siege of media publicity. The author recycles an ancient idea: biology is destiny, or perhaps, testosterone is destiny. Yet she presents this premise with a creative twist and a fierce intelligence. Although she does not specifically focus on sexual harassment in this book, she does take the position that men's sexual aggression is natural and inevitable, rejecting the feminist notion that rape is about power rather than a natural expression of sexuality.

> Modern feminism's most naive formulation is its assertion that rape is a crime of violence but not of sex, that it is merely power masquerading as sex. But sex *is* power, and all power is inherently aggressive. Rape is male power fighting female power. It is no more to be excused than is murder or any other assault on another's civil rights. Society is woman's protection against rape, not, as some

feminists absurdly maintain, the cause of rape. . . . Therefore, the
rapist is a man with too little socialization rather than too much.

In this densely written, difficult, but absolutely original work, Paglia
argues that rather than society causing sex discrimination, sexual harassment, and rape, society holds these natural forces in check. In general,
she identifies some of the major patterns that have endured with regard
to sex and sex roles in western culture from ancient Egypt and Greece to
the present. She discusses sex and nature as brutal, demonic forces, and
she criticizes feminists for sentimentality or wishful thinking about the
causes of rape, violence, and poor relations between the sexes.

> Feminists, seeking to drive power relations out of sex, have set
> themselves against nature. Sex *is* power. Identity is power. In western
> culture, there are no nonexploitative relationships. Everyone has
> killed in order to live. . . . The sexes are eternally at war. There is an
> element of attack, of search-and-destroy in male sex, in which there
> will always be a potential for rape. There is an element of entrapment
> in female sex, a subliminal manipulation leading to physical and
> emotional infantilization of the male. . . . It is in nature's best in-
> terests to goad dominant males into indiscriminate spreading of
> their seed.

This is a much discussed book, unique in the literature of sex roles
and gender issues.

Tannen, Deborah. **You Just Don't Understand: Women and Men in
Conversation.** New York: William Morrow, 1990. 330p. Index, bibliography. ISBN 0-688-07822-2.

Dr. Tannen, a sociolinguist, professor, and author of a number of
scholarly books, has written a readable and popular account, based on
evidence from her own extensive studies, of why and how conversations
between men and women are like cross-cultural communication. Tannen's thesis is that, from an early age, girls play with one best friend or
a small group and use language to seek confirmation and reinforce
intimacy, whereas boys use language to protect their independence and
negotiate status in large-group activities. Using the same styles as adults,
women and men hear completely different things in the same conversation. Backed by lively examples and anecdotes, this book suggests that
understanding can do much to help bridge the gap between the two
sexes as well as to help men and women find a common language for
communication. An internationally recognized scholar, Tannen has
managed to translate her academic work into books and articles accessible to the general reading public. This best-selling book is a must-read
for anyone attempting to understand how men and women may have
different ideas about what is—or is not—sexual harassment and why it

occurs. As Tannen concludes, "If you understand gender differences in what I call conversational style, you may not be able to prevent disagreements from arising, but you stand a better chance of preventing them from spiraling out of control."

Related Legal Issues

Friedman, Scott E. **Sex Law: A Legal Sourcebook on Critical Sexual Issues for the Non-Lawyer.** Jefferson, NC and London: McFarland, 1990. 167p. Index. ISBN 0-89950-540-6.

Intended to be a resource guide for lawyers and nonlawyers alike, this book steers the reader through the complicated maze of laws governing individual sexual rights and responsibilities in the United States. As the author notes,

> [t]his maze has grown wider and more complex over the past several decades as society grapples with the continuing sexual revolution that poses many novel and often unexpected problems for individuals and society at large. It seems to me that the legal aspects emerging from the sexual revolution are not generally understood, and many of us are often confused about our legal rights and responsibilities concerning sexually related subjects.

Friedman, a lawyer practicing in New York, clearly and concisely tackles such thorny questions as abortion, surrogate motherhood, protection of fetuses from their pregnant mothers' drug and alcohol abuse, and legal remedies for victims of AIDS and other sexually transmitted diseases. Sex discrimination and sexual harassment are also addressed. The rights of gay males and lesbians, paternity, and other issues are also clarified. Leading judicial precedents on these subjects are discussed, and many citations to case and statutory authority are supplied to assist readers who would like to engage in further research. A summary question-and-answer format starts each section to give readers a useful, quick answer to their questions on that particular subject. Although, as the author emphasizes, no single book can substitute for legal research of primary sources of the particular state or federal laws, this book serves as a useful aid for placing the whole issue of sexual harassment in the broader context of sexual issues in the law.

Olsen, Walter. **The Litigation Explosion.** New York: Dutton, 1991. 388p. Index, biographical references. ISBN 0-525-24911-7.

Olsen, a graduate of Yale University who studied economics at UCLA, is a senior fellow at the Manhattan Institute. In this book, he traces what happened when "America Unleashed the Lawsuit." He argues that 20 years ago, Americans saw lawsuits as a last resort; now we are the world's most litigious people. In *The Litigation Explosion,* he explains how this trend developed, what it means, who profits, and how it can be contained. He uses actual examples of lawsuits to make his points. Aggressive lawyers who draw out lawsuits, so that even innocent defendants are forced to settle, and expert witnesses who will say anything for a fee are particularly responsible for the growth of costly and unnecessary litigation, Olsen believes. Although he does not mention sexual harassment cases in particular, he argues that the law should not be used as a tool to correct every perceived social ill. Interviewed recently on the television show *Sally Jessy Raphael* (October 14, 1992) for a program on sexual harassment and schools, Olsen lamented the idea of bringing in lawyers to deal with this "old problem." He stated, "We have decided in the last year that we're going to bring in the lawyers and we're going to make it a matter of money, and that is slowly going to change the way kids in schools interrelate with each other, and I think it's going to change it for the worse." Such suits, he argues, will simply lead to increased expenses for schools and an increase in taxes. Olsen's book is a good resource for those who wish to track the rise and influence of the lawsuit in this country as a tool for resolving social problems such as sexual harassment.

The Women's Legal Defense Fund. **Sex Discrimination in the Workplace.** 3d ed. Washington, DC: Women's Legal Defense Fund, 1988. 71p.

This handbook explains federal laws prohibiting sex discrimination in employment and the administrative procedures for enforcing those laws. Designed to provide information for employees throughout the United States, it also includes more detailed data about Washington, D.C., Maryland, and Virginia law, as well as technical information for lawyers. Particularly useful is the section about the EEOC process, including a flowchart detailing EEOC procedures in private sector cases. Among the topics covered are sexual harassment, wage discrimination, pregnancy discrimination, and other forms of sex-based discrimination in the workplace; administrative procedures for filing a discrimination charge with the EEOC; procedures for federal employees; and an overview of state and local laws prohibiting discrimination in employment. Also offered are the list of Equal Employment Opportunity Commission offices nationwide. Written in a straightforward style, this book provides a broader canvas for viewing sexual harassment claims as one species of sex discrimination in the workplace.

Loose-Leaf Services

Larson, Arthur, and Lex K. Larson. **Employment Discrimination.** New York: Matthew Bender, 1992. Index. ISBN 0-8205-1626-0.

This five-volume set includes an entire volume (vol. 1) on sex discrimination in employment. Written for lawyers, the volumes are actually part of a loose-leaf service, so that the pages can be continually removed and updated when necessary to keep the material current. Such services are the only way to make sure that the legal material presented is accurate and timely. In these volumes, extensive detail is presented on the case law and statutes relating to employment discrimination. The lay person may find these books difficult reading, but for in-depth legal analysis and research such services are the best source. A useful pamphlet on the Civil Rights Act of 1991 is included. The volume on sex discrimination provides discussions on everything from Title VII to sexual harassment to unions and discrimination. This service is available in most large law libraries.

National Employment Lawyers' Association. **Employee Rights Litigation.** New York: Matthew Bender, 1992. ISBN 0-8205-1137-4.

This three-volume loose-leaf service is written and published by the National Employment Lawyers Association (NELA), a group devoted to representing individual plaintiffs in employment litigation. This service is one of NELA's attempts to help bring information and knowledge of employee rights to practitioners throughout the country. It covers the basic legal standards for the statutory and common law claims that could be raised on behalf of employees who believe they have been unjustly terminated. It also includes sections on antidiscrimination laws, plus chapters on the various emerging causes of action for wrongful discharge. Designed for lawyers, the book emphasizes pretrial advice about litigation, including extensive sample forms for use in actual lawsuits. A detailed section on sexual harassment and other forms of sex discrimination is included, as well as related subjects such as the Equal Pay Act. The extensive legal analysis of cases and statutes may be boring and confusing to the general researcher, but this service will prove highly useful for those needing to do more in-depth legal research. The loose-leaf format ensures that the most current information will be included, as pages are periodically removed and replaced when new cases or information become available. Most large law libraries will have these volumes.

Periodicals

Most of the organizations described in chapter 5 publish newsletters. Many also publish journals or other periodicals with articles of interest to their members. The following periodical is the only one devoted entirely to the issue of sexual harassment.

The Webb Report
Premiere Publishing, Ltd.
145 Northwest 85th Street, Suite 201
Seattle, WA 98117
(202) 782-8310 or (800) 767-3062
Monthly. $96/year; $144 for two years; $192 for three years.

The *Webb Report* is the only monthly newsletter to focus exclusively on sexual harassment. Each report includes news items, summaries of new cases on the issue, and recent studies and commentary. Articles usually balance a feminist perspective with a recognition of the problems and needs of management.

7

Selected Nonprint Resources

Films and Videocassettes

New videos on sexual harassment are being produced continually; therefore, it is not possible to write a comprehensive review of all of them. Following is a sample of the better known and more readily available selections. The accompanying annotations are intended to evaluate the films in terms of content as well as production value (writing, acting or presentation quality, camera work, editing, and graphics). Most of the videos were produced for use in training employees and managers and may come with training manuals. These written materials tend to be continually updated and revised, and sometimes even produced for specific companies; therefore, they are not separately reviewed here. Check with the source of each video to find out if the company offers any current manuals or other material.

A Costly Proposition
Type: Videocassette
Length: 32 min.
Date: 1986
Cost: $350–$875, depending on the exact combination of tapes and other training materials purchased or rented. Cost includes trainer's and participants' manuals.

Source: BNA Communications Inc.
9439 Key West Avenue
Rockville, MD 20850-3396
(800) 233-6067

This video-based training program is designed to prevent sexual harassment. Five well-produced vignettes address different kinds of sexual harassment while focusing primarily on media-related companies. A hostile work environment scenario is illustrated through a camera crew on location. An example of quid pro quo sexual harassment is shown through the guise of a record company environment. In scenario number three, a secretary is harassed by a client. She complains to her boss, who avoids doing anything to stop the harassment. After the secretary leaves and files a lawsuit, the employer's liability for acts of nonemployees when the employer knew (or should have known) of the harassing conduct and failed to take appropriate action is discussed. The fourth dramatization illustrates that when employment opportunities or benefits are granted because of an individual's submission to a superior's sexual advances, the employer may be liable to other persons who were qualified for but denied the opportunity. Finally, in a scene entitled "Gray Areas," the video seeks to emphasize how subtle sexual harassment occurs, especially when workers are traveling or socializing after hours and an act of friendliness may be misconstrued as a sexual invitation. The video emphasizes hostile work environment claims because, after the Supreme Court decision in *Meritor Savings Bank v. Vinson*, this is the type of sexual harassment claimed in 70 percent of the cases. This is a professionally produced set of stories, but the scenes lack resolution without the materials presented in the corresponding manuals. The current manuals are well designed and integrated with the video, and contain resource information, including relevant court cases and references. The video provides employees with a clear definition of sexual harassment and its legal implications, as well as exploring sexual harassment issues as they relate to working relationships within the organization.

Handling the Sexual Harassment Complaint
Type: Videocassette
Length: 15 min.
Date: 1990
Cost: Purchase $495, including workbooks; rental starts at $130.
Source: American Media, Incorporated
1454 30th Street, West
Des Moines, IA 50265
(800) 262-2557

This video is a follow-up to "Sexual Harassment in the Workplace . . . Identify. Stop. Prevent" (also reviewed in this section). The objective is to provide management with specific procedures to follow when receiving, investigating, and taking action on a sexual harassment complaint. The program offers information and techniques for answering the question, "What do I say and do when I receive a sexual harassment complaint?" Following the same format of the previous video, this tape dramatizes a meeting of managers with a sexual harassment trainer. The group discusses a step-by-step process to follow when investigating a complaint. The trainer also shows her own video with a dramatization of an employee bringing a complaint to a supervisor: a secretary whose boss implies that she must accompany him on a business trip or risk losing her job. The idea that her companionship is desired for reasons other than strictly business is never specifically stated, but is clearly implied. Thus, this scenario provides fertile ground for managers to discuss whether this implied message should be considered sexual harassment and how to deal with the complaint. The video vignettes include a dramatization of how the complaint proceeds and how the supervisor investigates it. The storyline emphasizes how those investigating a complaint must invest a lot of time and be prepared to use maximum creativity to ensure that all avenues are explored, thus limiting the company's exposure to lawsuits and low productivity. The tape suggests that managers consult with the supervisor's supervisor, the human resources department, and the legal department. A well-produced piece that meets its stated goals.

How Far Is Too Far?
Type: Videocassette
Length: 20 min.
Date: 1987
Cost: Purchase $275; rental $75
Source: Coronet/MTI Film & Video
108 Wilmot Road
Deerfield, IL 60015-9925
(800) 621-2131

In this ABC News *20/20* segment, hosts Hugh Downs and Barbara Walters explore the issue of sexual harassment in the workplace. Produced after the 1986 Supreme Court decision in *Meritor Savings Bank v. Vinson* on sexual harassment, reporter Lynn Sherr interviews women whose victories in court have helped establish higher standards for behavior on the job. The segment includes a clear explanation of the complex issue of hostile work environments. Sherr interviews several successful plaintiffs in sexual harassment cases, including Elizabeth Reese, who sued a major architectural firm; an all-woman jury awarded her $250,000. She also speaks with Virginia Delgado, who successfully sued her brokerage-firm employer for sexual harassment; even though there was no mention of sex, she was able to prove that men and women were treated differently. The segment also shows a training session with experts Stephen Anderson and Trisha Brinkman. Brinkman's advice on how to determine if behavior is sexual harassment: "If you don't want your actions reported on the evening news, don't do it." The show is informative and has the usual excellent *20/20* production value.

Intent vs. Impact. A two-tape series.

Type:	Videocassettes
Length:	41 min. 27 sec. (management); 26 min. (employee)
Date:	1988
Cost:	$298–$1,495, depending on the exact combination of videos and training materials rented or purchased; most packages include training manuals.
Source:	BNA Communications Inc.
	9439 Key West Avenue
	Rockville, MD 20850-3396
	(800) 233-6076

These two stand-alone videos, designed by sexual harassment trainer Stephen Anderson, address sexual harassment from both management and employee levels. This series was produced before *Myth vs. Fact* (also reviewed in this section), Anderson's more recent offering. The management video is intended to go beyond awareness, showing managers and supervisors how to recognize subtle sexual harassment, how to prevent it, and how to deal with sexual harassment situations if they do occur. Several dramatizations cover quid pro quo harassment and legal and financial liabilities for managers and organizations under Title VII, Title IX, and other fair employment laws. Other vignettes address identifying a hostile work environment; identifying sexual harassment by distinguishing when harmless hazing becomes sexual harassment; receiving a sexual harassment complaint; talking with the alleged harasser; and dealing with thorny issues such as false charges, sexual visuals, and provocative clothing. The dramatizations include retaliation when an employee refuses a supervisor's advances on a business trip and hazing that escalates to a hostile work environment. Narrated by popular Denver television anchor Reynalda Muse, the video is particularly adept at helping participants sort out the confusing issue of what is flirtation versus sexual harassment; the scenarios illustrate a three-step process to determine the difference between flirtation and subtle sexual harassment. Anderson's point is that subtle sexual harassment, if allowed to continue unchecked by a supervisor, can escalate into a claim of hostile work environment. The basic premise of the video is that of intent v. impact—that the intent of the perpetrator is irrelevant because the law focuses on the impact on the victim. The entire effect is a sophisticated interweaving of actual training and dramatizations. The video comes with a trainer's manual and a participants' manual, complete with pre- and post-tests, background information, legal definitions, examples of sexual harassment, and checklists to identify subtle harassment.

The video for employees takes the position that employees are sometimes in the best position to stop sexual harassment, and provides the skills and information employees need to identify sexual harassment and stop it. The video covers hostile work environment and what is flirtation or harassment, and has a self-test for employees to show that some people may not realize that the way they have always acted in the workplace is now sexual harassment. A short assertiveness training segment is offered to help employees stop unwanted attention. The narrative answers the most frequently asked questions regarding sexual visuals, provocative clothing, no-win situations for men and women, and the changing rules of the workplace. A companion training manual for employees is also offered.

Both these videos go beyond awareness and focus on how to resolve harassment situations. What makes these videos different from many others is that they assume that most managers and employees can now recognize blatant sexual harassment, but that the boundaries are less clear when it comes to identifying subtle sexual harassment. The focus of these offerings is on changing behavior rather than just providing information.

Making Advances: What Organizations Must Do about Sexual Harassment

Type: Videocassette
Length: 36 min. 14 sec.
Date: 1988
Cost: Purchase $600; rental $125
Source: Coronet/MTI Film & Video
108 Wilmot Road
Deerfield, IL 60015-9925
(800) 621-2131

This video is a straightforward, if somewhat dry, presentation of the cases and law on sexual harassment. Interviews with EEOC officials, who explain the law and EEOC guidelines, are interspersed with written lists of the principles of various cases. The presentation emphasizes the decrease in productivity and morale caused by sexual harassment and explains how to prevent claims and how to organize complaint and training procedures within an organization. The video does present a few dramatizations of various sexual harassment scenarios and makes it clear that if someone complains of sexual harassment, the organization has a legal duty to respond. A workbook for training purposes is also offered.

Myths vs. Facts. A two-tape series: (1) *How To Recognize and Confront Subtle Sexual Harassment* and (2) *How To Manage Sexual Harassment Situations*

Type: Videocassette
Length: 26 min. 14 sec. (each)
Date: 1992
Cost: $358–$1,595, depending on the exact combination of videos and training materials rented or purchased. Packages includes trainer's and participants' manuals.
Source: BNA Communications, Inc.
            9439 Key West Avenue
            Rockville, MD 20850-3396
            (800) 233-6067

The first video focuses on where to draw the line between subtle sexual harassment and flirtation. The production is a fairly recent offering from trainer Stephen Anderson, who also developed *Intent vs. Impact* (see preceding review). This production emphasizes that the rules in the workplace have changed. Through dramatizations and interviews with Anderson, conducted by Denver radio and television personality Tom Martino, the video discusses and defines sexism, sex discrimination, sexual harassment, and quid pro quo harassment and hostile work environment. This is one of the few commercial videos to use a female narrator, who continues the discussion of the issues. Among the types of subtle sexual harassment depicted are discussions of sexual material, sexual comments, hanging around or following workers, telling sexual jokes, asking about sexual fantasies, and leering looks. Stephen Anderson presents the following definition of subtle sexual harassment, which he emphasizes is not a legal definition but a practical one: "unwelcome sexual or sex based behavior that, if allowed to continue, could create a quid pro quo or hostile work environment." He also identifies a five-step method to decide if something is sexual harassment rather than flirting: (1) identify the persons in the situation, (2) determine the relationship between the persons, (3) look at the behavior itself, (4) decide if the behavior is welcome or unwelcome (that is, is there equal initiation and participation), and (5) ask if the behavior is sexual or sex-based. The analysis helps people sort out an issue that many find confusing, especially in the wake of the Anita Hill/Clarence Thomas hearings. Another new issue that is discussed in a good way is the reasonable woman standard. The video clarifies the sense behind the recent court decisions on this issue by emphasizing that women are still more vulnerable to sexual violence in our society. The presentation also dramatizes same-sex, third-party, nonverbal, previous-relationship, hostile work environment, and female-to-male sexual harassment situations, and shows how a supervisor can maintain a friendly work relationship when confronting a subtle sexual harasser. Finally, the video answers a question men frequently ask: "Don't women harass men by wearing sexy clothing?" While emphasizing that men have no right to harass anyone, no matter what they wear, the narrator concludes that both sexes have a responsibility to dress professionally. The bottom line, which the narrator stresses, is that we all want to be treated with dignity in the workplace. A well-produced video. Comprehensive training manuals are also offered, but the video can be used alone.

The second video provides management personnel with effective techniques for interviewing alleged victims of sexual harassment, including advice on what to do if the recipient requests that no action be taken or if she says she wants to deal with the situation on her own. It also demonstrates how an organization's sexual harassment resource person should talk with an alleged harasser and how a supervisor can intervene when he or she observes a subtle sexual harassment situation, even though there has been no complaint. A mature, confident female narrator introduces the various dramatizations, including examples of how a supervisor should *not* respond when an employee complains of sexual harassment. The tape emphasizes that the manager's role should be that of a supportive fact finder. The video is very specific in explaining how a supervisor should react, including suggested questions. After the dramatizations, the narrator introduces trainer Stephen Anderson, who answers questions and details management mistakes. Anderson also explains why many managers do not take the appropriate action—usually because they are unsure what to do and find the situation embarrassing. The video goes beyond most others in explaining a supervisor's responsibilities, especially if he or she observes sexual harassment. The presentation concludes with suggestions about how to evaluate a workplace to prevent sexual harassment. It emphasizes the potential legal liability of failing to police the workplace. An effective presentation; corresponding training manuals are also available, but the video can be used alone.

No Laughing Matter: High School Students and Sexual Harassment

Type: Originally a filmstrip; now available on videocassette
Length: 25 min.
Date: 1982
Cost: Purchase $45; rental $24
Source: Massachusetts Educational Television
           MET-Office of Educational Technologies
           Massachusetts Department of Education
           1385 Hancock Street
           Quincy, MA 02169
           (617) 770-7509

Produced by the Boston Women's Teachers Collective and Media Works, Inc., this filmstrip (which was transferred to videotape) explores sexual harassment as experienced by high school students in school and at work. Three female students, played by professional actresses, explain the harassment they received from fellow students and from an employer. Their narration is interspersed with scenes of a workshop in which student participants struggle to define harassment and to distinguish it from behavior that is acceptable, such as flirting. The leader stresses the need for a strong school policy. Students are advised to talk with someone if they experience behavior they think is harassing, to tell the harasser that they are uncomfortable with the behavior, and to identify the person at their school responsible for helping with sex discrimination problems. The producers recommend the tape for grades 7 through 12, school personnel, and parents. Because it was originally produced as a filmstrip, the video is not of high visual quality, but it is one of the few available for high school students.

The Power Pinch
Type: Videocassette
Length: 27 min. 31 sec.
Date: 1981
Cost: $575
Source: Coronet/MTI Film & Video
             108 Wilmot Road
             Deerfield, IL 60015-9925
             (800) 621-2131

Narrated by actor Ken Howard, this video explores what sexual harassment is and how it can be prevented. Dramatized vignettes portray three types of harassers: the power player, the office adapter, and the victim of mixed signals. Executives, attorneys, psychologists, and victims discuss the emotional, economic, and legal repercussions of harassment, and advice is given on how managers and employees can deal with the problem. The video seeks to answer the question of why sexual harassment exists, but overall it suffers somewhat from a lack of focus and a lack of orderly progress. Once again, this video emphasizes that sexual harassment can be costly for business in terms of lost productivity, morale, and legal fees and awards. Overhead transparencies, a manager's handbook, and employee guides are also available for use as part of the training. The video itself is now somewhat out of date, as it was produced before many important cases.

Preventing Sexual Harassment: A Management Responsibility (Part I—The Risk, Part II—Minimizing the Risk [for management], and **Preventing Sexual Harassment: A Shared Responsibility** [Part III, for employees])
Type: Videocassette
Length: Part I: 27 min.; Part II: 24 min.; Part III: 13 min.

Date: Parts I and II: 1991; Part III: 1992
Cost: (of three-tape series) Varies from $220–$1,595, depending
            on the exact combination of tapes and other training
            materials ordered
Source: BNA Communications Inc.
            9439 Key West Avenue
            Rockville, MD 20850
            (800) 233-6067 or (301) 948-0540

This three-tape series, complete with a comprehensive trainer's manual and participants' manual, is an integrated video-based training system designed to help organizations educate management and employees about sexual harassment. The goals of the series are: to prevent sexual harassment complaints and lawsuits; resolve complaints internally should harassment occur; limit the organization's legal liability for harassment; demonstrate the organization's efforts to prevent harassment; highlight internal resolution procedures to employees and support disciplinary action should employees engage in harassment; show managers how they can be held personally liable for harassment; prevent other types of harassment based on race, age, national origin, or disability; and place all employees on notice that harassment will not be tolerated. The first video opens with a dramatic courtroom scene at the point the jury brings in a million-dollar verdict for a sexual harassment claim. The three videos then intersperse scenes of the trial with discussion and background dramatizations. These methods illustrate both the right and wrong way to handle a sexual harassment claim.

The only problem with this technique is that the scenario becomes a bit old after watching all three videos. The creators have purposely picked an ambiguous situation to illustrate a number of points. An employee has a brief affair with a supervisor. During the affair, she is promoted, to the consternation of other employees who feel they were better qualified. After the affair is ended (it is never clear by whom), the employee feels that she is treated unfairly by her former lover and eventually resigns and sues the company. Whether the initial affair was consensual is never shown; this allows the presentation to emphasize that office romances can be tricky, no matter how innocently they begin. In this office, the supervisor also had a habit of flirting with other workers, telling sexual jokes, and making other sexual comments, all of which were used against him at the trial. Part I of the management video shows the wrong way to handle the situation from a management point of view; Part II shows the right way; and the employee tapes illustrate how to handle the situation from an employee's perspective.

Preventing Sexual Harassment was produced following the confirmation hearings of Clarence Thomas and includes a discussion of the just-passed Civil Rights Act of 1991, along with an explanation of the reasonable woman standard. The program emphasizes how differently actions can be interpreted in a courtroom setting and makes supervisors aware that they themselves can be held personally liable. Three real-life experts—a human resource manager and two attorneys—comment periodically on the storyline. The videos also cover the standard definitions of sexual harassment as they show how to handle complaints. In all, the series provides accurate information in a well-produced manner.

Preventing Sexual Harassment in the Workplace

Type: Videocassette
Length: 27 min.
Date: 1991
Cost: $495 (nonmember; includes workbooks and instructor
             manual) $395 (members, includes workbooks and instructor
             manual) $50 preview
Source: Society for Human Resource Management
             Distribution Center
             1600 West 82nd Street, Suite 200
             Minneapolis, MN 55431
             (612) 885-5500
             (800) 444-5006

This comprehensive training program includes a video and instructor's guides and participants' workbooks designed to enhance the video presentation. The video dramatizes real-life scenarios and focuses on common questions and answers. The first part of the video is an overview of sexual harassment, dramatized through a managers' meeting. The managers then watch a video-within-a-video: a special "news report" on sexual harassment. Definitions of sexual harassment, its causes, and its costs are addressed. In Part 2, the managers discuss distinguishing sexual harassment from other forms of discrimination based on sex; in Part 3, various types of sexual harassment are defined. In Part 4, liability for sexual harassment in the workplace is considered, and in Part 5 the question of how an employee may pursue a complaint, both formally and informally, is addressed, as well as how to communicate the responsibilities of managers, supervisors, employees, and co-workers in preventing and responding to incidents of sexual harassment. Finally, how to investigate a sexual harassment complaint is dramatized by the managers in the video through a role-playing exercise. This video is not as comprehensive as some others in defining the difference between sexual harassment and other more subtle types of flirting or sexual behavior, but it does cover the basics. The video-within-a-video format of a news report becomes a bit forced at times. Dramatizations of workers talking, discussing the kinds of sexual harassment they have experienced, however, lends an air of reality to the video. The presentation addresses who is most vulnerable to sexual harassment (i.e., women who work in nontraditional jobs, in a male environment, have attended college, and are

single or divorced). Potential legal costs and the human resource costs—
turnover, absenteeism and reduced morale—are also emphasized. The
video generally has a fairly high production value.

Sexual Harassment in Schools
Type: Videocassette
Length: 16 min.
Date: 1984
Cost: $60; price includes copy of the Law Center's booklet *Sexual
           Harassment in Employment and Education.* Video alone is
           available for $45.
Source: Northwest Women's Law Center
           119 South Main Street, Suite 330
           Seattle, WA 98104
           (206) 621-7691

This video production is actually a video of still photographs with a
voiceover narrative. The program focuses on the myths and realities of
sexual harassment; defines the term; presents studies on harassment in
employment and education; delineates harassment's effects and costs;
and provides steps for students and education employees to take to stop
sexual harassment. The video is intended for use with the center's
150-page resource manual. Shot in black and white, the video is not
particularly engaging, nor of high-quality production, yet it does offer
basic information on a subject that has not yet been extensively covered
in other videos: sexual harassment in schools. Produced before the
Supreme Court case finding that sexual harassment in schools is clearly
a violation of Title IX for which schools can be held liable for monetary
damages (*Franklin v. Gwinnett County Public Schools*), the video presents
several dramatizations of possible instances of sexual harassment to
make its point. The narration seems to be directed more at teachers,
administrators, or employees than at students. The tape does a thorough, if somewhat stilted, job of explaining both formal and informal
means of resolving a sexual harassment complaint. Though it is now out
of date, the video is included here because it is one of the few available
for schools facing the issue.

Sexual Harassment in the Workplace . . . Identify. Stop. Prevent.
Type: Videocassette
Length: 21 min.
Date: 1990
Cost: $57; includes written materials
Source: American Media, Inc.
           1454 30th Street West
           Des Moines, IA 50265
           (800) 262-2557

This video is meant as a training device for managers and employees on the issue of sexual harassment. In a series of dramatizations, the video introduces the fictional Mr. Wright, who has recently heard that another company similar to his lost a sexual harassment lawsuit. Not only was the publicity embarrassing, the settlement was sizeable. To avoid this problem in his own company, Mr. Wright decides to provide management and employees with the latest information and instill in them the attitude that sexual harassment will not be tolerated. To do so, Mr. Wright hires a consultant, Ms. Hanson, and then schedules a meeting with his top management. The video proceeds with a dramatization of this realistic meeting. Actors portraying top management are diverse in terms of race, sex, and points of view. The trainer shows her own video within this video, dramatizing various sexual harassment scenarios; then she stops the tape and asks the assembled managers to discuss the implications of each vignette. A variety of scenes are presented, including how sexual relationships at the office can spur third-party complaints of preference and same-sex harassment. The trainer's explanation of the law is woven into her discussions of each scenario in a natural, realistic way. Some of the managers do not hesitate to express their disbelief about some of the rules of sexual harassment, such as when one manager explains that he has a problem when women dress in a way that he believes attracts this kind of attention. A depiction of workers looking at a magazine with pin-ups and then making remarks to another worker spurs a discussion of the theory of hostile work environment. The trainer also presents parts of her video to illustrate how workers can stand up to sexual harassment, and explains that harassers do not respect any kind of boundaries of type or class.

The acting and production values are fairly high in this video and the presentation offers the basic information in an engaging format. The trainer's style is natural and pleasant and she emphasizes that the underlying reason for sensitizing managers and workers to sexual harassment is to make certain that each worker has an opportunity to be valued for his or her work, not sex. The trainer emphasizes that sexual harassment is a misuse of power, not an expression of sexual desire. Workers are also shown how to prevent sexual harassment through dress and a professional manner, as well as what to do if they must confront a harasser and ultimately complain.

Sexual Harassment Is Bad Business

Type: Videocassette
Length: 22 min.
Date: 1987
Cost: $495 purchase; $45 preview (full credit if purchased); $175, three-day rental

Source: J. M. Glass, Inc.
PO Box 90999
Spokane, WA 99209
(509) 326-4989

This video and its companion training guide emphasize the cost to business of sexual harassment, including the loss of employee morale and the costs of litigation. The winner of six national and international awards, this video was designed primarily for managers and supervisors and examines the issue of sexual harassment through the experiences of its victims. Based on dramatizations of actual cases, it allows the audience to become personally involved with the problem. The production does a thorough job of defining sexual harassment legally, but is so detailed that this part sometimes drags. The video emphasizes the employer's responsibility and the fact that "you can't afford to be confused about this issue." The script includes a clear explanation of the new paramour-preference type of case. A thoroughly professional presentation, although now somewhat out of date.

Sexual Harassment: Issues and Answers
Type: Videocassette
Length: 19 min. 40 sec.
Date: 1991
Cost: $60
Source: College and University Personnel Association
1233 20th Street, NW
Washington, DC 20036
(202) 429-0311

This video, narrated by a pleasant female broadcasting professional, focuses on sexual harassment on college campuses. The narration begins with a comparison of myths versus facts in the area of sexual harassment, and includes a review of the surveys showing the prevalence of sexual harassment. The script goes on to examine the definitions and look at examples of sexual harassment. The video outlines what supervisors or employees should do if sexual harassment occurs and makes it clear that educational institutions have a responsibility to protect faculty, staff, and students. One dramatization is of a rather blatant—and perhaps outdated—quid pro quo situation between an administrator and his staff. There is also a dramatization of a student and a dean discussing a consensual relationship in which the student had been seeing a professor but then broke it off. Now the student feels that the professor is retaliating. Another scenario shows a female graduate student harassing other students. The video emphasizes that professional ethics must be addressed when power and authority clash and that universities are responsible for student-to-student harassment. There is a brief discussion of how to investigate both formal and informal complaints. The video takes the position that power, rather than male/female relationships, is the issue in sexual harassment. Although this production is not as high in quality as some videos produced for the corporate workplace, it is one of the few to focus exclusively on college campuses, and therefore will be particularly useful for those dealing with that environment. CUPA produces a corresponding booklet, "Issues and Answers," with legal definitions and sample policies.

Sexual Harassment: It's No Game

Type: Videocassette
Length: 30 min.
Date: 1988 (curriculum revised in 1992)
Cost: $250 (includes 50-page curriculum in binder); $60 for one week package preview/rental
Source: Center for Women in Government
University of Albany
Draper Hall 310
Albany, NY 12222
(518) 442-3900

This video-based training program was developed especially for the public sector. It includes segments from the popular TV program "Cagney and Lacey," repeating parts of an award-winning episode that dramatized the issue of sexual harassment in the show's fictional police department. The engaging format opens on a sexual harassment training session attended by a diverse group of public employees. The trainees are watching the "Cagney and Lacey" show to examine the behaviors and issues involved. The situation is powerful—and objectionable—enough to make the employees uncomfortable. In the ensuing lunchroom scenes, the workshop participants share their reactions to the television episodes. Some of the participants have experienced sexual harassment, while even the "nice guys" have been its perpetrators. Personal anecdotes are shared, illustrating the range of sexual harassment behaviors for the viewer. The training scenes are packed with information and answers to frequent questions, but it is the lunchtime interactions that defy stereotypes and illustrate how subtle and complex the issue of sexual harassment can be. The video also outlines the legal rights of employees and the legal responsibilities of employers, while suggesting procedures for complaints and problems. The video does a good job of illustrating both the professional damage and the personal anguish sexual harassment causes its victims. The leader of the training session takes the feminist position that sexual harassment is not about sex but about power. Although the men in the group issue the standard complaint that there are no set rules, the trainer emphasizes that after ten years of court cases, it is clear that the victim has the right to define unwanted sexual harassment. The video also makes the subtle but important point that any woman—young or old, pretty or plain—can be a victim of sexual harassment. The companion curriculum provides questions to stimulate group discussion, expands on the issues raised by the video, and addresses common viewer questions and concerns.

Shades of Gray. A five-tape series: (1) *What Are We Doing Here?*, (2) *What Is Sexual Harassment?*, (3) *Why Should I Worry about It?*, (4) *What Does the Law Say?*, and (5) *What Am I Supposed To Do?*

Type:	Videocassette
Length:	15 min. (each tape)
Date:	1989
Cost:	Varies from $300–$1,495, depending on the exact combination of tapes and training materials purchased or sold
Source:	Premiere Publishing, Ltd.
	145 Northwest 85th Street, Suite 201
	Seattle, WA 98117
	(206) 782-8310
	(800) 767-3062

This five-tape training series, developed by Seattle sexual harassment trainer Susan Webb, uses dramatizations of real problems from real stories to make its point. The video is one of the few to deal realistically with the concerns of workers (usually men) who feel threatened by the imposition of workplace standards that they do not understand. Serving as the narrator, Webb emphasizes that harassment is not a new concern. Webb takes the position that the "trainees" often become defensive and resistant to the subject; in spite of, or perhaps because of, people's resistance, the problem of harassment is as great today as ever. Because of this, Webb takes care to ensure that the information is complete and accurate, yet presented in such a way that people will pay attention and learn—breaking through their initial defensiveness or resistance.

Video 1: "What Are We Doing Here?" reviews all five tapes and is an introduction to and overview of the problem of sexual harassment in the workplace. Video 2: "What Is Sexual Harassment?" defines sexual harassment in behavioral terms with a common-sense definition, using a continuum from light gray to dark gray harassment. It also discusses why certain behaviors must be repeated before they constitute harassment and the responsibility of the recipient to speak up about unwelcome behaviors. Video 3: "Why Should I Worry about It?" details and emphasizes the costs to employers, victims, co-workers, and harassers. Included are consequences such as lowered productivity, absenteeism, turnover, lawsuits, and court awards and settlements. It also emphasizes the personal as well as professional liability of each employee. Video 4: "What

Does the Law Say?" first covers the *Vinson* U.S. Supreme Court case and then examines the EEOC guidelines, to explain the responsibilities of individuals in the workplace and to show how recent court decisions support those guidelines. Video 5: "What Am I Supposed To Do?" tells employees at all levels what their responsibilities are. These comprehensive videos present accurate information in a nonthreatening way. One of the most detailed and complete packages available, resource manuals, training manuals, a leader's guide, and participants' handbooks also come with the video. Because the tapes were produced in 1989, however, a few of the more recent cases are not covered.

So Like You
Type: Videocassette
Length: 22 min.
Date: 1990
Cost: Purchase $350; rental $85
Source: Coronet/MTI Film & Video
            108 Wilmot Road
            Deerfield, IL 60015-9925
            (800) 621-2131

This comprehensive program, set in a fictional company, explores the issue of sexual harassment and shows what happens when a harassment accusation has been made. Individuals experiencing sexual harassment and managers who are investigating harassment are shown steps they can take to achieve resolution. The program examines the same situation from two different points of view, those of the man and woman involved. Meant to provoke discussion, it allows managers and employees to explore sexual harassment issues that may be unspoken or misunderstood. Each program includes leader's guides and participants' workbooks that provide exercises, role plays, guidelines, materials for discussion, and details of actual sexual harassment cases. Unlike some videos, this one would not be complete or provide adequate information without the accompanying manuals. The video serves mainly to spark discussion on the issues raised in the written materials. In addition, because the video examines the same fact situation from both a female and a male point of view, it tends to drag in places. Still, the script is realistic and intelligent and the dialogue and setting have a truthful ring.

The Workplace Hustle
Type: Film/videocassette
Length: 30 min.
Date: 1980
Cost: $520, 16mm film; $520, videocassette

Source: Woody Clark Productions
            943 Howard Street
            San Francisco, CA 94103
            (415) 777-1668

This documentary, narrated by Ed Asner and including commentary by Lin Farley, author of *Sexual Shakedown,* the first book to use the term *sexual harassment,* won awards at both the San Francisco and New York Film Festivals. The film stresses the social and emotional dimensions of sexual harassment, especially the different ways men and women define the behavior. Dramatized vignettes and interviews with a victim and an employer underscore the personal and organizational consequences of harassment, and advice is given on steps women should take when harassed. Asner wisely acknowledges the oddity of having a male narrator, but explains that those men who have been taught not to listen to women should "consider me our translator." The film does a good job of dramatizing the difference in men's and women's perceptions, with groups of both sexes discussing the issue. Farley emphasizes that much harassment occurs when women enter previously all-male professions and when men have economic incentives to "communicate power expressed sexually," but stresses that she knows "most men don't want to behave this way." Farley notes that men are trained, while growing up, to show their manhood through intimidation. Asner's narration adds a nice touch as he notes that although men have used sexuality as power, sexuality is an expression of intimacy and love, not power, and that women want to separate sex and work to improve both. An effective, well-produced film, albeit now somewhat out of date.

Would You Let Someone Do This to Your Sister?
Type: Videocassette
Length: 33 min. 38 sec.
Date: 1984
Cost: Purchase $50; rental $10 for two weeks.
Source: Women's Rights Department
            United Auto Workers
            8000 East Jefferson Avenue
            Detroit, MI 48214
            (313) 926-5271

This video includes interviews with female workers who have been harassed and suggests steps for victims. Focusing on the plight of office, factory, and other union workers, the presentation offers emotional and persuasive interviews with actual harassment victims. One especially effective segment shows a black factory worker describing the details of her harassment experience, while her husband listens with tears in his eyes. The women describe the embarrassment and the physical and psychological effects of harassment. Male viewers may be surprised by the pain caused by sexual harassment that is revealed in this video. The speakers also emphasize how dressing unattractively did nothing to stop their harassers. Various UAW union officials pledge to uphold the union's "no tolerance" stance on harassment. The speakers take the position that sexual harassment is not about passion but is caused by hostile aggression. An appearance by the UAW president, stating that sexual harassment is an insult to the worker and a barrier to equal employment for men and women, delivers a powerful message from the top to union workers. Another UAW vice-president emphasizes that sexual harassment policies should be raised at the bargaining table and included in union contracts. Although the production consists mostly of talking heads, the documentary style and impassioned feelings of the presenters make this video especially effective.

Glossary

agency   The relationship in which one individual (the *agent*) acts for or on the behalf of or represents another (the *principal*) under the authority granted to the actor by the principal.

assault and battery   Actually two separate legal wrongs, but because they frequently occur together, they are often paired in legal complaints. To prove assault, the victim must show that the person who allegedly assaulted him or her intended to cause physical contact and that the victim feared the contact. *Battery* is actual physical contact that is harmful, offensive, or insulting. The victim must show that the person intended to touch the victim, and that he or she did contact the victim physically.

common law negligence claims   Negligence actions based on English common law, the foundation of the American legal system. *Negligence* is failing to do what a reasonably careful person would do under the same circumstances, or doing what a reasonable person in similar circumstances would not.

compensatory damages   The amount of money awarded to individuals to make them whole or to place them in the position in which they would have been if the situation complained of had never occurred; actual losses.

constructive discharge   The theory that a resignation from employment may actually be a dismissal (and legally treated as such), because the employer's imposition of intolerable terms and conditions of employment gave the resigning employee no choice but to leave.

defamation   An oral ("slander") or written ("libel") false statement that damages another's reputation.

defendant   The person, employer, or entity (such as a school) charged with the complaint or wrong. Usually, an individual employee, student, or supervisor will be accused because of his or her own conduct. An employer or school may be liable through *respondeat superior* or agency theories.

disparate impact   In discrimination cases, discriminatory effect that results unintentionally from the use of a requirement—for example, a preemployment test—that is neutral on its face.

hostile environment   One of the two types of sexual harassment claims; requires a showing of frequent, serious acts of a sexual nature that create the effect of a hostile, offensive, or intimidating working or educational atmosphere. The victim need not show money damages.

injunctive relief   Usually, an equitable remedy ordered by the court requiring that certain activities stop, such as that an organization refrain from discrimination against women in the future. A *mandatory* injunction (*mandamus*) requires that a defendant take certain actions, such as in a sexual harassment case in which the court orders that an employer or school implement certain policies or training.

intentional infliction of emotional distress   A claim that the actor or defendant intentionally acted in a way that he, she, or it knew, or should have known, would cause nontrivial emotional pain to another. The conduct must be so shocking or extreme that a person of normal sensibilities would consider the action outrageous.

invasion of privacy   A claim that the defendant intruded upon another person's solitude or into his or her private affairs; usually requires the public disclosure of embarrassing facts about the person.

negligent hiring or retention   Tort action against employers that fail to protect employees from foreseeable harm by carefully checking references of new employees or that fail to terminate employees who they know have caused harm in the past.

paramour preference   Term used to refer to the preference of a supervisor for the individual with whom he or she has an ongoing social or sexual relationship over others in the workplace or educational institution.

plaintiff   The person bringing the lawsuit or EEOC claim; usually, the victim in a sexual harassment case.

punitive damages   The money amount awarded to an individual by the jury, or specified by statute, so that the defendant is punished for its conduct and so that all potential defendants will be effectively deterred from acting in the same manner.

quid pro quo   In Latin, literally, "this for that." One of two types of sexual harassment claims; requires a showing of unwelcome activity of a sexual nature in exchange for tangible employment or educational benefits, or the loss of tangible job benefits because of the rejection of such activity.

reasonable person/woman   A legal standard for behavior; the judicial construct of an individual who thinks and responds the way an ordinary, logical, and careful person or woman would under the same circumstances and conditions.

respondeat superior   Literally, Latin for "let the master answer." The principle that the master is responsible for the acts of the servant; usually meaning that an employer is responsible for the acts of an employee, whether or not the employer has actual knowledge of that employee's acts.

sex discrimination   The cause of action recognized by Title VII and many state statutes; the favoring of one individual or group over another on the basis of gender or stereotypes associated with gender.

sexual harassment   A cause of action grounded in sex discrimination; the imposition of unwelcome sexual conduct on an employee in the workplace or a student in an educational institution, which conduct affects the student or employee's performance.

strict liability   The automatic imposition of liability, regardless of extenuating circumstances, knowledge, or intent.

tort   A wrong committed by one person or institution against another, redressed by money damages; defined by state common law rather than by statute.

Index